INKLINGS

INKLINGS

A MEMOIR

Jeffrey Koterba

HOUGHTON MIFFLIN HARCOURT

BOSTON • NEW YORK

2009

For information about permission to reproduce selections from this book,
write to Permissions, Houghton Mifflin Harcourt Publishing Company,
215 Park Avenue South, New York, New York 10003.

www.hmhbooks.com

Library of Congress Cataloging-in-Publication Data
Koterba, Jeffrey.
Inklings : a memoir / Jeffrey Koterba.
p. cm.
ISBN 978-0-15-101492-7
1. Koterba, Jeffrey. 2. Koterba, Jeffrey — Childhood and youth. 3. Koterba,
Jeffrey — Family. 4. Cartoonists — United States — Biography. 5. Editorial car-
toonists — United States — Biography. 6. Tourette syndrome — Patients — United
States — Biography. 7. Creative ability — United States — Case studies. 8. South
Omaha (Omaha, Neb.) — Biography. 9. Omaha (Neb.) — Biography. 10. United
States — Politics and government — Caricatures and cartoons. I. Title.
NC1429.K64A2 2009
741.5'6973 — dc22 [B]   2009012505

Illustrations by Jeffrey Koterba
Book design by Brian Moore

Printed in the United States of America

DOC 10 9 8 7 6 5 4 3 2 1

For my father

Prologue

I'M ON DEADLINE. I should be working on tomorrow's cartoon, but my mind drifts. I'm sketching a man. He's the man I always sketch when I can't think of anything else to draw. He's not me, but he is me. He is smiling, calm. In the next frame, one of his eyes is squeezed tight, his mouth stretched grotesquely to one side. The third frame: he is again smiling. This is how I draw the man with Tourette's.

PART ONE

Rough Sketches

THE PLYMOUTH RATTLES UP the driveway, its headlights beaming through the blinds of our living room window, illuminating the dark canyons of broken TVs and boxes. I want to leap, but instead I slide off the scratchy davenport and ease through a minefield of screws, bolts, and wires to the front door. He barges in, bringing with him the October night, the scent of fresh ink and newsprint.

"Hi, Daddy."

He doesn't respond because he's worried. I don't mind. I know how important his ad is. It's Saturday night, and he's cradling the early edition of the *Sunday World-Herald*. The newspaper, every other day known as the *Omaha World-Herald*, comes wrapped in comics. He flicks on the overhead light and discards the comics; they land partly open at his feet, forming a color-splashed tent.

I drop to all fours. I'm at eye level with Dagwood Bumstead. He's running, leaving behind puffs of cartoon smoke. It's not yet safe to move.

Other sections of the newspaper fall to the floor, on top of boxes and TVs. A squeak—a single hiccup—comes from my father's throat as he spreads open the want ads like a bird's wings. All he ever wants from the newspaper is confirmation his weekly ad has made it into print and is accurate.

"Damn it," he says to himself. "Where the hell is it?" He gives the paper a quick snap, attempting to shake his ad into the open.

He's the tallest thing in the room, taller than his stacks of TVs. I watch as his face makes a wide circle, drawing the letter "O" in the air with his nose. He focuses again, squinting with concentration.

Please let his ad be okay.

Finally, he smiles. "Perfect," he says, tossing the want ads onto the davenport. He leaves the room singing "I'm in the Mood for Love."

I scramble for the comics.

Although the paper comes to our door, every Saturday night after *The Jackie Gleason Show* my father makes the drive downtown to the *World-Herald*'s headquarters to buy an early edition from a toothless man on the corner. The round-trip takes no longer than a half hour.

On rare occasions he invites me along. I ride up front where my mother and brother, Artie, usually sit. Even after eight on a Saturday night, downtown Omaha bustles with trains, Greyhound buses. As far as I'm concerned, the W.O.W. Building—Omaha's tallest at nineteen stories—is a New York skyscraper I'd once seen on the late movie. During these drives I watch as the lights of the city reflect, move across the passenger-side window. Once, I licked the cool glass, my tongue following a streak of red neon into the gooey crevice where the window sinks into the door.

"You'll catch germs if you do that," my father warned, "and then you'll get sick and we'll have big doctor bills we can't afford."

"I'm sorry," I said.

"That's okay. You have nervous habits just like me."

On the dusty wood floor of my room, I devour *Peanuts, Dennis the Menace, The Wizard of Id.* I'm convinced I'm a time traveler, reading tomorrow's funny pages. As I scan *Prince Valiant* and the strips that remind me of my mother's soap operas, I dislodge a nugget of gravel that became embedded in my right palm while crawling on the floor.

4

From my dresser I retrieve a black Flair pen and a handful of typing paper. In the other room, TVs are blaring. The music and laughter make me wish we're throwing a party, but we never have visitors. It's back to the floor, on my stomach. I position *Peanuts* to my left, a sheet of paper to my right. Often, the early-edition comics are blurry, the black outlines and colors not quite in register. Tonight everything is aligned as perfectly as in a comic book.

Charlie Brown.

His eyes are two black dots bracketed by parentheses.

I always start with the eyes.

Back and forth I go, shaking my head in slow motion, studying, sketching. Left. Right. I'm in a trance.

There's a spot of blood next to my Charlie Brown. It's from picking out the gravel. I ignore the blood and keep going. The paper is smooth, its surface soothing, healing.

After a quick scribble of hair, I'm ready for the mouth. Even when the Charlie Brown in the newspaper comes with a wavy line, I change it to a smile. This time I want my Charlie Brown to look *exactly* like the Charlie Brown in the newspaper.

I lick my lips. I make the wavy line.

I move on to Snoopy, then the King and Spook from *The Wizard of Id*. When I'm drawing, time stands still.

I finish and come up for air. On my elbows, I study my efforts.

Silence.

When did the house get quiet? I can't hear my father's TVs. I want to show my mother what I've drawn, but I'm paralyzed by the utter lack of sound. If not for my lamp casting an orange glow through its tasseled shade, our house might've blown another fuse. I can hear nothing but my own breathing. I'm used to my parents' yelling, and as much as yelling scares me, hearing nothing frightens me more. Somehow I must stay this way, frozen, until I hear a sound. Otherwise, I believe, my parents, my brother, might die.

I focus on Spook, his hairy body and his bulbous nose. Together,

5

we keep everyone alive. A short while later, relief tingles my body as I detect my mother's voice through the wall. She must be talking to Artie. He's almost two, four years younger than I, but still sleeps in a crib alongside my parents' bed, as if in a motorcycle sidecar.

Clutching my drawings, I step into the dark hallway. From the dining room comes a faint but reassuring snapping—the sound of electricity. My father is tinkering, which also means electricity didn't kill him. He *controls* electricity.

As I enter my parents' bedroom, my mother is on her bed, Artie at her breast. The other breast stares at me, a heavy, surprised cartoon eye. She makes no attempt to cover herself.

I divert my attention to the floor.

"It's okay," she says, "you can come in."

Keeping my head lowered, I close the door behind me and from under my brow I watch as Artie leaps from her chest to the bed. Her flesh disappears as she fastens her bra, her blouse.

"How's my Jeffrey?" she asks.

"The house was quiet."

"Oh?" she says, patting the bed. Her face is framed by black bangs, swoops of hair on either side of her flushed cheeks.

I sit next to her, my drawings on my lap. I watch our reflection—all three of us—in the blank, silver-gray screen of their Magnavox. I'm grateful for the image of us, the movement of us.

"What's this?" she asks, reaching for my drawings.

I shrug.

"I'm so proud of you!" She always makes a fuss over my drawings.

"Artie, look!" she says. "See what your brother did? See Snoopy?"

"Snoopy!" he repeats, bouncing on the bed, a piston.

"Honey," she says to him, "you're going to fall. Why don't you read a book in *your* bed?" He obeys, and climbs over the railing. He dominates his crib.

She guides my head to her chest, cradles it. We rock slowly as I count the wigs on her dresser, all with expressionless Styrofoam faces. Four. There is nothing wrong with her own hair, it's just that she likes to pretend she's a movie star, a diplomat's wife, an airline stewardess.

The hallway fills with heavy footsteps and the bedroom door swings open, but not angrily. My father asks if anyone has seen his Phillips screwdriver. We shake our heads. He's gripping a fistful of black licorice whips, maybe a treat for me.

"Why can't I ever find anything in this house?" he says sadly, pocketing what I now realize is a nest of wire.

"Because we have too much junk," my mother says.

Ignoring her, he opens one of her dresser drawers, reaching in, sorting through her flowery underwear. "One Phillips screwdriver is all I ask."

"Why on earth would I keep a screwdriver in there?"

"All I know is that someone keeps stealing my tools." He clinks open another drawer, this one full of perfume bottles. The bottles come in different shapes and sizes and are huddled toward the back of the drawer. In the commotion, bottles tip over, scenting the air. A wig and its head somersault to the floor. My father's almost out of the room.

"Wait," she tells him.

"I'm busy." He scowls.

"Isn't Jeffrey such an artist?" She holds up my sketches.

"Can't I do this later?"

But he relents, taking the pages. He shuffles; his brow furrows. "Damn it," he says to me, exasperated. "Be different, kid. Be *original*. Don't you know what a sin it is to not be original?"

I can't look at anyone. My eyes well up and I maneuver around him, leaving with my drawings.

My mother calls, "Jeffrey, please . . ."

I'm in my room, on my bed.

"Oh, for God's sake!" His voice reverberates through the wall. I can't make out my mother's words.

I cover my head with a pillow.

"Hey, kid!"

I can't drown him out.

"Come back," he calls. There's a chuckle in his words. "Don't let your feelings get hurt so easily!" He laughs. "That boy is too sensitive."

I don't want my father to be right. "Original" and "sin" bounce around in my head.

His voice is closer, in the hallway. "Please, hon," he asks my mother cheerfully. "Why won't you come see what I've done with the RCA?"

I curl into a ball, clasping my hands. My brain insists that my eyes flicker.

My messy hands disappear.

Now they're back, my inky fingers.

Everything goes dark.

Again, here is my room, my lamp.

It's hard to make the nervous habits stop, and nearly impossible when I'm frightened or worried about my family.

I try to think of something else; I crawl across the bed, pressing my forehead against the window. The night presses back. Our back patio, our yard, is all shadow. The garage, the dead peach tree, and the other bony trees in the ravine beyond the garage don't exist.

Later, I sneak into the kitchen. My father is in the dining room, flipping channels. Quietly I crumple the tainted drawings, forcing them deep into the trash, hoping my hands don't touch old meat. The tomato-red canister is overflowing with garbage. There are chicken bones and crumbs on the linoleum.

My father is talking to himself. "All I do around here is work, work, work," he says. It comes out *workworkwork*.

Something crackles, more electricity.

"Don't know why," he sings, "there's no sun up in the sky. Stormy weather."

The Damn Depression

THE MORE TVs my father stuffs into our house, the more my mother is "tired of living this way." He clutches his chest, gasping, "I'm just trying to make a goddamned living." They go on like that, throwing around the word "living."

"Do you think I enjoy fixing TVs?" he often asks.

I stare at my sneakers.

My father has an eight-to-five office job with the Union Pacific Railroad. He works on budgets and operates a comptometer, which he calls a giant adding machine. I've never seen it, but I can picture his fast-moving fingers clacking away on rows of keys as wide as a piano. Occasionally he's hired through the musicians' union to play drums — "jobs," he calls them — in various local orchestras and combos. If he carried a violin case instead of lugging around bulky drums, taking a "job" might make him sound like a hit man. Especially when he wears a heavy overcoat and fedora.

"But the money's best in TVs," he tells me with a wink, letting me in on his secret.

He repairs most of his TVs on the main floor of our tiny house. Our enclosed front porch doubles as his "showroom." In spite of a space heater, the porch is cold enough to store leftover Thanksgiving turkey. Customers come and go in the evenings and at all hours on Sundays, my father rubbing his hands together, making his sales pitch.

When my mother is weary she turns to me and asks why my father can't work in the basement.

I don't have an answer.

The basement is a mountain range of picture tubes and gutted Zeniths, RCAs, and Motorolas stacked precariously on the concrete floor, up to the dark and woody beams. Wires and cords dangle from the cobwebbed ceiling like roots. Paths snake around cliffs of TVs and boxes marked PARTS and MISC. One such path leads to my mother's dryer and off-balance washer while another meanders to my father's drum set, where he bangs away, letting everyone know he's getting out his frustrations. (Sometimes the washer's *ka-thump ka-thump ka-thump* mimics his drumming.) Otherwise, every trail is a dead end, as our basement has long before become an unmanageable graveyard, his workshop spilling out on our main floor.

The attic is out of the question. My father refers to it as a furnace in summer, a freezer in winter. Besides, even the attic is beginning to fill up with his other garage sale finds of clarinets and saxophones, winter coats, and dusty lamps.

Lately he's been accepting more Friday night jobs, "for Christmas money," he explains. When he's away, my mother makes popcorn and we play board games. I'm usually still awake when he returns. I help bring in his drums. His suit brings home the smells of the bar, the cheering and the laughter, the ghosts of the dance floor.

The next day he collects more TVs and parts, storing up for winter. I help in any way I can, carrying the lighter items or running ahead to hold open the porch door. This happens at night. He doesn't want the neighbors observing what we're up to. In the moonlight I watch for signs in his face that he's happy with me, that he approves of me.

While we work, he whispers stories. He was the youngest of nine children, and "you do what you have to," he says, "when you grow up without a father and have no money." Underage, he snuck into stale taverns to play drums with "doped-up" musicians. He and his older brother Ed delivered the other newspaper in town, the *Omaha Bee-News*. After finishing their route, they practiced music to warm their hands — Ed on clarinet, my father on snare.

"There were many times I got sick," he says, "and thought about falling in the middle of Brown Park in the snow, letting myself die." Brown Park is a ball field surrounded by a stadium of trees. I know it well because my father has driven us around on a tour of all the places he "nearly died."

The attic door is cracked open; my mother sits on the steps. She's holding herself, rocking slightly. Today she's a redhead. On the landing behind her there's a box marked CHRISTMAS BALLS.

"What's wrong?" I ask, making the steep climb.

"Just thinking."

"Oh."

She sighs and stares blankly, squeezing herself tighter.

I nestle onto the step next to her and let her hold me. It's all I can ever think to do. The palm of her hand is cool against my face.

"Well," she says, "I guess we should sort through our decorations, don't you think?"

"Yep."

We drag boxes down the steps and stack them in the hallway as a staging area.

"Can I hang lights?"

"No," my father says, eavesdropping from the other room. "Maybe later."

"How about tomorrow," my mother says to me reassuringly, "after school? Tonight we can make sure all the lights are working."

Later, after she and Artie are asleep, I go to my father. He's on his haunches at the back of a console in the dining room. I stand behind him, unable to speak the question that rattles inside my head.

He detects me from the corner of his eye, but keeps soldering. "Yes?" he says impatiently. His nose is strong, his jaw sunken, resting against his throat—an extra Adam's apple.

I survey the crowded landscape of our home.

"What already?" he says.

"Where are we going to put the Christmas tree?" The words slip out as I stare past him, past everything, to the fireplace. A stack of bills is piled on the mantel, next to framed pictures of Artie and me.

"Is that all? For crying out loud, kid, we'll find room." He leans into his work. The inside of the TV is a dark cave. Glass tubes protrude above and below him. "By the way," he says, "I'm glad you're here. I could use your help."

"But where?" I ask.

"I don't know right now. Somewhere." He refuses to stop what he's doing, leaving me to stare at the back of his mad-scientist head, his hair on the verge of shooting sparks, his bald spot reflecting the flickering sets that encircle us. His odor is a mix of burning wire and Old Spice.

"Why do we have to have all this junk?" I ask, echoing my mother. I immediately want to reclaim my words.

"Kid, this isn't junk! This is how I feed my family. Now, are you going to help me or pick on me?"

I want to escape to my room.

I want a clean house for my mother.

I want to help him.

I can't move.

"Well?" he says.

"Okay."

Without looking, he reaches for and grabs a flashlight near his feet. Twisting his arm backward, he hands it to me. "I can't see a damn thing in here."

I switch on the flashlight and lean in, attempting to illuminate where he's poking around with his soldering gun. He might be playing Operation except that everything inside looks authentically sharp and dangerous. If I could shrink myself, it's a place I'd be too afraid to live.

"Here," he says, pointing with the tip of the soldering gun. "I have to reattach *this* green wire to *that* resistor." I'm not sure exactly where I'm supposed to direct the light — I have no idea what a resistor is. The beam of light wiggles.

"Hold still," he says, the fingers of his other hand a spider uncoiling a spool of soldering wire.

I'm trying to.

"Now to the left."

I must have stumbled onto the correct spot because he says nothing more as he works; the light becomes smoky.

"Do you know what the Depression was?" He pulls his head out, glares over his shoulder. His gray eyes, already deep-set under the heavy ledge of his brow, disappear even further as he pushes down his forehead. Maybe this scrunched look is his way of underlining the importance of what he's saying, but it frightens me, as though he could crush me with his expression. "Well, do you?"

I've always known about it. The word ties my stomach into a knot, making me believe that the Depression followed him — us — into the late 1960s. Once, I got into trouble for using "damn" — the D-word, as he calls it. But to me, the D-word is "Depression." And when my father really drives home his point, "Great Depression" is interchangeable with "God Damn."

He swivels around toward the guts of the TV. Something inside the set buzzes.

"Shit!" He jerks his body away.

I fear he's been shocked. I hold my breath. I'm frozen. *Please let him live.* Slowly, he pivots, now facing me, his weight on his knees.

Relieved, I release the air from my chest. I do not know what happened inside the set. Maybe it was an electrical short, or maybe he accidentally joined the wrong wires together. What matters is that he's looking at me, breathing.

"We had nothing when I was a kid," he continues. "Did you know that my father died before I was born?"

I am sorrowful every time he mentions it.

"Well, did you?"

I nod my head. It's rare for him to stop like this. Maybe if I can keep his full attention, I can persuade him to clean the house.

"He worked in a packing plant and I never knew him. After he lost that job, he straightened bent nails for six cents an hour."

This chance to hold his attention is fleeting. He again lowers his brow, but this time his eyes counter by darting upward—he's trying to peek inside his head. This is his monster face, his death face. He keeps talking but I'm focused on the whites of his eyes. He returns to his tinkering, taking his odd stares with him.

"Can I go now, please?"

Maybe he didn't hear me.

I leave anyway. In the living room, in front of a broken Sylvania table model, I make faces of my own. It's satisfying to stretch my mouth wide, even if my lips crack and bleed. I force down my eyebrows; I'm surprised by my distorted face. I slowly roll my eyes to the ceiling, straining as hard as I can until all I see is warm darkness.

My Secret Wish

MY TOOTH IS THROBBING, and my mother's on the phone with my father, who's at the office. He's not allowed to take personal calls at his desk, so earlier she left an urgent message with his boss. He calls from a booth in the lobby for privacy, even though he suspects the pay phone is bugged.

"Jeffrey's suffering," she says to him. "He needs a dentist. You can tell me how you hate your job later."

I'm on the davenport, home from Hawthorn School. My mother's on the other side of the living room, tethered to the flesh-toned receiver. Behind her, in the hallway, are boxes containing our Christmas decorations, including lights that no longer work. My father won't let us throw out the broken lights. The boxes have remained there for over a week. We have yet to buy a tree.

"No," she says, her voice raised. "I'm not going to sing to him. Don't you understand? Singing won't help. He needs to see Len."

She holds the receiver at arm's length, the cord swinging, a jump rope. I can hear him.

"It's not worth it," he yells. "Len's a cheap sonofabitch. We don't need his charity. Please, if you'd just sing to the kid!" He breaks into song. "Oh, the weather outside is frightful, but the fire is so delightful."

Uncle Len is married to Ann, one of my father's sisters. His dental office takes up a corner on the twelfth floor of the W.O.W. Building, which my father calls the "Wow Building." I've never been in an airplane, but when I visit Uncle Len, I look out his large window and see the tops of buildings, including the one where my father works. To the north, what could be model trains pull slowly from a switchyard. I squint into the hazy west hoping to find the farm where my mother grew up. My parents' conversation ends, and with a lengthy sigh my mother settles next to me, pen in hand, leafing through the Yellow Pages.

"Can I have another baby aspirin?" I ask.

"Sorry, sweetie. You're at the limit. I wouldn't want you to go into convulsions."

She worries about her children dying. Together, we worry. This is how we love each other.

I'm pressing my fist against my jaw in a feeble attempt to make the pain go away. Her finger draws a circle in the phone book. "This one's close by," she says optimistically.

She makes a call, and within minutes she's bundling Artie and me. She warms the Buick and we're off. My father recently purchased this second car because when one car is full, he can come home and quickly head back to garage sales without first unloading. We leave our neighborhood of bungalows and follow the same route we take to my grandparents', rambling past the Chief Theater, its rusted marquee and neon Indian head looming over the sidewalk. I plug my nose as we drive near the stockyards. Before we get to Grandma and Grandpa's, my mother takes an unfamiliar street and veers into a parking lot.

The exterior of Dr. S's office building couldn't be more different from Len's. This red brick and concrete shoebox claims only one floor. Once I'm inside Dr. S's, my mood brightens. Unlike the "antique" furniture in Len's office, the furniture in this waiting area is new and clean — something from a sitcom living room. We move into the examination room. The reclining chair and the gangly mechanical arm glisten. At the same time an antiseptic heaviness weighs everything down. More than the scent of cleanliness, it's the starkness of the place, the lone cardboard Christmas tree taped on a wall, that makes me uneasy.

This dentist is a stump of a man. He flicks on an overhead light as bright as the sun. "What happened to your mouth, young man?" Even his breath is antiseptic.

"Chapped lips," my mother offers.

"I see that," he says with a note of suspicion.

My mother and Artie are made to stand in the hallway as x-rays are taken. While we wait for him to return with the developed film, she's back at my side, stroking my hair. Looking up, I imagine that the white ceiling is the largest sheet of paper on Earth. Dr. S comes in holding the x-rays to the light. "Two cavities," he says without emotion, escorting my mother and Artie to the lobby.

Unlike Uncle Len, Dr. S offers no preemptive shot of Novocain. I'm thrilled to be spared the shot. I'm getting away with something, cheating pain, but when he begins drilling, the sting is piercing. My lower jaw, my face, rattles. The lamp is blinding. Everything is white. My eyes flicker out of control. On, off, on,

16

off. It hurts so much I can't get a squeak out of my throat. I'm holding my breath.

Without warning, he makes his move on the other tooth.

"Almost finished," he says, the odor of burning enamel lingering around us. "What's Santa bringing for Christmas?"

"A yawg," I say around his fingers, not able to get out "dog." I've never spoken my wish to anyone. The pain forced it out of me.

"Uh-huh, that's nice." He seems unaware of the tears streaming past my temple into my ears. He pulls his hands away, his fingers bloody. "Spit," he commands, motioning to a porcelain bowl, a trickle of water spinning inside, making me nauseated. I gag. He forces a Dixie cup of water into my hand.

He finishes with the fillings, and afterward in the waiting room I find my worried mother at the receptionist's desk. I don't complain how much I hurt.

"All done?" she asks, smiling an artificial smile.

I nod, my cheeks full of cotton. Artie's paging through a book, sitting on a chair in the corner. He appears out of place in this waiting area so spare and clean.

She rubs my shoulder. "Yes," she tells the receptionist. "If you wouldn't mind billing us. I forgot my checkbook."

That night, my father taps lightly on my bedroom door. "Feeling better?" he asks.

I'm up on one elbow. A dull ache throbs in my jaw, but I want to appear brave.

"Would you like to hear a story?" His voice is low, mesmerizing.

"Okay."

My father's bedtime visits are sporadic. Most of the time it's my mother's job to tuck me in. She reads me stories from Golden Books; other times she lies next to me, holding my hand until I fall asleep.

"How about 'Puffy the Cloud'?" my father asks, reclining next to me.

17

"Puffy," he always starts out, "is a little cloud in the sky. He floats down, down, down, and comes in through the side door of our house, through the kitchen, through the hallway, to this bedroom.

"Hi, Jeffrey!" My father's voice now high-pitched, breathy. The voice of Puffy. "Climb aboard!"

Back in his narrator's voice, my father tells me I climb aboard. I shift under the covers as though I *am* climbing aboard. "Puffy's body is fluffy and soft like a big pillow," he continues. "Together, Jeffrey and Puffy float out of the bedroom, through the kitchen, through the hallway, out the side door, and into the night sky. They go up and up and up, and the night is clear."

I allow my head to sink into the pillow, closing my eyes to the dim, cobwebbed ceiling.

"Look, Jeffrey," says Puffy. "See down there? That's your school."

Although it's a December night, I imagine the story takes place on a warm spring afternoon. Children skip and dance on the playground.

"They keep floating," my father tells me, through the night sky. "Puffy is cozy."

I'm struggling against sleep.

"And see that tiny house down there?" says Puffy. "That's where your father grew up. And that big brown circle? That's the baseball field at Brown Park."

Puffy takes me on a flight high above the business district of South Omaha, above Seig Drugs, Hinky Dinky, and the Salvation Army, where we buy clothes. In my mind, I see squares and rectangles, building after building.

"Well," says Puffy, "it's time I got you home and into bed."

Together, I am told, we return to our neighborhood, past the ravine, over our backyard and house, floating "down, down, down, through the side door, through the kitchen, through the hallway, into this bedroom," where I "crawl back into bed."

As my father stands, he asks if I'd like a "parachute." Before I can answer, he grabs one end of my bed sheet, softly snapping it in the air, allowing it to unfurl into a rectangle. Slowly, he allows the sheet to float to the bed, to my body, covering me, my face.

Holiday Cheer

WINTER'S IN THE AIR," my father says, sneaking a TV from the Buick to the porch. He's taking a chance, not waiting for nightfall. The late-afternoon sky is a blank slate of whitish gray.

The throbbing of yesterday's tooth drilling is mostly gone; I'm stringing Christmas lights on our bushes out front. The bushes are strikingly green against the onset of winter. I make up a song.

"Christmas lights, are so bright! On the Japanese, Japanese, Japanese Jews!"

"Keep it down," he scolds under his breath. "And they're not Jews, dummy. They're yews. Japanese yews! Now get the door."

I'm embarrassed and release the tangle of lights to the frozen dirt. I run, and before I round the corner of our house, I see my father on the front steps, balancing the TV on one knee. He's glaring, but doesn't yell.

I go to the backyard, sprinting past the garage and storage shed to the edge of the ravine. Because the leaves are gone, I can spot the discarded washers, dryers, refrigerators, and tires that populate the ditch. Below me, a concentration of picture tubes and chassis, empty TVs, evidence of what my father and I discard in the night.

I speak my wish to my father.

"Not old enough," he says, hovering over a pan on the stove.

"Yes I am!" I'll be seven next May.

"Not old enough to be *responsible*."

"A *nice* dog," I emphasize. "Please? It won't bite!"

"You think I'm afraid of some little mutt? Besides, we can't afford another mouth to feed." He flips over a thick slice of ham.

19

"Hell, not even Santa can carry a year's worth of dog food on his sleigh."

"I had a dog," my mother says to him, coming into the kitchen, squeezing a paper bag of groceries.

He doesn't seem to hear her.

She shakes her platinum-blond head, frustrated.

I know I'm supposed to help retrieve the other bags from the car, but I plop to the linoleum where there's grease and bones and crumbs. "Ruff!" I hang my tongue, drooling.

"Damn it, kid," he says, "get off that filthy floor."

"Well, why not?" she demands.

He clanks his spatula.

"Dad? Did you hear what I said?" She never calls him Art or Arthur. "Are you listening? *I* had a dog growing up!"

"Yes, I'm listening, damn it. You had a dog growing up. But you lived on a farm. Well, we were too poor to have a dog. Or to live on a farm." My father often compares his childhood to my mother's. My father always wins. He insists his childhood was always worse.

"What does that have to do with now?" she says, letting the heavy bag slip to the counter. I'm grateful that my mother sticks up for me, but I don't want a fight. I know the routine. He'll pull out his worn wallet, flapping it open, snapping it closed, over and over, the wallet mimicking a hungry animal. They'll argue, and the TVs will get into the action. He'll yell "Shit!" like Fred Flintstone cries "Wilma!"

Most of their fights fizzle away. My father's emotions explode and quickly dissipate — a fast-moving storm. Soon, as he unscrews the back of another set, he's again whistling or singing, "The sun is out, the sky is blue, but it's raining, raining in my heart." He takes on the personality of his TVs — loud and jumpy one moment, his plug pulled the next. My mother, on the other hand, is sullen for hours or even days afterward.

"I say, hell no," he continues. "No dog. Not unless money

starts falling from the sky." He tilts his head and squints toward the grease-splattered ceiling. I never should have asked.

My mother leaves the kitchen and I get up, following her to the car, brushing off my clothes. Together we carry in the rest of the groceries, past my father, who is now in the dining room, working on a blond table model.

Without speaking, my mother and I put away the meats, the canned fruits and vegetables.

"Would you be a dear and sweep the kitchen?" she asks, going off to check on Artie.

I reach for the broom under the table. A torn Life cereal box will double for a dustpan. We haven't seen our dustpan in nearly a year. Meanwhile, around the corner, my father's in an argument with himself.

"Money," he mutters aloud. "Everything comes down to moneygoddamnedmoney."

"Well, Art," he says, "why the hell is that?"

"That's not what God wants!"

"It sure isn't."

"What's religion done for me?"

Two days before Christmas and still no tree. My mother and I have pleaded with him.

"We're broke."

After dark, without explanation, he leaves in the Plymouth. I can see from the window by the davenport that the car has left deep tracks on the driveway, the grooves filling in with snowflakes.

"Where'd Daddy go?" I ask my mother.

She doesn't know.

The empty driveway makes me lonely. The Buick is there, but it's the Plymouth's sea-green fins I love running my hands over. I think of the Plymouth as I use my tongue to make drawings in the moisture of the living room window, creating a snowman, a candle.

A half hour later, he's back, stomping into the house, bringing with him a tree, leaving a trail of needles and melting snow on the only bare path in the living room. The air comes alive with fresh evergreen.

"Ta-da!" He balances the tree against his recliner.

"Mommy, c'mon," I call. "We need to make room!" I see an opening near the fireplace. But we'll need to push a few sets out of the way.

"Later," he says, rubbing his purple gloveless hands together. "First, come help."

He's wearing his monster face and he's out the door. I'm hesitant, but grab my coat and follow.

Snow-covered trees hang over the roof of the Plymouth. Protruding from the car's trunk, more trees, already decorated with tiny red warning flags.

"They were on clearance," he says under his breath. "Guess how much?"

I shrug. I'm too excited to guess.

"C'mon, guess! You have to."

"A hundred million dollars!"

"Don't be stupid," he says, his volume turned up. "Think! How much?"

I take another look at the trees on the car, in the trunk. "Five dollars?"

"Five dollars?" His mouth is elastic and stretched wide, his breath steaming out. "No, I got the whole batch for eight. Eight bucks. Can you believe it? Can you believe how cheap they were?"

My mouth stretches, too. He begins snipping rope with his pocketknife, and one by one the trees spring to life and are removed from the car, lined against the house and chimney. There are eleven in all. As happy as I am to have these trees, I can't understand where we'll put them.

"Grab that end," he says, tipping the point of a tree toward the driveway. My fingers are quickly met by the pin-sharpness of the needles — I forgot my mittens.

I retract my hands. "Ouch!"

"Be a man!"

"It hurts."

"Oh, forget it," he says, raising the tree. "I'll do it myself." He grabs a second tree and proceeds into the backyard. The snow has eased up and I follow his footprints, my prints in his, me leaping to keep up with his stride.

He "plants" the first tree into a snowdrift as though claiming a mountain with a flag. He does the same with the second tree. I wait while he retrieves four more in one trip. Again he jabs them into the thick snow of the yard, near the swing set and near where my mother's tulips will bloom in spring. Eventually, all the trees are planted here. I run circles around and through our instant forest. I'm giggling, singing "Jingle Bells," and my father laughs, too. I can't stop running. Everything is white and evergreen, crisp and alive.

"We need decorations!" he decides. "Do we have enough decorations?"

I nod wildly.

"What are you waiting for?"

With numb toes I run toward the house, singing.

"And lights," he shouts. "Lots of lights."

We Get Along

NEAR THE TREE, among the TVs: unwrapped Matchbox cars, boxes of candy, pairs of socks. Packages of typing paper, felt-tip markers. I'm drawn to a pair of fins. The fins belong to something almost as large as my wagon—a Batmobile, its shiny dark plastic reflecting the tree's twinkling lights like stars in black water.

"Oh, my God!" I say. I step around everything to get to my new car. As I scrunch inside, my knees to my chest, disappointment sinks in. Although I can reach around my legs to grasp the steering wheel, it's immediately clear I'm too big.

My parents come into the living room grinning. My father calls, "Hooray for Batman!" He sings the theme from the TV show, Bing Crosby style. "Bu-bu-bu-Batman!"

"Shhh." My mother's voice is gentle. "You'll wake Artie."

"Sorry, honey," he says. I love that he calls her that.

My mother's in her pink robe. Her real hair, black as the Batmobile, falls into her tired eyes. My father's in the same red robe he wears every day, not just on Christmas. What he calls his "pee-pee" accidentally pokes out. "Oops," he jokes. "I'm a skinny apple with a worm." My mother laughs and teases him, making him pull his robe tighter. He laughs, too, as he fixes himself. I'm heartened by this display of affection.

"Do you like your Batmobile?" she asks me.

"I love it!" I say, shifting in the small seat. "Can you sew me a Batman outfit?"

"We'll see," she says.

"Did you see your Etch A Sketch?" my father asks, gesturing to the top of a table model, next to me.

I reach and find the flat toy, still in the box. I'm not used to getting new toys. This has the same red frame and gray screen I know from commercials. I remove the toy from its box and move my fingers over and around the embossed *Etch A Sketch* logo as though reading Braille.

"You can draw with it," he says, "and make pictures. It's practically a TV. See? It even has knobs!"

"He can play with it later," she says. "First I want to take his picture in the Batmobile!"

She reveals her Kodak Instamatic, holding the camera to her face, obscuring her eyes. As she says "Smile!" she smiles herself. It's all I can do not to exaggerate my mouth beyond a wide grin into something grotesque. But I don't want to ruin her snapshot. A white flash explodes from the ice-cube bulb and I briefly turn away to open wide, giving my mouth some relief.

"Try it," she says. "Push the pedal."

As my eyes adjust, I blindly search with my bare toes, tapping gently at first. Nothing. I press harder and lurch forward. Another camera flash goes off as I bump into a console, the motor whirring louder than my mother's blender.

"Maybe not in here, kid," my father says. "You're going to scratch all my sets."

I lift my foot off the pedal.

"How about you wait to ride that thing outside," he says. "Maybe in spring."

"No!" I protest.

"If we didn't have all this —" she says, not finishing her thought.

He goes off to the dining room. "Well, I'm going to enjoy *my* Christmas." I can hear him fiddling with the hi-fi. Soon, Bing Crosby is singing "White Christmas." My father joins in and together they form a duet.

"Don't worry," she says, winking at me from across the room. "We'll make room. But right now I have to make breakfast."

I get out of the Batmobile and drag it sideways to a path, then squeeze back inside. There are throw rugs creating a patchwork of streets; I imagine it's Saturday night and I'm about to head downtown for the early edition.

My father has stopped singing but Bing Crosby keeps going. My mother is clanging in the kitchen. I smell coffee.

"Like hell," she says.

There are lowered voices.

"My junk paid for Christmas." His voice picks up steam.

"We're suffering."

A pan is slammed against the stove. My father comes into the living room. His eyes dart to and from a corner of the ceiling. He makes a sound like he can't catch his breath.

"Your folks hate me!" he shouts to my mother. "They've hated me from day one."

I shake my head no.

"And do you know why?" he growls. "Because I'm not rich."

"Daddy, stop!" I yell.

My mother returns to the room.

"Go on," he says, gesturing. "Tell Jeffrey."

Tell me what?

"You're terrible," she says to him. "It's Christmas."

In my direction, he says, "Your grandmother wants me out of the way so your mother can go off and marry someone with a lot of money."

"My God," she pleads, in a voice under a scream. "That's not true."

"They want me goddamned dead."

"Daddy, please!"

My mother's eyes fill.

To get him to stop, I scream, "I'm Batman!" No one takes notice. My father's recliner is patched with duct tape. I burrow my pinkie around the tape, into a hole. I want to *be* my pinkie, deep inside the chair.

"I'm just trying to take care of my family," he says. "Is that such a sin?" He gazes past me, past his TVs, past Christmas, staring off into . . . I don't know what he's focused on. "Goddamn it, I try so hard!"

Even though it's winter and our windows are closed, I worry that the neighbors can hear. I'm covered in shame; shame is a blanket smothering me and is somehow also under my skin, in my heart and stomach. I'm suffocating. I don't want anyone to know about us, our arguments.

"Have you ever spent a night in jail?" he asks me.

I don't understand the question.

"Have you ever been humiliated?"

"You're insane!" my mother screams at him. "Leave him out of this!" I see myself driving to Mexico in my Batmobile.

She stomps off to check on my brother. My father bolts to the porch. When my mother returns with Artie, she instructs me to show him his new toys. There's a train. Blocks. Crayons. Or are the crayons for me? It doesn't matter; he's already scattering the crayons on the davenport.

Minutes later, we poke somberly at scrambled eggs and sausages at the dining room table, partially cleaned for the occasion. My mother takes exactly one bite. Before she can clear the dishes, my father guides everyone to the davenport. I remain standing. Artie is between them, rolling his toy car over his leg, over my father's leg. My father presents my mother with a tear-shaped gift, haphazardly wrapped in *World-Herald* newsprint, the words BLUE STREAK SPORTS stretched across the wide part of the gift. She carefully tears at the paper to reveal a frying pan. The pan rests on her lap, and inside the pan is taped a twenty-dollar bill. She says nothing, her eyes blankly fixed on the money. He reaches, hugging her.

"C'mon," he says, pulling close. "Let's forget the whole thing."

She only stares into the pan, at the money.

"Do you know how much I love your mother?" he says to me. His face is kind, calm. "But look, she doesn't even want me hugging her."

Although this attempt by my father to show my mother affection should reassure me, I take a step back. Maybe I'm picking up

on how shut down my mother is. On the other hand, there's a part of me that craves for her to say that she loves him, too.

"Hug him back, please," I say to her.

She doesn't look up from her lap.

I hand him his gifts of screwdrivers, Bic pens, batteries, and a flashlight. This is what he wants. This is what he always wants.

When my mother puts Artie and me in our Christmas outfits — matching white shirts, black pants, red vests, red bow ties — I'm proud to dress up; Artie squirms. For her part, she dabs on makeup and transforms into a brunette. But she can't camouflage her defeated expression. As a family, we attend Mass at St. Agnes Catholic Church. It's rare to have my father in the pew next to me — he did enough praying as a kid to last a lifetime, he says. He sings boldly and his voice resonates where my heart beats. My mother doesn't smile, not even at the end of Mass, while singing "Joy to the World."

The Relatives

A S WE DRIVE, Artie and I try out the walkie-talkies, another Christmas gift, but we're too close to each other and the toy's feedback is too loud for my father. "Try the Etch A Sketch," he says.

"Okay, Daddy." I twist the knobs of the toy, coordinating my hands, turning both knobs to create Santa, to keep Artie entertained in the back seat. He's getting too big for my mother's lap. I let him shake the screen.

"Bye-bye," he says to Santa, shrieking happily.

I make a bunny and let him repeat the game.

"Bye-bye, bunny!"

I do the same with a car, then a kitty. Artie giggles but our parents aren't speaking. In the rearview mirror, my father's eyes wink in tandem, causing his nose to wiggle.

My grandparents are pleasant to my father, and my father pats my grandfather's shoulder, wiping away the things he said earlier, like forgetting a bad dream. My mother's sisters are here. Their husbands and children, too. The house is brimming with the aroma of kolaches, roasted duck. We open our presents of bubble soap and candy and hug Grandma and Grandpa. My mother receives perfume — she spritzes a little on her wrist, on my wrist — my father, a set of screwdrivers.

"Wonderful!" he shouts. "Just what I need!"

Our family also receives a bulky leather-bound Catholic Bible.

"This is the nicest Bible we've ever had," my father declares. He is sincere. As far as I know, we have no other Bibles in our house. After all, we only joined St. Agnes last year so we could get Artie baptized.

We eat, and afterward my father sips from a beer bottle at one end of the table, the rest of the men telling jokes at the other. He laughs with his entire body, but my uncles turn their chairs, their backs to him. A replica of *The Last Supper* hangs askew on a wall behind my father.

In the other room, my aunts chatter on about distant cousins and which great-uncle is having surgery, which great-aunt is dying. My mother plays her role, nodding when everyone else nods.

"Let's play with your walkie-talkies," my cousin Dickie suggests.

I'm glad for the attention, even though he once bit my arm for no reason.

"Go to the basement," he commands. The basement is home to my grandfather's workshop, but it's also where my uncle Jethro dwells. The door is always shut, a yellow line underneath all that glows in the musty darkness. The big silence behind his door makes my heart race. Sometimes I just barely hear the mournful strumming of a guitar. Jethro is my mother's oldest brother. He's always lived with my grandparents, but rarely makes an appearance, especially during large gatherings. When he does come out, he doesn't speak. "He's a damn recluse," my father says.

My mother can't help but notice that Jethro dresses like Charles Starkweather. He even wears his hair in a pompadour, and there's always a cigarette dangling from his lips. She lived on the family farm during the Starkweather murder spree, the farm less than fifty miles from Lincoln, where Starkweather claimed his first victim. For as long as I can remember, my mother has spoken of Starkweather, but also of "bad weather," and from time to time I confuse the two.

Gathering my courage, I sneak down the wooden steps and duck into the brown darkness of the workshop. To ease my fears, I pretend I'm in a submarine on a secret mission.

I squeeze the red light of the talk button.

"Come in," I say. "Do you read me?"

No answer.

Above, the sound of feet, both heavy and light, pacing, running.

"Come in," I repeat.

An electronic crackle.

"I'm here," whispers Dickie.

"What's your location?" I ask.

"Under the table," he says. "Spying on your dad."

"What's he doing?"

"I don't know."

Simultaneously I hear my father's laughter through the walkie-talkie and through the ceiling. "What else do you see?"

While I wait for an answer, my eyes adjust, allowing my grandfather's tools to emerge on the walls, unearthly shapes forming out of the darkness.

"Come in," I say, holding down the button.

Above, the sound of a hailstorm in the dining room. A spilled bag of marbles?

"Hello?" I press the button as hard as I can. The red light radiates through my skin, making my thumb a pink x-ray.

I stand, peering around the corner. The light from under the door reassures me that Jethro is in his room, but I still climb the stairs two at a time.

I wander through the house and find Dickie in the living room, watching TV with the other cousins.

"Where's my walkie-talkie?" I ask.

He ignores me.

"Mommy," I say, "Dickie won't give me back my walkie-talkie!"

"What's that son of mine done now?" asks Dickie's mother.

"Maybe it's under the table," Dickie says.

My father slides his chair back, bending, searching at his ankles.

"Hey!" he cheers, holding up the toy. "It's right here!" A wire hangs loose, the antenna nothing more than a broken finger. I break into tears.

"Don't worry," my father insists. "I'll fix it good as new!"

My mother escorts me outside.

"But Mommy."

In the biting wind she brushes my grandfather's sawdust from my pants. My face is freezing cold from my tears. "If you were a girl," she says gently, "I wouldn't have to worry about you getting into so much trouble, would I?" She kisses the top of my head and gives me a pat on the butt.

We head indoors, and my mother tells me I'd better round up Artie so we can get going. I run ahead, past my father, who's alone at the table, my cracked walkie-talkie a pile of plastic and wire next to his empty beer bottles.

"C'mon, Daddy," I say, "Mommy wants to go!"

"I'll fix this later," he says, his eyes red. "I promise."

We drive west across Omaha, to the nicer and newer part of town, where there are, according to my father, "good" garage sales. Aunt Jean lives here, with my father's mother, "Granny." Jean opens the front door, releasing the smell of Vicks VapoRub. Her carpeted floor is expansive, but plastic rugs and runners direct visitors' movements. I do not stray from these paths. It would worry me to do otherwise.

31

There are paintings on nearly every wall, paintings of forests, mountains, and wet city streets filled with people and horse-drawn carriages. It's as if her house is filled with frozen TV screens. Aunt Jean had once been a Sunday painter. One of her paintings hangs in our dining room—a seascape my father says was painted from a photograph of Granny's village in Czechoslovakia. In the painting, an old woman carries a heavy basket on a dirt path that leads to a white and foamy ocean—the "Czech Ocean," my father calls it, though there is no such thing.

"Dobry den, Mother." My father speaks to her partly in Czech. She responds in Czech, words I can't follow they go by so fast, the sounds thick and running together, a vowelless train.

"Jeffrey," she says, rolling the "r" in my name. She grins kindly, her cheekbones stretching her wrinkly skin. From under a shawl she produces a small Popeye toy. The toy is a plastic figurine on a round pedestal, its limbs held together with rubber bands, maybe, or strings. When she presses a button underneath his legs, his body trembles and contorts, a strange dance.

Granny worked hard all her life, my father always says, and her hands bear him out as her knobby fingers squeeze the toy.

We go back home, and from the street our simple white house, with its twinkling lights, appears warm and inviting. The yellow house next door is dark, undecorated. I used to think Frank and Mary were neighbors we didn't get along with until my father explained that Frank is my uncle—my father's older and only living brother. He says that Mary, Frank's wife, is a witch, and to this even my mother agrees. I am told that my father hasn't spoken to his brother since Frank and Mary ran from our house when I was two, Mary gagging at the smell of my mother changing my diaper. The only time Frank acknowledges me is when he calls me "bastard," when I make ovals with my bike on our driveway, the narrow and oily cement strip that separates our houses. I don't know what a bastard is, only that my father never uses the word. Yet the mere sound of "bastard" tells me that I'm something awful.

32

Dogie

I T'S NEW YEAR'S DAY, 1968, and as I watch two networks' parade coverage at once, I overhear my father theorize to my mother that with Super Bowl II only two weeks away, we're bound to have a taste of good fortune. My father never talks sports and never gambles—he doesn't know the teams in the Super Bowl. Yet he loves to make predictions about the weather and our finances, and this time his vision for TV sales comes true. In a few days he nearly empties the porch of all his finest TVs, black-and-white and color. "Thank God above for the Super Bowl," he says, gazing upward, clasping his hands. He squeaks.

Whatever the reason, the TVs sell, which means more cash in his pocket, which allows him to buy more broken sets to fix and resell, which ultimately makes him happy enough to go around the house singing "Sentimental Journey."

A few days of Christmas break remain, and I'm rejuvenated, wearing down the tips of Flair pens, filling sheets of paper. I always have an ample supply of paper in my dresser. And what I draw, over and over, are dogs.

I sketch dogs from my head and dogs from our neighborhood.

I've probably seen more people on TV than I have in real life. Same for animals. I don't know much about breeds—dogs are simply small, medium, or large. I experiment, creating the kind of pet I would love to have.

It's on the last day of Christmas break that Dogie the Doggie makes his appearance. I don't know how the name comes to me. Maybe from hearing my father sing "Whoopie-ti-yi-yo, git along you little dogies." Dogie, like Snoopy, walks upright. He's also confident like Snoopy. But he's different enough from Snoopy to

33

make him "original." He's tall as a man, his fur a pale brown. His contour is made of rough and scratchy lines. All weekend I sketch him. In Dogie's world, he makes nice with squirrels, talks to birds and bunnies. He cruises in a convertible, his scarf fluttering behind him. Most of the time I draw him in profile—I can't quite figure out how to draw him straight on. His eye is always a simple black dot, a period at the end of a sentence. And when he's content, his eye is a brief, happy dash.

My mother dotes on my dog character. Much as I love making my mother smile, what I really want is to exist within my drawings. If I can make my characters perfect, if I can make my characters real enough, maybe I can join them in their world of clean white paper. As I draw, I want to get as close as possible to the lines I create. I often nap on the floor of my room, on top of my sketches, my drool smudging my pencil marks, making my pen lines bleed. The paper is my second skin.

Midnight Oil

A T HAWTHORN MY TEACHER thinks I'm not getting enough sleep. The reason she thinks this is that I'm always yawning. And while it's true that I have no set bedtime and can stay up as late as I want watching TV, not all of my yawns are real yawns. Sometimes a craving bubbles up from deep within me and makes its way to my face, or my neck, or my limbs. If I ignore it, the craving cries out for attention. So when she sees my mouth open like a cave and asks in front of the class if I'm sleepy, I nod. This is my way of hiding my nervous habits in plain sight. But when I can't stop my mouth, I lift my desk lid and stick my head inside, pretending to look for something for a long time. And when we have air-raid drills and are made to "duck and cover," I'm most content. Because in the shadow of my desk, I'm free to move my face however I please.

· · ·

Bobby Thompson comes out of nowhere. The tallest kid in first grade, he sits unnoticed in the back of the room. After Christmas break, it's a different story.

Yesterday, the teacher hung my drawing of a rocket on the bulletin board. We'd been instructed to keep ourselves busy — doing puzzles, reading, most anything so long as we sit quietly at our desks. I asked for a large sheet of manila paper and sketched, as best I could recall, a three-stage rocket. The launch pad gave me the most trouble — I thought of my Erector Set as I sketched and colored a tower made of crisscrosses. In black lettering I wrote "U.S.A." vertically, top to bottom, on the rocket. Last, I added an American flag to the capsule. As soon as I finished the drawing, I raised my hand.

"Yes, Jeffrey?"

My mouth went dry. It was unusual for me to raise my hand. I fixated on the floor, wanting to disappear into its wooden crevices.

"What is it?" she said.

Instead of words, all that came from my throat was a quick, shrill note.

"Do you need a drink of water?"

The habits that make noise are more difficult to conceal. "I made a drawing."

"Why don't you bring it up?"

Hesitantly, I got up from my desk in the middle of the room and approached her. I could feel my classmates eyeing me, trying to figure me out as if I were a puzzle. As they usually do when I make the sounds.

"That's very nice," she said, studying my efforts. "May I hang this on our bulletin board?"

I nodded.

When I returned to my seat, she cleared her throat, which made me clear my throat. "Class, I have an announcement." She held up my sketch. "See what Jeffrey made for us?"

The blood rushed to my ears; I hadn't thought ahead, hadn't

counted on this attention. But it made me happy to see her holding up my drawing, to get her approval.

"Do we have any other artists who want to share their work? Anyone with a story or a poem?"

No one responded, and she proceeded to tack my rocket at each corner onto the corky surface. I was grateful everyone was now scrutinizing my drawing, and not me.

It was this morning, as I entered the classroom, that I noticed a larger, sleeker version of a three-stage rocket hanging next to mine. This rocket's stages were numbered—1, 2, 3—which bothered me because real spaceships don't come that way. Yet the rocket itself was striking, everything large and bright, detailed with hatches and bolts—far more complete than my version, which now, in contrast, seemed to have come from the kindergarten room.

Before our first subject, math, the teacher addressed the class: "As you can see, we have *two* artists in this room. Last night, our own Bobby Thompson went home and came up with the masterpiece you see before you."

We turned and faced the last row, near the aquarium, where big Bobby Thompson's awkward body was wedged into his desk. Through the thick glare of his glasses, I could not see his eyes. Bobby Thompson was reserved and mysterious, and I admired the way he accepted our teacher's compliment with quiet confidence. While everyone else continued to stare at Bobby, I slid down in my seat, stretching my hand to the floor, digging my pinkie's nail into a groove.

"Bobby," she continued, "you must have stayed up quite late working on this, burning the midnight oil." *The midnight oil.*

"Yes, ma'am," he said shyly.

I dug my nail a little deeper into the gooeyness between the planks.

Did midnight oil help you draw better? I wondered. And if so, where could I get it? I could almost taste it—licoricey, warm, soothing. Black syrup with sugar.

Times Square

AFTER THE SUPER BOWL, in celebration of all of his sales, my father sets up a little bar in the dining room, which he's begun calling the family room. The bar is an old wooden cabinet he stocks with bottles of whiskey and sweet wine. A chrome ice bucket sits atop the bar, reflecting the party lights that surround it. I'm mesmerized by a Miller High Life decoration, its white blips of light bouncing, chasing each other. Above the bar, hanging from the ceiling, there's a spinning blue orb encircled by a white ring. At one time there must have been an advertisement wrapped around the white ring, but all that's left is glue. I imagine my father's bar is Times Square.

As his sales wane, his visits to Times Square increase. So do the fights with my mother. When my mother yells back, he clutches his chest, claiming he's going to "keel over."

Now and then someone leaves our frigid porch with a TV, but for the most part the phone stops ringing. My father rereads his ads every Saturday night to make sure the printed phone number is correct.

"See?" he says. "Haven't I always said February is the worst month?" He glares at the phone, willing it to ring. Every few minutes he picks up the receiver and listens for the dial tone. "Still working," he says. He hangs up, pauses, lifts the receiver again, pressing it against his ear, keeping it there, making it part of his head. He nods. *Still* working. He again hangs up. "I'll bet anything we're wiretapped."

He complains that spring is a long way off. He reassures us that warmer weather will be good for sales. "Everybody's broke because of Christmas and the Super Bowl," he reasons.

One day, after he comes home from the Union Pacific—the U.P., he calls it—he rushes to Times Square and chugs from a tall green bottle.

"That damn hellhole," he says. "The U.P. is *pee-you.*" He pinches the tip of his nose.

"Maybe we'd all be better off if I jumped off the bridge," he says nonchalantly, taking stock of what's left in the bottle. He stands over his recliner. The only time he uses it is when he's passed out. Right now it contains a stack of boxes.

I know what "the bridge" means.

We live a block from the entrance of the South Omaha Bridge, which crosses the Missouri River. When we hear sirens and run to the corner to find that police have blocked off the bridge, we know something bad has happened in the netherworld between Nebraska and Iowa. Maybe it's a car accident. Or worse, maybe someone has leapt into the muddy and churning waters below. A neighbor died that way last summer. I can never ride my bike around his house without feeling sorry for the widow, who keeps up her flowers as if nothing happened. When my mother and I drive home by way of Missouri Avenue—my father calls it Misery Avenue—I'm relieved not to see police blocking the bridge, and every night I pray my father won't jump.

Blowing Up

BESIDES THE ADDITION of Times Square, our home begins to see other changes. Around the time I turn seven, my father somehow squeezes his drum kit into the middle of the living room.

When he plays, he closes his eyes to this world—our world —making all of us go away. His limbs kick, tap, smack. But his face is at peace, the drums taking him back to when he played dance halls with his orchestra. His slogan in the 1940s was "Dance and be gay with Artie Kay." He must daydream about the nights he played the drums with Johnny Carson, when Johnny was a traveling magician in the Midwest. My father rarely misses *The Tonight Show*, always reminding us that his drums were set up behind Johnny, allowing him to see how Johnny's tricks were accomplished. "I know all his secrets," he'll say, recalling his carefree days on the road.

When he's not playing, he insists Artie and I practice.

"Both of my boys are going to be drummers, by God," he declares. "If there's one thing I'm going to do in my life, if I can't be rich, it's to teach my kids to play drums."

"I don't want to," I say.

"Be a man."

"No."

"I'll teach you paradiddles!" He laughs at my stubbornness, speaking "paradiddles" as if it's a magic word, like "abracadabra." He guides me through the house by my shoulders, sits me on his stool, and hovers behind me, the smell of his whiskey on my neck, tutoring me on how to hold the sticks, how to keep time, one, two, one, two. If I miss a beat he'll grunt, "No, goddamn it. Like this!" He wraps his hands around mine, strangling them, pressing the sticks into my palms until my palms turn red.

Together we pound the tom-toms, crash cymbals, create a circus-style drumroll. And when he imitates a walking bass line with his voice, we form a rhythm section.

He's begging my mother to sit at his drums.

"C'mon, Lennie," he says. It's always "Lennie," "hon," "honey-bunch," "Ma." Never "Helen."

"I'm too busy to play music," she explains.

"Look how she ignores me," he addresses the ceiling while attempting to massage her shoulders. She nudges him away. He tries to kiss her cheek, but she shakes her head so much, I worry she'll lose her brown wig.

He hugs her from behind, asks again; reluctantly, and with great effort, she makes her way to the drums. At first she appears awkward. Gently, she tinkles a cymbal. The cymbal barely moves, and I imagine a flying saucer hovering in the sky.

"C'mon," he groans. "You can do better than that."

She strikes the snare once.

"That's better!"

She hits it again.

"Good!" He claps.

Then again, harder.

She bursts with energy, her hands crisscrossing, randomly banging on the snare and tom-toms and on the golden cymbals, making them go blurry. The house fills with clicking and pounding, crashing. She grins proudly and shouts, "Look at me!" Artie covers his ears and screams.

"No!" my father scolds, his hands now clasped in prayer. He goes to her, stands behind her, choking her hands as he does with me.

"No *yourself!*" She twists away. He takes a step back, against a box. Calmly, she places the sticks on the snare. A cymbal continues to ring as she makes her way from the living room. It scares me how calm she is. I've never before seen such an act of defiance toward my father.

• • •

40

He tells me to turn off *The Flintstones.* "This is more important!" he says. It's unusual for him to tell anyone to turn off a TV.

"No."

"It's for your future! Don't you want to get rich and famous and go on Johnny Carson?"

I shake my head, my lips pressed tight.

"Open your mouth," he says. When he's not forcing drum lessons on us, he's making us sing.

Please don't make me.

"C'mon, let's hear your scales. *Bu-bu-bu-bu.*" The notes rise higher with each *bu*. And down, like going into a basement. "*Bu-bu-bu-buuuum.*"

It's not that I hate singing; it's that I hate singing in front of him.

"Ba, ba, ba," I say flatly, keeping my eye on the TV. Fred and Barney are going bowling.

"No, no, no. *Buuuuuuuum.*" His low voice is rich and resonant.

"Baaah," I say, in the voice of a lamb.

"Don't get smart with me!" He clicks off the set.

"I'm not!" I watch the screen, a pinprick of light holding steady — a solitary star.

He slumps his shoulders. "Do you know I once sang live on the radio with a big band? That was in Memphis, back in the late forties."

"Yes."

"Do you know I was once asked to join a band that headed off to New York?"

I watch the blank screen, the reflection of his legs. I have no idea what Memphis looks like. I can't remember seeing anything on TV about Memphis. But New York is a place full of sound and light and commotion.

"Oh, you don't give a shit."

"Yes I do!"

"Did you know radio waves never die out? They just keep going into space? One day, astronauts will travel into space to retrieve old radio signals. I'll be dead and gone but you'll be able to listen to me sing. Think about it. Somewhere in deep space, I'm still singing. I'm still somebody."

"You're going to ruin your eyes, sitting that close," my mother warns from the other room, even though the TV is off. She moves toward my father, her hand gripping Artie's. "Here," she says, arranging Artie's hair. "He's your son, too."

"You think I don't know that? He's going to be a drummer!" He leans, takes Artie's chubby hand, placing it firmly against his shirt pocket.

"*Bu-bu-bu, boo,*" he sings. "Can you feel my chest vibrate?"

"*Booo!*" Artie sings.

At least when Artie pays attention to him, I don't have to worry about my father dying. All it takes is for one of us to listen — one of us to play the drums or sing.

It's a summer afternoon, a Saturday, and my mother is in the living room, pushing the vacuum cleaner here and there in short, quick bursts, almost scrubbing at the narrow paths. My father's back from his collecting, leaning over Times Square, pouring a second drink. He's also brought home an opened bag of colorful balloons, which he instructs us to inflate. We blow until we're dizzy, then bat around the balloons, playing "keep it up," bouncing them off the obstacles of the room. Once in a while I press a balloon to my face, peering in, imagining I am small enough to live inside these bright balls of air.

When he drinks, he might clobber out an ear-thumping solo. Or might pass out in his recliner. I am grateful for any option that doesn't end in a fight.

"Here," he tells us, grabbing at a blue balloon. "Have I ever taught you boys about static electricity?" He rubs the balloon against his shirtsleeve, steadies the balloon on a wall, making it stick. "Now you try!"

We wildly rub balloons on our clothes, but because of the junk, we can't reach the walls. Balloons won't stay put on the brick of the fireplace. Again my parents yell at each other about not having grocery money. Artie yells, too.

"Stop it!" I demand, leaping from the davenport.

"Why don't you all just kill me now," my father shouts.

"You're crazy," my mother says, her face turning red.

"Stop. It!" If only I were loud enough, louder than either of them, maybe I could get them to stop.

There's a pause. A pause is not good.

"Goddamn it!" He spanks a TV with his hand.

My throat is nervously chirping, but I attempt a scale. *"Bu-bu-bu-boo!* Come on, Daddy, sing!"

He ignores me. I scurry to his drum set to retrieve a pair of drumsticks I will hand him, but it's too late. My father heaves a box of tubes across the room; the tubes, as fragile as eggs, shatter against the wall, spraying glass. Balloons scatter.

The house goes still, dead silent, even though TVs continue to run. A white balloon defies gravity, hovers near him.

"Why does everyone hate me?" he shouts, his voice making his snare sizzle. "Why are you all against me?" Glass is everywhere, on the tops of TVs, inside boxes. Everything glistens with the sheen of fresh sleet. The balloon bounces off a TV, landing on my shoes. The floor is also sprayed with glass. My toes curl inside my shoes, afraid of getting cut.

My mother tries to talk sense: "No one's against you!"

"Like hell!" He kicks the side of the TV to make one last point, leaving a dent in the wood-grain metal. Artie takes a swipe at a red balloon that teeters on the top of a TV, sending the balloon to the ceiling. When my father hoists big Artie to his chest, I know the fight is over. "At least Artie still loves Daddy, don't you?" Artie kisses my father's cheek. My father smiles.

I take another look at the fragments of glass before moving carefully from the room, outside.

Our backyard. At one time, the patio was free and clear to ride my rusting blue Schwinn and to bounce black Super Balls the size of baseballs. Now an army-green tarpaulin hides more junk. Behind our old garage? Our newly constructed redwood garage. And past that, past my mother's garden at the edge of our yard, lies the TV cemetery. When we discard worthless picture tubes into the dark ravine, sometimes they explode. My father even allows me to throw bricks into the blackness of the ditch, as a treat, to make the picture tubes go off like bombs. But because these deeds are performed at night, I am never able to see the glass fly.

Beyond the ravine, to the west through a brigade of trees, I see a sliver of orange sunlight. In the distance a dog barks. I imagine it licking my hand.

Above, I search the purple and choppy sky for the first star of the evening. Too cloudy. I become aware that our yard is swarming in lightning bugs. A train whistles. Crickets are in full symphony. As I run circles through the weedy yard, I imagine the lightning bugs are stars and I'm in a rocket ship hurtling through space where my father sings.

Now Playing

AS MY MOTHER, Artie, and I return from Mass, my father greets us on the porch. He's hiding something behind his back. "I have a surprise," he says.

"What is it?" I ask. Artie grabs at my father's arms.

"We had some luck," he says, stopping us.

"That's nice," my mother says, not interested.

"Show us!" I say. From his smile I can tell something good is going to happen.

"Let's celebrate!" My father reveals twenty-dollar bills, seven in all, fanned like playing cards.

"How about a movie!" I shout. I've been asking all summer, but his answer is always "Hell no!"

"Why not!" he says. How easily his answer comes. "How about the drive-in?"

"Are you kidding?" my mother says, taken aback.

"Dead serious," he says.

"I don't know." She moves into the house, past a Motorola as large as a stove. "It's expensive," she calls from inside.

"We'll want to leave before dusk," he tells me, ignoring my mother's concerns.

Artie and I jump and I ask which movie, but he says we'll be surprised when we get there. I hug my father at the waist; his hands are preoccupied with the money so he can't hug back. Artie and I hug. If my mother becomes happy about the movie, we'll all be happy forever.

"Now," my father says to me, "go clean your room."

I pull on a red-and-white-striped T-shirt and a pair of shorts and stuff my other clothes from the floor into my closet, gathering my drawings, hiding them wherever I can. I've never been to a drive-in, and only once have I seen a movie in a theater. One summer day, my mother and I took a bus to the Chief. I was three, maybe four. The instant we entered, my eyes went fuzzy. As we inched forward through the blackness, I gripped her hand tightly; her flesh, after the bus trip and the heat of the day, was warm and damp. I held my breath and frantically searched above, but except for her palm, she had dissolved into the darkness. Music swirled. I searched for my feet, but my feet were gone, too. Finally, when we were in our seats, my sight reignited, and bright colors jumped from the screen and the music became friendly. But it is the darkness, the dissolving, that I remember most from that day.

In the back seat of the Plymouth, the interstate trembling beneath, I stretch out, my head on the pillow my mother brought in case I don't make it through the movie. "It'll be late by the time we get home," she cautions.

"We're getting closer," my father says, exiting and taking us under the bridge that carries the traffic that had rushed behind us moments before. Two blocks later, my father stops unexpectedly at a lone filling station that appears to have been dropped into the middle of a cornfield. Suburban houses sprout on the horizon.

"I have to make a call," he says.

"Why?" my mother asks.

"That guy lives out this way, down, let's see, which county road was it?" He's unraveling a scrap of paper.

"Guy?"

"That guy who wasn't answering his phone earlier. His ad says he has a color console. 'Needs work. Best offer.' What if I can get it for ten bucks? What if I don't have to do very much to it? Think how much I could make on it."

"But the movie," I interject.

"I just want to make sure he has it, so he can hold it for me until we get there."

My father strides to a pay phone, hand in pocket, digging for a dime. Artie is half singing words that don't exist. *Please stop singing.* I need an ally besides my mother. I need Artie to worry also. If only he would cry. We wait, the three of us, in the stifling heat of the car. The vinyl seat sticks to my bare legs. My mother, cracking her window, lets in the heavy warmth that lingers outside. Rows of corn barely move in the thick air, in the growing shadows.

Artie quiets his singing and teethes the vinyl of the seat. I'm watching my father wiggle a pen on a paper scrap when I hear the metallic crunch behind us, some distance away. The accident happens in an instant. Missing is the long announcement of screeching tires I'm used to hearing on Misery Avenue. I roll down my window and poke my head out to get a better view—nothing. My father throws himself inside the Plymouth and we rumble from the parking lot.

A cluster of people has already gathered under the bridge, a community forming like strangers in church, and we move to take our places among them. A car lies on its side, a mammoth made of metal and chrome, bleeding fluids that could have been any color, but in the tailspin toward nightfall, in the wide underbelly of the bridge, are shiny black.

The air under the bridge isn't moving—it's stale and oily, and I tug at the neck of my T-shirt to loosen myself from its tightness.

Shards of window glass remain frozen in their tracks not far from our feet. Above, what was once the guardrail is now a thick, crinkled rope of metal dangling from the bridge, revealing the place where the car had barged through and taken flight.

An object that might be a large warped suitcase, or part of the car's seat, a mere leap from the car, has attracted its own half halo of a crowd, which keeps its distance, as if moving too close were somehow dangerous. We wait from where we stand. A figure moves toward the suitcase or seat or whatever it is. A figure I realize is my mother. How had I missed her leaving my side?

She kneels beside the lumpish form and a splash of light illuminates her, her hands folded in the way she holds them in church. My hands are clasped tightly against my chest, too. *Please God.* But I'm not sure what I'm praying for. Despite the roar of traffic above, a bubble of imperfect silence envelops us, how St. Agnes Church sounds on its busy street.

A man moves toward my mother and places his hand on her shoulder. They merge, forming a single silhouette. In the distance, a siren. And another. Now a red light rotates above, at the open gash of the bridge.

I squint hard against a sudden flash. It's different from that of my mother's camera—this white light burns on, an errant star floating under the bridge, lost from its constellation in the young night sky. The light moves away and I blink, squinting at the cameraman who is panning the crowd, his spotlight sweeping, searching.

A stretcher is slipped from the ambulance; I'm asked to spin away by my father. "Don't turn around until I tell you, okay?" he

47

says gently. He manages to hold Artie, Artie's legs dangling, his thick arms around my father's neck.

I'm squinting again, this time to distort the lights, and it comes to me that we are in the street, an unnatural place to stand. It's as though I am suspended mere inches above an ocean without a boat or life jacket, floating in air, waiting to fall in. At my side, I sense my father. If only he would speak again, even a single word to hold me.

"We prayed for him," I hear my mother tell my father. "And the minister prayed, too." Her voice is low and calm. Her bedtime voice.

Back in our car, a hush floods over me. A watery quiet, small and languid. My father says he's taking a different route home, to avoid the interstate, and that's all that's said for several minutes. Without a fuss, Artie has fallen asleep in my mother's lap. My eyes are blinking rapidly, making our drive flicker, an old movie.

"Why don't we stop at your parents'?" my father asks my mother brightly, taking his eyes from the road, glancing at her. "We'll never make it home in time for the news."

I wait for her response, which never comes. Maybe she's as thrown off as I am by his suggestion.

"They should still be up, right?"

We creak into my grandparents' driveway, behind Jethro's '57 Chevy. My grandfather answers the door, rosary beads clicking, dripping from his fingers. He always prays at night.

"No time," my father says, rushing ahead to warm up their TV.

My grandmother appears from her bedroom, tying her robe; there's no sign of Jethro. We go to their living room, where my father stands over their console, and the rest of us settle into their davenport. The Motorola's picture comes into view, showing an announcer in a suit.

"I hope we didn't miss it," my father says.

My grandparents listen patiently as my father recounts the accident, all while fiddling with their set. I learn details. The man's

48

legs were buckled under his body. My mother gets caught up in the story and explains that she asked the man if he was Roman Catholic, but he couldn't speak. "I wish a priest could have given him last rites."

"Tsk," my grandmother says. "How awful."

My grandfather worries the rosary beads in his hand.

My father changes the subject. "I can get you a nice color table model," he tells them. He's a puppeteer behind the set, making the announcer in the suit go from black to disintegrating white. "Wouldn't color be nice? Maybe a Philips?" He adjusts the picture to somewhere in the middle, where it was before his tweaking.

"At the top of our broadcast," the announcer says, "we reported that a man had been thrown from his car during a serious accident."

"Thank God we didn't miss it!" my father says.

"We now know," the announcer continues, "that the man was pronounced dead at Clarkson Hospital. His identity is being withheld pending notification of relatives."

The image of a smashed-up car, on its side, fills the screen. "Look," my father says, reaching for my shoulder. "It's our accident!" Even lit up, the car is unrecognizable for what it once was.

A shot of the crowd flashes on the screen.

"Oh, my God! Look, Jeffrey," he says proudly, patting my back, "there you are!"

But I catch only a glimpse. I almost don't recognize myself — my striped shirt is in black and white. I see my father's pant leg, his elbow, Artie's foot.

"What's it like to be famous?" he asks me.

I shrug. I thought famous was sitting next to Johnny Carson, and afterward going to the beach with beautiful women. All I can think about is the man who fell and died.

We get home and I can't sleep. All night, I sketch a car accident over and over, never quite getting it right.

Halloween Heart

THE SCHOOL YEAR starts and there's no sign of Bobby Thompson. We were never friends—both of us were too shy—but I am sad that he is gone. I look around my second-grade classroom, and those I recognize appear older, bigger. The girls are prettier. Everyone, I'm convinced, has matured over the summer except for me.

During our first recess I discover that some students have gone through more than physical changes.

"I hear your dad's a junk dealer," says a boy who was nice to me last year.

"Yeah," says another. "Koterbutt lives in a junkyard."

"It's Jeffrey Koterjunk!" declares yet another, a boy with a gap in his teeth.

Laughter.

My eyes want to flutter, beg to flutter. I can't let them. Not now. But these tics have a mind of their own, a will I cannot fight.

"Hey Queerbutt, you winking at me?" says toothless boy.

I want to shove my finger into the gap between his teeth. Not to hurt him, but because my finger might enjoy the sensation.

"You want a fist in your face, Queerbutt?"

This time I'm spared getting hit, yet my stomach burns from phantom punches. I'm a recurring playground spectacle. And some days the ridicule shadows me back to my neighborhood, where many of these same kids live, and they chase me down, tackling me, kicking and punching me. I'm relieved when the bell rings, and slowly I follow my classmates to our new room, our new teacher. She is pretty, her jet-black hair like Mary Tyler Moore's on *The Dick Van Dyke Show*. My stomach's still queasy, and to comfort myself I reach for the floor like an old friend, digging in my nail. The floor isn't as far away as last year. Next to me, a girl with a platinum bob giggles softly. Nancy. I'm not sure why she's giggling. She reminds me of Goldie Hawn. Maybe it's the hair. I sit up, not wanting her to see my pinkie in the hard-wood's groove.

Sitting next to Nancy, watching her raise her hand, listening as she answers a geography question, helps me forget about the names I am called, the threats made by other boys. At night, when trying to sleep, she's all I think about.

Nancy never makes fun of me for my facial expressions or my sounds.

I love her and I want her to love me back.

I don't know how to make her love me.

When the boys and the girls form separate lines to go to the bathroom, she always tries to stand next to me, but we are not al-lowed to speak.

On the playground, the boys don't mix with the girls.

All I can do is watch her, at her desk next to me, digging my pinkie into the floor.

It's the end of September, and in my bedroom I sketch pump-kins, black cats, vampire bats, and skeletons for Nancy. I create a connect-the-dots puzzle that will outline the shape of a heart. The idea came from my mother, who slips homemade puzzles under my pillow in place of money when I lose a tooth. From a box in the basement, I find a tarnished ring.

"Dear Nancy," I write on a sheet of paper. "Here are some drawings and a puzzle. I love you." I place everything inside an envelope and, last, drop in the ring. I lick the gluey strip five times. It's so wet it won't stick; I tape it shut.

The next morning, when the teacher is writing subtraction problems on the blackboard, I hand Nancy the envelope. I'm so nervous I could throw up. I ground myself with my other hand, running my fingers between the floorboards.

She smiles as though she's been expecting the envelope. Carefully, she slips it into her math book. The best part is that she jots *me* a note, sneaks it to me. It reads: "I'll open it when I get home."

After school, I linger in my classroom.

"Yes?" my Mary Tyler Moore says, smiling, wondering why I'm still sitting at my desk. "You're not in trouble, Jeffrey. You may go."

I take my time. I'm relieved the front of the school is nearly deserted, and I walk in the steady mist that coats everything, making everything slick.

A block from Hawthorn, on the sidewalk, a lump of rusty leaves reveals something white, something that didn't fall from a tree. The envelope is smeared with muddy footprints. The writing looks familiar. "To: Nancy."

In the street, in the rotting leaves curled along the curb, wet drawings of pumpkins, black cats, bats, a skeleton.

I scoop them up, cradling them against my windbreaker — leaves are mixed in — and take them home to my room, where I shove them under my bed to dry. I don't tell my parents about Nancy. I don't tell them about the other boys, the names, the hitting. They have enough to worry about as it is.

Glass Rocket

STORIES ABOUT UNCLE ED fill me up, fill my bones with air. Lately, because of the space race, my father talks a lot about his brother.

Uncle Ed, I am told, began his career in the 1930s at the *World-Herald*. After that, he was off to Washington, D.C., where, my father says, he wrote columns for Scripps-Howard and later interviewed Eisenhower and Nixon and others. I don't know who Scripps-Howard or Eisenhower are. Nixon I know from Walter Cronkite and *My Weekly Reader*. He's running for president.

"Of course," my father laments, "the *World-Herald* didn't print his column, so I didn't often get to read it."

Uncle Ed investigated the Soviets, he explains, at a time when the Communists were pointing their missiles at Strategic Air Command headquarters, south of Omaha. When John F. Kennedy became president, Uncle Ed joined the White House press corps, which sounds like an army. My father stretches his arms wide, almost knocking over a lamp and my mother's knickknacks, when he says, "Ed traveled the country, the world. Did you know he made two attempts to become the first journalist to land in Antarctica? Both times, the weather was so bad, navy pilots had to turn around."

What I hold on to most: Uncle Ed interviewed Wernher von Braun, the mastermind behind the Saturn rocket, the same rocket that will someday launch a man to the lunar surface.

"Ed was there when Kennedy gave his speech about landing a man on the moon," my father says. "That was a few weeks after you were born."

"Gosh," I say. For a moment, I suspend what I know about how the story will end. I will hope for a different outcome, as I do when watching reruns of *Gilligan's Island*. But my excitement evaporates as my father continues with what comes next. It's what always comes next. Two months later, Uncle Ed died in a plane crash in Puget Sound, a place that sounds mysterious but loud.

"I was right over there when I got the news," my father says, pointing his screwdriver to a corner of the living room. His face fills with disbelief as he time-travels to the exact moment. "I'm fixing a big console when the phone rings." He pauses.

I hold my breath.

His face scrunches in anger. "I think the goddamned Soviets had something to do with it. Of course, you could never prove it. He wrote columns about the Soviets, you know."

I sigh.

Next comes the punch line. "There was only one odd thing he ever told me," he says. "That there was evidence that we were visited."

"By UFOs?" I always ask.

He shrugs.

When it comes to Uncle Ed, my father is a headline man, short on details. I've never seen a photograph of Uncle Ed, or his widow. Did Communists remove all the photographic evidence? My father hasn't kept any of Ed's newspaper clippings. And I've never met Ed's only son, Eddie, who is ten years older than I. Eddie lives with his mother and stepfather "back east." My father holds it against my cousin that he took his stepfather's name, that he's no longer a Koterba. With the exception of annual Christmas cards, we never hear from them.

"Jeffrey!"

It's an October morning, and I'm sprawled on the floor of my bedroom sketching Dogie. I've again stayed home from school. My father says he doesn't blame me for not wanting to go because of the rocket launch, but it's my mother who makes the calls to Hawthorn, explaining I have a stomachache.

"Jeffrey," my father shouts again. "Hurry!"

I jump up, slipping on one of my drawings, nearly doing a split. He's taken a sick day, too, and I follow his voice into the living room, my heart racing.

"Hurry, hurry, hurry!" In our house, everything is an emergency, even good news. I scrape my leg on something. I climb over boxes to get to him.

"Shhh," he says, even though I haven't spoken.

He stands in front of a Zenith color console, the latest set we consider *our* set. On the screen is a special report announcing the successful liftoff of *Apollo 7*.

I have memories of watching reports on the Gemini program. Now, whenever there's news on Apollo, we stop what we're doing and together monitor the latest developments.

Demonstrating with a plastic model, the man on TV explains how the Saturn IB rocket's stages will separate on its way to entering Earth's orbit.

"I wish I had a rocket," I say, referring to the plastic model.

"Shhh. Maybe we have one around here someplace."

"Really?"

"Maybe."

"Where?"

"Hell if I know. Maybe the basement."

"Can we find it?"

"Later."

"When?"

"Not now," he says sharply, cranking up the volume. I can't blame him for being concerned. After all, it was only last year we watched the reports of a fire that killed three astronauts on a Kennedy Space Center launch pad.

"So far so good," he says. The network returns to regular programming, one of the soap operas my mother watches. He turns down the volume.

"I wish my brother was around for this," he says wistfully.

I slip off to the basement in search of a model rocket. As I rummage, I come across old radios, broken lamps, dead bugs, marbles—I hold nine small marbles, one large marble. I'm grasping the solar system. There are Barbie dolls. My hands caress a triangular-shaped piece of glass, longer than a Bic pen, thicker than my wrist. The object, smooth and heavy, looks like a glass pyramid that has been pulled and stretched. Disappointed in not finding a model rocket, I swoop it over my head as I return to my room, placing it on my dresser for a paperweight.

55

I think of Uncle Ed, imagining him typing away, a pencil tucked behind his ear.

That evening, I plop to the floor of my bedroom, filling sheets of typing paper with drawings, creating my first newspaper, the *Dogie the Doggie News*. My mother calls me three times to dinner, but gives up, allowing me to eat cold hot dogs, mac and cheese, and canned peas in my room.

The front page of the *Dogie the Doggie News* features a sketch of Dogie, a bubble around his head for an astronaut's helmet. The headline reads, "Dogie the Doggie to Land on the Moon." My newspaper consists of four pages stapled together.

After I finish, I listen at my mother's door, but her room is quiet. My father's in the living room, at the edge of the davenport. I call, "Extra!"

"Shhh, goddamn it," he says, leaning toward the TV a few feet in front of him. "Weather."

When it comes to the ten o'clock news, my father has little interest in the news itself, unless it's space-related. For the weather he puts down his drink and cups both hands around his ears to better hear the forecast. He also frequently kneels in front of whatever TV he's watching. He kneels more often in front of the weatherman than he does in front of our priest, Father Kleffman. The weather—watching the sky—plays a role in my father's business. A rainy or snowy day might get people in the mood to watch TV, he reasons. Too much rain or snow and they might not want to travel all the way to South Omaha for a used set. Tomorrow's forecast promises a crisp, sunny autumn day.

During a commercial, I again shout, "Extra, extra!" I parade in tiny circles at his feet, on the only clear floor space. "Dogie the Doggie to land on the moon! Only a dime!"

I wait for my father to reach into his pocket, produce a coin.

"Move," he growls. "I'm trying to watch."

"But the weather's over!" I protest, waving my newspaper in his face.

"Damn it, kid, not so close. Johnny's almost on." He slaps away my *News* the way he shoos away flies.

I pull back. "But Dogie's going to the moon!"

"If he could have, my brother would have flown to the god-damned moon." His Adam's apple seesaws as he gulps from a golden-brown bottle of beer. "Do you know who Wernher von Braun is?"

Yes. I know. I always know.

I also know we are a family filled with regret. We are the clouds of smoke left behind on the launch pad as the rocket soars sky-ward. But even in our fog of disappointment, the rocket itself, its power and speed, gives us hope and makes us believe that at any moment our luck might change.

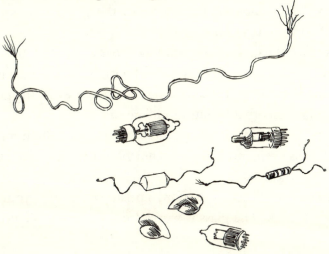

The next morning, a Saturday, my father is at the dining table, mapping out his garage sale route. The table is covered with tools and a spray of tiny electrical parts and wires, the bugs and worms of the unseen life of TVs.

"Want to come along?"

I glance out the window; it's drizzling. My father sees what I see — that the weatherman got it wrong.

"It's the Soviets, you know," he tells me. "They're controlling our weather. Read about it in the newspaper years ago. I'm pretty sure there's even a weather machine in western Nebraska."

I imagine a factory, clouds, real clouds, spewing from smokestacks.

"Ready?"

As much as I love to go anywhere, I am short of breath at the idea of being stuck in a cramped car.

"They might have toys," he says. "Maybe even a rocket."

But I have a rocket. The glass in my hand.

"What is that?" he says, reading my mind. "Is that a prism? Where did you find it?"

My throat tightens. "Downstairs," I say.

"Here." He snaps his fingers, takes the glass from me. My empty hands clench into fists.

He carries the glass to the window, moves it around, tilts it this way and that. A burst of reds and yellows, blues and purples—a spectrum of color ignites across the ceiling, the walls, the piles of everything. "Isn't that beeuuutiful?" he sings.

The colors vibrate. I can see them wiggling a million miles an hour. This is even better than Technicolor. I want to go into the colors, live in them.

"We sure as hell couldn't afford a prism when I was your age." He gives it back. The glass is warm from his hand. "C'mon, get in the car."

"I don't want to."

"You're going."

"You can't make me."

"Spoiled kid."

Minutes later, the car squeals away. My mother and Artie are in the kitchen, but I remain in the living room, where I bring the prism to my eyes, to learn where the color is coming from. Inside, auras of rainbows dance around TVs and boxes, around the drums. I move it again, and everything flips upside down. In place of junk, what I see before me is—the ceiling.

I step through our house, the prism against the bridge of my nose, ignoring what I bump into, doing my best to imagine I'm walking on the ceiling. The prism is magic, not Johnny Carson magic but *magic* magic. Until I'm old enough to become an astronaut, I decide, I will live on the ceiling. And when I'm not up *there*, I'm down *here*, where I draw.

Butterball

Two DAYS AFTER my brother turns three, my father comes home with a twin mattress and box spring tied to the roof of the Buick.

"It's time Butterball had a big-boy bed," my mother tells me. She calls Artie Butterball because he was born on Thanksgiving.

"Pick up your mess," my father says, surveying my room. "We might have to do some rearranging."

To ensure a smooth transition, when she comes to tuck us in, my mother lets Artie and me each pick a story for her to read. She also takes turns lying in each of our beds, holding our hands. One night it's Artie's bed, the next night mine. My father still tells us Puffy stories, but lately he's come up with "The Adventures of Jep and Marty."

Jep is a boy my age who has a brother, Marty, who happens to be Artie's age. Together they ramble around a neighborhood that sounds very much like ours. These boys *are* us, existing in this parallel universe, climbing trees, exploring the ravine, riding bicycles and go-carts. Unlike Puffy stories, which have a clear ending when we return to our beds, these stories are random adventures pieced together; no one flies, no one travels to exotic lands. Maybe that's what makes them seem plausible, like something that could really happen.

Often, Artie crawls into bed with me and my father, the two of us drowsily taking in my father's tales. I always wait for Artie to fall asleep first, and except for the rising, falling of his chest, Artie doesn't move and I don't wake him. It's when he's awake that he pesters me. Although he followed me around before, sharing a room only encourages Artie to mimic everything I say. If I lean against the refrigerator, he leans against the refrigerator. If I sing "Winston tastes good, like a cigarette should," he sings it, too.

"Don't copy," I tell him. *Be original.*

He doesn't understand. "Original sin!" I say. "Do you want to go to hell?"

This makes him cry, which fills me with regret.

One afternoon, I discover that Artie has ruined a stack of my drawings, including the next in-progress edition of the *Dogie the Doggie News*. I scream, running to my mother. She's at the stove. Bacon sizzles in a pan.

"Look what he did!" I shout.

"What happened?"

I present the defaced front page of the *News*. Under Artie's swirls of green crayon, Dogie's gripping a hose, spraying a house filled with red and orange flames.

"Is Dogie fighting a fire?" She puts down the spatula, taking the page. "That's so cute!"

"But Mommy—"

"I know, sweetie," my mother says, "I know. I see what he did to your picture. You have to remember that he wants to be an artist like you."

This doesn't make me feel better.

My father comes in from the backyard.

"What the hell's going on in here?" his voice booms. "Jeffrey, did you know I can hear you all the way to the ditch?" He's dressed in his hit man's attire—long, bulky coat and fedora. He tries to keep warm when he's moving TVs around outside, covering his sets with tarpaulins and blankets in cold weather, heaving TVs into the ravine.

"Jeffrey's upset about what happened to his work," she tells him.

60

She flaps around the *News,* but he doesn't grab it in horror as I hope he will. Briskly, he rubs his bare hands together.

"For God's sake, is that all?" He peers at my mother. "You need to control him better."

"Butterball can't help it."

"No, the other one."

"But he's upset about his drawing." She's on the defensive, shaking the ruined page, placing it in his cold hands. She presses the spatula, making the grease pop.

"Look," he says to me.

I stare at the paper, attempting to see beyond Artie's scribbles.

"No, not at the goddamned drawing, dummy. At me." He lifts his black hat from his head. Strands of hair rise from his scalp, following the hat. Static electricity.

I don't know what he wants me to see.

He returns the hat to his head, tugging at the brim.

He lifts it again.

I glance at the stove, where my mother is battling a smoky flare-up.

"Goddamn it," he says. "Pay attention." His mouth stretches in silence. He's a roaring lion on *Mutual of Omaha's Wild Kingdom* when the volume is off.

I squeak.

"Watch!" He lifts the hat, returns it yet again to his head. Lifts. Puts it back. "See how my hat covers the top of my head?" He's waving around the *News* in his other hand. Under Butterball's green crayon storm, there's Dogie's fire helmet, floating above his head.

I don't know what my father means.

"What are you doing?" my mother asks him.

"Trying to explain to the little dummy what it looks like when someone wears a hat. Do you see me going around with a hat this far off my head?" He holds the fedora above him, almost to the ceiling.

He hands me the *News*. But I want no part of it. I now understand: I have no idea how to draw a hat or a helmet on someone's
head. I run from the room.

"Damn ingrate," he shouts, half laughing.

"You hurt his feelings," she says.

"He needs to grow up. Or he'll never make it in this world."

In my room, in my bed, I press the prism against my face,
squinting. The harder I press, and the harder I squint, the farther
away from home I will travel.

Adjustments

ALL AFTERNOON, IT SEEMS, we've been learning multipli-
cation tables. The spring air coming through the windows
doesn't help my concentration, nor does a wasp that lazily skims
the tin ceiling. I love the tin ceiling, how high up it is. Also, the
ceiling comes in handy during math. The rows of panels act as
a sort of abacus — I can do all sorts of math up there: counting,
subtracting, multiplying the panels. Other times I envision cross-
word puzzle designs, imagining which panels I would color in if
I were up there. And of course I am attracted to the corners of
the room.

I'll shift gears and focus once it's time for art. Today we're
making Easter baskets from construction paper. But for now I
home in on one corner in particular, the one toward the front
of the room near the windows. I want my eyes to be like my
fingers, somehow reaching up there, penetrating deeply into the
very point of the triangle where wall meets wall meets ceiling.

"Hey, Cobra," whispers the boy behind me, tapping the back of
my head with a pencil. "What do you keep looking at up there?"

I glance down at my handout, pretending I didn't hear him.
Still, the corner of the ceiling is irresistible.

"Stop it," the boy says.

Trying not to stare at the corner is like being thirsty on the hottest day of the school year but not being allowed to leave the room to get a drink. The more you can't get a drink, the thirstier you become. You raise your hand and ask your teacher if you can be excused to get a drink, but she says no, you just had a drink a little while ago. You'll have to learn patience, she says. But your mouth is so dry and you just know you're going to die. In this moment it's the corner I thirst for.

"I said stop it," he says, jabbing me in the back. "What's wrong with you, Cobra?"

I never know if kids call me Cobra to make fun of my last name or because I'm always sticking out my tongue. I can't look away from the corner.

He grinds the pencil into my back. I worry that the point will break off under my skin and cause lead poisoning. I begin to tear up. But I dare not cry—then I'd really have problems on the playground.

I notice my teacher glaring. "Will I have to separate you two?"

I don't want her to think I'm a troublemaker. I shake my head no.

To put the corner out of my mind, I try to distract myself. Closer to ground level, the wasp is bouncing off the glass of the tall double-hung windows, attempting to get out, unaware that just a little ways down, where the window is open, the coast is clear. The wasp takes a breather on one of the paper eggs taped to the windows. It isn't my egg. My egg is striped in lavender and yellow. The egg the wasp prefers is scribbled over, like something Artie would draw.

On Easter, my basket is filled with candy and a new set of markers. My mother also makes a pair of bunny ears from a plastic Clorox container. She says I'm cute, but my father playfully disagrees.

"They're rabbit ears," he says. "See? You're a TV! Let me adjust your picture!" He attempts to grab my nose, calling it a knob.

I show my teeth, chomping, pretending I'm a fierce bunny that doesn't want his nose tugged on. "Watch out," I say, "I'm a mad bunny!" My teeth briefly catch in his skin; it's enough for him to whip his belt from his pants. He threatens to strap me, cracking his belt on TVs, swatting at boxes and the davenport — thud! — as I run from him, zigzagging through the house. He chases me, hitting everything *but* me.

My mother begs him to stop. He's never hit me before; he doesn't hit me now. He gets madder when his pants slide down around his thighs, then his feet. He isn't wearing boxers. I run to my bed, sobbing.

My mother comes in with her camera, hoping that will make me want to smile.

"Oh, my poor bunny," she says.

With my new markers, I draw until one day I run out of paper.

I doodle in the margins of the *Omaha World-Herald,* but newsprint bleeds. I make comic strips on my forearm and keep the drawings covered with long sleeves, as we are allowed to bathe only once a week. I ransack my room, uncovering my Etch A Sketch. I've always been suspicious of playing with the toy, because making pictures with it isn't real drawing. Real drawing, I believe, happens with pencils, pens, and paper. The Etch A Sketch is almost *cheating.* Not to mention I can't touch the lines that are made under the screen. I escape Artie and clear a place at the dining table, twiddling the knobs, making dogs, birds, a rocket. If I make a mistake, I shake away my error and begin again. I try a city scene of downtown Omaha. Omaha's buildings aren't tall enough. *Shakeshakeshakeshake.* Next, New York City. There are angles and windows and one tower is topped with a spire.

The Buick comes up the driveway. I can practically *hear* how packed it is. I'm almost finished with New York, but I don't want my father watching me over my shoulder. I'm afraid to carry the Etch A Sketch too far, out of fear I'll accidentally erase it. I slide it under a newspaper on the table.

He plops a box on the table, inviting me to look inside. I stand on a chair and lean over, opening the lid. Inside, stacks of orange cardboard. I'm thrilled. Now I can draw again, even if that means my animals, cities, rockets will be cast in monochromatic sameness.

It's not until days later that I realize my Etch A Sketch has gone missing. Maybe it was swept away in the tide on the table. By now it could be anywhere.

Under Construction

TWO SATURDAYS AFTER Easter, my father insists we join him in his search across town for garage sales. Today the ads are "lousy," he says. I know the drill. We'll venture haphazardly around the city, looking for sales that haven't been advertised. "It's better, anyway," he says of these aimless journeys, "because the merchandise won't be picked over."

We make our way west on the interstate, past the bridge where the car fell, to the suburbs where all the houses repeat like Monopoly pieces. I dream of living in one of these "cookie-cutter houses," as my father calls them. The lawns are perfectly manicured, the sidewalks and driveways spotless, uncracked. I imagine what these houses are like inside; I know they must be clean and orderly. If I'm lucky I catch a glimpse, from a garage, of a rec room or a finished basement. On rare occasions, if Artie or I have to use the bathroom, the sellers invite us in. We might go through the kitchen, the appliances white and gleaming. I might pass a child's bedroom, the bed made, baseball pennants hanging on the wall. There are no canyons inside these houses, only open fields of carpet.

Out here, we are frequently held up in traffic. Construction horses and rubber cones announce another street-widening project. I adore construction horses, with their four legs, striped bodies, yellow winking eyes. I also want an orange cone to wear on my head.

"The price of progress," my father grumbles.

I don't mind paying the price, getting stuck in traffic. I would be happy to pay the price every day if it meant living in the suburbs.

We search and pull over for anything that has the potential for secondhand merchandise. We even stop at a house where the people are "spring cleaning" their garage, and yet my father persuades them to sell an old pole lamp. After a few hours, the Buick is spilling over with TVs, hi-fis, clothes for me, clothes for Artie, a box of tangled marionettes.

My mother says our car is the "junkiest thing" in these neighborhoods. As the car becomes more crowded, I fill with more shame. One thing leads to another, until my tongue begins to go wild. I'm grateful we're far enough away from our neighborhood so that no one I know can see our car, or me darting my tongue in and out.

"Dad," she asks him, "when are we going to be done?"

"Huh?" he says, with other things on his mind. We keep going.

"Daddy!" I say. "Listen to Mommy!"

"Don't!" Artie slaps me. He loves garage sales.

I can't make my tongue stop its jabbing.

A motorcycle rumbles past us.

"That's all we need," my father says, "is for a gang of Hell's Angels to think the kid in the back seat is sticking his tongue out at them." He glances over his shoulder, giving me what I think is a dirty look. But I can't always tell if he's really mad or if it's one of his faces.

Loaded down, we lumber into the driveway at a garage sale that looks good to my father. My mother waits in the car while my father, Artie, and I scope things out. In the blue coolness of the garage, I discover a box of *Archie* comic books and *Mad Magazines*, all marked "5 cents each." My father is already dickering with the people over the price of two TVs. Jingly money is exchanged. He specializes in haggling with Kennedy silver half dollars. He picks up a new roll of the magic coins from the bank every Friday, leaving his pockets heavy, noisy.

66

"Jeffrey," he orders, motioning to the smaller of the two sets, a portable. "Think you can carry that?"

"Me!" cries Artie, struggling, unable to lift the TV.

My father grins proudly at Artie. "One of these days you'll lift that thing over your head."

I nudge Artie out of the way, bending, hugging the TV. Hoisting the set, I strain the tiny muscles in my stomach and arms, struggling to the car, lowering it carefully to the sidewalk.

"Wow! Look at Jeffrey!" my father proclaims, lugging the other set. He's wiry but strong. He gracefully rests his TV on the grass. He lets out a whistle, a fragment of a tune. The wind blows a thread of hair across his forehead as he surveys the contents of the Buick. The car's trunk is stretched open, TVs huddled inside, waiting to be devoured. The pole lamp is jabbed in there, too, next to the marionettes, all of them grinning, staring at me, waiting to get loose. In the back seat, more "bargains."

"What about wigs?" my mother calls to my father. Her door is open; Artie's crawling onto her lap.

He takes a few seconds to answer; he's studying the trunk. "Didn't see any," he responds.

"Artie has to go to the bathroom," she says.

"I have to go poopy!" Artie cries.

"Car's out of room," my father says sharply, without missing a beat. He runs his hand over his scalp, trying to keep his wild hair from flying away. "Looks like we'll have to head home."

He gets into the driver's seat and speaks in low tones to my mother.

Artie throws a tantrum. "I. Have. To. Go. Poopy!"

Behind me, the people who live in the house are packing up, dragging boxes of clothes, tables, and a baby swing back inside the garage, next to their Chrysler. The thin metal legs of the swing make a long scraping sound as they drag it, pulling at it as if it's a stubborn animal.

There is some discussion inside the car, but I can't hear what's being said. My mother rubs her temples as Artie attempts to crawl out the window. "Then you tell Jeffrey," she says to my father, loud enough for me to hear.

Tell me what?

He's out of the car, striding toward the house. "Excuse me," I hear him call to the people.

The wind is picking up and I can't hear what's spoken in the garage. Artie keeps complaining.

My father returns to the car. "There's no room for you and the TV," he says to me. "And the people who live here have to leave right away. So you can't wait in their house. You'll have to stay right here until I can come back."

More words are spoken in the car as my father cranks the engine; a burst of dirty white smoke coughs from the tailpipe and hovers, ghostlike, until disintegrated by a breeze. It's late April, and the air is still cool from winter. The three of them, in the car, disappear around a corner.

Gone. Abandoned at a garage sale in an unfamiliar neighborhood.

Behind me, the garage door is now sealed shut. The driveway is barren except for a fresh oil stain in the shape of a strange and faraway continent. To comfort myself, I want to go and stand in that oil stain, in its colorful filminess. I want to run my pinkie along the clean crevice of the sidewalk and driveway. I want to run my tongue along there, too. I can't make myself move. This is the farthest I've been from home, alone.

Minutes pass, but the people inside the house haven't left. There's no sign of movement in their windows. I regret not having brought along my prism.

I'm a dummy for not bringing it.

My knees are weak, almost as if I don't have legs.

Cars come and go, nicer, newer, freshly waxed cars, none of them my family's. What if a stranger kidnaps me? Kills me? At least then, sadness will bring my parents closer together.

A boy I fear might be a bully approaches on his bike; I hold my breath, trying to suppress a squeak, but it comes out, just like that, echoing off the houses. I worry my sounds will annoy him and he will throw down his bike and beat me up, but he doesn't notice me. I'm invisible, I don't exist here in the suburbs, without my parents. This at once relieves me, but also unnerves me.

When our Plymouth finally appears, my father's alone. I'm thrilled for the chrome grille's smile, the car's wide-set eyes. My father puts the Philco into the back seat, next to boxes and other TVs. He must've stopped at sales on the way back.

We drive and he whistles. I watch the neighborhoods go by as the houses devolve, become hunched over, until we pull onto 14th Street, our street.

My mother greets me at the front door, placing her hand on my cheek. "You're freezing," she says. "Are you hungry? Do you want some Campbell's?"

In the warmth of my bed, I draw construction sites of new buildings and big houses. I draw miniature construction horses adorned with cautionary stripes and the words DETOUR and ROAD CLOSED. I cut out the construction horses, making them stand, posting them on the hallway floor in front of my bedroom.

Mysteriously, typing paper begins appearing again, and it's so white, compared to the orange cardboard, it hurts my eyes. I become a nomad, searching the various man-made nooks and spaces of our house. My mother suggests the kitchen table. She even sits with me, and together we read John Gnagy's *Learn to Draw,* which she found in a box in the attic. She wants us to attempt the step-by-step approach of creating the railyard scene from the book. First we're instructed to draw a "horizon line," and on it we are to make a small dot, the "vanishing point." Skeletal cylinders and cones and cubes transform into the engine, water tower, buildings. This is cheating. Real artists draw what they see in their mind, or, at least, what they see in real life. Or on TV. My mother follows the directions, but I venture off on my own, skipping the steps, attempting to replicate the final version of the railyard *my* way.

It quickly becomes clear that my mother's drawing is the better of the two. In my boredom, I page through the book. It's the self-portrait of John Gnagy that makes me worried. Sporting a Vandyke beard and wearing a plaid shirt with upturned collar, he's the type of man my father dislikes. My father hates cowboys, sailors, lumberjacks, anyone who would fit the "strong and silent" description. The next time my father accuses my mother of wanting to run off with another man, I'll picture John Gnagy.

I draw at the kitchen table, but too often I have to compete with the meals of the day (we eat in shifts) and the flies that defy winter and congregate in our kitchen and grow in numbers with the spring weather. The flies come because my father has a habit of leaving fried meat in the skillet day and night. No matter how hard my mother tries to fix a nice meal, he rarely joins us for dinner, eating instead at odd hours, cranking up the burner, reheating whatever remnant of meat has been left out. The eating, the flies, force me out; I return to my bedroom, to Artie.

I clear a space on the floor and encircle myself with miniature construction horses.

"This is my area," I tell him. "Stay out."

To enforce my point, I tape a discarded TV cord to a red flashing light I discovered in the new garage; placing the light on my head, I tie the cord under my chin. Although I have to hold my head steady to keep the heavy light from sliding off, a red strobe blinks from my scalp. This makes Artie giggle uncontrollably. I also can't keep from laughing. We both giggle harder, the light crashing to the floor, red plastic breaking into slices. I brush aside the pieces of plastic and before long we are dancing around the room, laughing, jumping on our beds. My construction horses have been knocked over and the light — now a disappointing white — continues flashing on the floor.

Artie screams, "Owie!"

"What's wrong?"

He's crying, grabbing his bare foot.

I study his foot but can't see anything.

"It hurts," he cries, "it hurts!"

I look again and remove a sliver of red plastic from his dirty but soft flesh. There's a smudge of blood, but nothing critical.

"All better?" I ask.

He rubs at his nose, a river of green goo stopping short of his mouth. I reach for a discarded Kleenex from under my bed. "Here," I say, dabbing above his upper lip. No matter what my father says, Artie is not invincible.

We settle onto the floor.

I'm sketching Dogie.

Artie colors in a Barbie coloring book.

He holds up the book to show me what he's accomplished. It's all ovals and meaningless lines, browns and yellows and pinks and reds, clashing over Barbie's face and her lean, narrow body.

"That's pretty," I say. "Very pretty."

He grins proudly.

Cindy

JOIN ME," MY MOTHER SAYS, mussing my hair. She's just returned from the drugstore with a batch of photographs, and I'm on the floor of the living room, my back against a TV while watching cartoons on another, munching a Hostess fruit pie.

She tells me to wash my hands and join her in her bedroom, where she will retrieve her photo albums. My mother collects photographs like my father hoards TVs. And freshly developed photographs are always an occasion to go through the old ones.

I sit next to her on the bed. Around us, dusty albums covered in fake leather.

"Look how cute you are as a bunny!" she says, removing the photographs from the envelope.

Upon close inspection, my bunny picture reveals watery red eyes. My mother doesn't mention what happened that day.

We look at other photographs, several of which were taken at my grandparents'. There are none of my parents. We finish, and soon we're flipping pages in one of her albums.

"You were such a cute baby," she says. "Such an obedient little boy." These pictures of me are nothing out of the ordinary—a chubby baby in diapers, a crawling toddler. I relish these photographs, if for no other reason than that they show our house—our floor—before my father discovered garage sales. Other photographs are more entertaining—a devilish Batman, a stern Superman, a snappy cowboy—all thanks to my mother's handiwork at the sewing machine. When I was a week old she made me pajamas with rockets on them. She likes to tell me that the day before I was born, Alan Shepard became the first American to fly into space. But there are no photos of me in the pajamas.

"As a baby, you slept all the time. I'd have to wake you so we could play."

We come across a familiar but undated Polaroid of a skinnier, more youthful version of her. The snapshot, as she always explains, is from her last days on the farm, before the family left for Omaha. She's leaning against her father's shiny black Chrysler. Her jeans are rolled high, above her ankles. She's barefoot. Between her fingers, a cigarette. In the corner of the photo, a partial view of a silo, a rocket ship that might carry cows and sheep into space.

"It was the next year we moved to Omaha" is the only other

72

thing she ever says about the photograph. I never know the age of my parents. They say it's a secret; my father says it's rude to ask. "I couldn't wait to move to the big city," she continues. "But then, our first apartment was infested with cockroaches."

"Oh."

"Then you came along. I smoked throughout my pregnancy with you." She looks concerned, stroking my hair. "I'm just grateful my smoking didn't damage you." It's rare for her to say anything about her pregnancy with me. I focus on the white stub she's holding in the picture, searching for any clues about her life before I came along.

Another photograph, its color faded, is of my mother in front of our Plymouth Fury. She's slightly heavier than in the first photograph, her breasts stretching the sheer material of her dress. Her hair is the color of a squirrel.

"Daddy took this," she says.

In my father's hand—the only time his writing exists in her photo albums—are the words "My wife: as beautiful as Dorothy Lamour."

"Who's that?" I ask, pointing at the name.

"Dorothy Lamour? A famous pinup," she says.

"What's a pinup?"

"You're too young to understand."

The Plymouth appears especially polished, the chrome gleaming with sunlight. I recognize the side of our house, our driveway, Frank and Mary's house next door.

I know these images by heart, and it gives me comfort knowing I can count on them to remain unchanged. Some are accompanied by a story; most are passed over without a word.

Here is "Cindy."

From my infancy until the age of five, my mother decorated me in her myriad wigs and makeup and clothing. She taught me everything I needed to know about lipstick, including the trick of pressing my lips together onto a Kleenex to remove the excess.

She captured each moment with her camera. Now that I'm almost eight, my memories of playing dress-up are kept fresh by these photographs. I again know the scratchiness of her wigs on my crew cut, the smell of her hair spray and perfume. As embarrassed as I am, I'm simultaneously attracted to the hair in these images—sometimes dark and bobbed, other times platinum, with two big curls enclosing my face in single quotes.

She explains it to me now as she always explains it: "I wanted a daughter so bad." She taps her index finger at a washed-out Polaroid of a two-year-old me, lost in the folds of a lavender dress. I'm bald save for a Charlie Brown wisp of hair. "If you'd been a girl, I would have named you Cindy. Look how cute you are! Are you my Cindy?" She pulls me to her bosom, kissing the top of my head. There's her spicy perfume.

Occasionally, she calls me by the more formal "Cynthia." "Cynthia," she'll say, "hand me that loaf of Wonder bread, please." My father's not in our game; he's never around when she says it.

"Do you remember anything about what happened after I took this picture?" Her finger conducts a symphony over the photograph. I recognize the gold drapes and brown carpet from my grandparents'. I can almost taste my grandmother's poppy-seed kolaches; I can nearly smell the sweet odor of chewing tobacco in my grandfather's plaid shirt as he talks about fishing. The child's expression—my expression—is a mystery.

I slowly shake my head against her breast.

"A minute or two later you pointed to a corner of the ceiling and said, 'Look, it's Jesus.' That's when the phone rang."

I wait for her to compose herself.

"The call was about my great-aunt Betty," she says. "She'd just passed away. Can you imagine?" she says. "My Cindy. My angel."

She pulls me tight and I listen to her breathing.

"When children are very young," she says, "they're free of sin and can see things, know things, that adults can't. You knew before any of us that Betty had died."

74

No matter how hard I squint at this photograph, I don't see an angel, only a two-year-old version of me in makeup and a lavender dress.

The last "Cindy" photograph was snapped days after my fifth birthday. I'm a brunette with rosy cheeks, bright red lipstick, wearing a T-shirt emblazoned with a growling tiger.

There's a familiarity about the smile, the puffy cheeks, the eyes. I study this image as I might the face of a long-lost sister, or any number of girls I once had a crush on at school.

Tonight I slip off to my bedroom and attempt to sketch from memory these images of me as a girl. I draw my face, the pretty hair and lips. I grow tired of drawing only my face. I want the whole body.

I remember the naked Barbie dolls in the basement. I sneak three into my room — one is missing a head. When Artie isn't around I draw their bodies. I draw the breasts, the arms, the legs. I draw Barbie's body with "Cindy's" face — my face.

I'm embarrassed for drawing Barbie without her clothes.

I can't help but chew on the foot of the headless naked Barbie. I gnaw all the way, until her foot falls to my lap. I conceal what I've done with a pair of G.I. Joe's boots. I keep the dolls, my sketches, in hiding. Artie's too young to know about such things.

Marlo

FOR MY EIGHTH BIRTHDAY I receive a sketch pad, which I immediately fill with drawings of starlets from *The Tonight Show Starring Johnny Carson,* the late movie, the Miss America pageant. And I can't get enough of the Golddiggers on the *Dean Martin Show.* I'm never barred from viewing any program, but my father goes on about how awful some of these shows are. Miss America? "Immodest." Dean Martin? "Un-Christian." Although my father believes Johnny Carson can do no wrong, he finds ways to backhandedly criticize Johnny's guests. "What a talented singer she is, but look how trashy she's dressed."

My mother agrees. "Tsk, tsk, tsk."

I'm never made to leave the room. Anyway, what would it matter? I have a TV of my own.

I store my starlet drawings under my bed, the catchall for everything shameful. When my father comes in to tell us bedtime stories, I worry he will somehow see under my bed, see my shame. But if he does, he never says anything.

Keeping these women in hiding is too much to bear. Under the guise of inventing a contest for my parents, I create a sweepstakes flyer promising the winner an all-expenses-paid trip to "the ocean." I don't want my handwriting giving me away; to make the form look official, I sneak one of our typewriters into my room.

"I want to type!" Artie says.

"No. Go play with your toys."

Artie turns on the TV; the glare from the setting May sun through the window obscures the TV's picture.

"Turn that thing down," I tell him. "I'm trying to draw." Besides, it's only the ABC Wednesday night movie. Tonight there are no beautiful women. *Boring.*

After several failed attempts, I peck out the form, sketching a beach scene around the text. I color in palm trees, a setting sun on the watery horizon. In the middle of the scene, I pencil out a woman. I think of Marlo Thomas as I draw, but she's different enough to make her "unique," as my father might say. The woman wears a red bikini. Her eyes are dots, the same dot I use for her navel. Her nose, the shape of the letter "L." Her mouth, a red oblong of a line. The woman's body is shapely, and if I ignore her face, she's *beeuuutiful.*

In spite of my clacking on the typewriter, Artie falls asleep on the floor, the screen flickering across his face.

As I get up to leave, second thoughts race through my head. In a frenzied moment I fill in Marlo's stomach with red crayon, transforming her bikini into a one-piece swimsuit.

"Stupid," I call myself, regretting my actions. I've ruined everything. I smack my forehead five times. I always count.

I consider starting over, but the ten o'clock news is under way, and I've already invested more than two hours in the flyer.

I take the form to my mother. She's on her bed reading the only books she ever reads, books about Admiral Byrd's travels to the North and South Poles. When I tease her that she loves the explorer, she blushes.

"Artie in bed?" she asks.

"He's sleeping on the floor."

"That Butterball," she says with a laugh, rolling her eyes, shaking her head. Her focus lands on my forehead.

"Do you want to win this contest?"

"Hmm?"

"You can go to the beach!" I say softly.

"That's pretty," she says, glancing at the entry form. She forces a smile and makes no effort to enter my contest, makes no mention of the woman in the swimsuit. "Aren't penguins fascinating?"

"Yes, Mommy."

She's reading her book again.

I waddle from the room, my arms at my sides.

"Close the door behind you."

I waddle to my father. He never reads books.

He's in the living room scooping through a box of tubes, mimicking the sound he makes when he digs into his Times Square ice bucket. He's singing: "The sun is out, the sky is blue, but it's raining, raining in my heart."

"Arf! Arf!"

"Hey, a dog!"

I shake my head no. "Arf!"

"Seal?"

"Arf! Penguin!"

"You sound like a seal."

"I'm a penguin! Here." I try handing him the form.

"I'm busy."

"Please."

Grunt.

I grunt, too; maybe nervous habits are contagious.

Laughter comes from the TV. Our TVs provide our home with a laugh track. Even if the laughter comes at the wrong time.

He pulls his large hand from the box, reaches for my flyer. "A free vacation? Why didn't you say so?"

My father never passes up the chance for anything free, even when the grand prize is imaginary. He asks for a pen, which I quickly produce from my back pocket. I watch over his shoulder as he turns the top of a Sylvania table model into a desk. *Name: Arthur G. Koterba. Address: 4718 South 14th Street.*

"I hope I win!" he says, his breath all singsong and whiskey. His enthusiasm is infectious. I begin to believe that the contest is authentic after all.

"And who's this?" he says, pointing to the cartoon woman, her bug-eyed breasts covered in red Crayola.

I lift my shoulders to my ears.

"Is this your girlfriend?"

"He's too young to have a girlfriend," my mother teases, coming into the family room. "Aren't you, my little penguin?" She pulls me close, her breasts pressing against my head.

"Well, she's very good-looking," my father says to me. "And I hope I win!"

"So you can go off with all the pretty girls?" She's quick with her response, as if she's been waiting with it. This is new. It's always my father who expresses jealousy.

I fear an argument is brewing, but he speaks softly: "No, I just want to *win* something for a change."

Although they rarely show affection for each other, in this moment there is an unidentifiable closeness between them that fills

78

me with the promise that they will never again argue. I want us to stay like this forever.

"I'd better check on Artie," she says.

Don't leave.

But she goes, the chance for them to hug gone.

"Wish me luck," he says with a wink, handing me the form. Sometimes his winks are winks and nothing more.

He sips from a sweaty tumbler that rests atop his set, hints of ice cubes floating in the brown liquid, melting from the warmth of the TV. I turn to leave, not sure what I'll do with the entry form. I haven't planned this far ahead. Do I construct a mailbox?

"One thing," he says, yanking the paper from my hands. "The angle is off on the — what do they call that? — perspective."

Perspective?

I read and ignored that word in the John Gnagy book. As my father holds up the drawing to get a better view, I'm left staring at the back of the translucent paper, the backward lettering pressing through, the colors muted.

"See?" He grabs me by the arm, pulling me next to him. In addition to whiskey, I'm now engulfed in the aromas of cologne and sweat. "Goddamn it. Right here." He pokes at the paper impatiently. "Your girlfriend's standing on the sand, but the beach looks like it's going uphill in the background. If this were real, the water would rush down and everyone would drown. Is that what you want?"

Dizzy

H E CALLS IT his experiment.

Just when I believe he only clacks away on a comptometer for the U.P., fixes TVs, and plays the drums, he tells us he's been off inventing a new toy. Bags of rubber bands, in every color and size, and spindles of string are mixed in with his glass tubes and wires on the dining table. I had thought nothing of the Hula-Hoops in pieces on his recliner.

It shouldn't come as a surprise. At times he's talked about his past inventions. He once claimed to have had the idea for the transistor twenty years before someone else took credit for it. "Think how rich we could have been!" He nearly came up with the Wankel engine, he told us — again, years ahead of its time. "But I don't give a shit. The Wankel engine never amounted to anything anyway." He lamented that he has yet to get us rich by coming up with a concept to cure the blind and deaf. And his holy grail? A perpetual motion machine.

We're in the deepest part of the backyard, our family ushered here by my father. We'd been watching *The Tonight Show*, waiting for all the neighbors' houses to go dark. Just to be sure, we gave it another fifteen minutes. Most of all, he was concerned about Frank and Mary. "Have to make sure they're all asleep, the damn spies." The ravine looms, a black vortex, a million bugs rubbing their legs together. It's a moonless night; my eyes have to adjust.

Like a magician pulling a rabbit from a hat, he removes his "experiment" from a grocery bag. He raises it above his head in the way a priest holds up the Communion wafer. This is my father's miracle. "Here it is," he whispers.

"What is it?" I ask.

"Hold on," he says.

"But what is it?"

"Shhh. Do you want the whole neighborhood to hear you?" He makes his lion face. My mother holds Artie against her chest, shifting his unruly weight in her arms.

"It" is a black tubular hoop fashioned from a larger Hula-Hoop, crisscrossed by a series of rubber bands. The rubber bands are pulled and stretched in a pattern my father claims is of great scientific significance. Hanging from the rubber circle is a string knotted to a plastic ring. He cradles the thing gently.

I peer through the trees above, into the Milky Way. I squeeze my eyes and make an oval with my head; I speed up, turning the stars into falling stars.

"This," he says, "is a Dizzy Wizzy."

"But *what* is it?" my mother asks, losing patience.

"It's a toy," he explains. "A toy that makes music."

"Oh," she says. "Is that all?"

The air goes out of my father; his shoulders slump. I wonder how old he is. Forty? Fifty?

He motions to us to stand back, to make room. Slipping his index finger into the ring, he tosses the toy into the black air, twirling the Dizzy Wizzy above his pinwheel head of hair.

Thud.

His toy smacks the side of the new garage.

"Not enough room," he says. "C'mon." We follow him into a clearing. I'm grateful to be away from the ravine. The light's better here. Again the Dizzy Wizzy is airborne. He twirls faster and I can barely see the hoop. The rubber bands quiver as the toy cuts through the humid air, emanating an eerie pulse. The sound is unearthly, stranger than the loud hum of the Goodyear blimp; the only time it came to Omaha, I watched it fight against a strong wind above the Missouri River. The toy also reminds me of a swarm of bees, or the locusts that live in the two big maples that shade our porch in late summer. It's a blimp and bees and locusts all at once, the sound rising, falling, depending on the toy's location above.

Wrzzzeeeooorrr wrzzzeeeooorrr wrzzzeeeooorrr.

Uneasiness fills my stomach. I imagine my father will accidentally contact secret creatures that dwell in the darkness of Earth and space. Maybe thick tree monsters will crawl from the ravine and chase after us.

My tongue is poking, retreating, a turtle head gone mad.

"May I try?" I ask, careful not to bite my tongue as I speak.

81

"Not yet!" he says loudly, over the noise of the toy, forgetting his worries about the neighbors.

WRZZZEEEOOORRR.

He goes even faster, sending the pitch higher, the spinning halo now invisible, the string completely dissolved, his hand and arm a blur. Everything's spinning out of control. He's a crazed rodeo clown with an imaginary lasso.

Artie shakes loose from my mother, wriggles to the ground. He's fully awake, running in circles, attempting to catch the sound.

"When can I do it?" I ask, swatting a mosquito on my bare leg.

WRZZZEEEOOORRR.

Artie's jumping, reaching.

"Please!" I call. "My turn!"

"No," Artie says, "it's my turn!"

My father gets distracted and the toy falls to the black grass. Artie leaps for it, but I get there first, holding it high above me.

"I want it, Daddy!" Artie cries.

"Wait," my father says, grabbing the Dizzy Wizzy, bringing it to his chest.

"But—" I stomp my foot; the ground is soft and damp; the effect is lost.

"For God's sake, I said. *Wait!*"

Artie yelps, but my mother quiets him.

My father cocks his head backward, casting a sheepish glance into the sky. A small plane glides across the Milky Way. I recall a time before Artie when the three of us would sit on the front steps, waiting for satellites to glide overhead.

"Be still," my father warns. "You never know who might be watching."

We don't move. I allow a mosquito to needle the skin of my neck. Finally, the buzz of the plane fades and we're left with the pulsating chorus of crickets.

"And who's going to buy this thing?" my mother asks. There's more worry than skepticism in her voice. Half of her face is covered in shadow.

"Who?" he says. "Kids. Goddamn kids of all ages!"

I take the toy from him and toss it into the air. It's heavier than I expect; the toy flops to the ground.

"Faster," he says, desperately wanting to raise his voice. "You have to do it way faster than that."

I try again, running as I might when attempting to get a kite off the ground.

"Not like that, dummy!" He forgets to keep his voice down.

I move my arm faster, putting the Dizzy Wizzy into orbit.

Wrzzzeeeooorrr wrzzzeeeooorrr.

I'm whipping my arm around while my father explains to my mother the low cost of manufacturing such a toy. I can't help but rub an itch on my neck; the rubber hoop pops my father in the temple.

"What the hell're you doing?"

"It was an accident," I say, the Dizzy Wizzy now in the grass and weeds, a dead thing, the end of the lame string still attached to my finger. Artie goes for the toy. "I'm sorry."

"Now the whole neighborhood's going to know about this. God, that hurt like a sonofabitch."

"Well, if you wouldn't yell so loud . . . ," my mother says under her breath. "We're going in." She removes the toy from Artie's hands, leads him toward the house.

"But I want to play," he demands, trying to squirm from her grip.

My father massages his injury. In the distance a dog comes alive, perhaps the same dog I've heard in this backyard for years. The dog's bark echoes. There's another small plane above, or maybe the same one circling.

"Why's everyone so against me?" he asks the Dizzy Wizzy, scooping it from the ground.

"I heard that," my mother calls before heading inside.

"I'm sorry," I say again to my father.

"I know you didn't mean it," he says.

"Airplane."

We turn to stone, church statues, waiting until the plane is out of range.

He again sends the Dizzy Wizzy into its trajectory.

Wrzzzeeeooorrr wrzzzeeeooorrr.

I allow my eyes to roll under my brow, making the sky disappear, the toy's nervous sound filling me up.

"Watching for more planes?" he asks.

"Yes," I lie.

"Great. Let me know if you see anything."

"I will, Daddy."

The Lot

JEFFREY!" My father is frantic. "I need you to mow the lot right away. It's an emergency!" He's come home from work and finds in the mail a yellow warning from the city. I'm usually the one who cuts our lawn—a mix of bluegrass and weeds in front; grass, weeds, wires, and knobs in back—but I've never mowed the lot, a mysterious rectangle of property on the corner of our block, five houses from where we live. He purchased the lot when I was four, when it was still part of the ravine that snaked through the neighborhood. Dump trucks filled the hole with dirt to create a playground, though I'm not allowed to go there alone. What I know of the lot comes from driving around it, to and from home.

"Lousy Communists," he says, tossing the notice onto the mantel.

We have three working mowers in the driveway. We also own a rider mower, but it's missing its blade. Last spring my father somehow brought it home in the trunk of the car. It's a behemoth, white and rusty, the skin of the cushioned seat cracked, exposing yellowed foam like rotting meat. My father says that one day we'll fix it up. I can't tell what brand it is. Everything about it is worn out.

We choose a mower fit for the job—our red, gasping Toro. Next, I follow him into the old garage, searching for yard tools. We climb over boxes and around a Wurlitzer organ, the heat raising a stale odor from stacks of worn tires.

"It's so goddamned hot," he complains, wiping his face with his arm. No matter how warm things get, he always wears long-sleeved shirts, long pants. His chest hair sprays from the top of his shirt. He has the body of a scarecrow, the mustache and wild hair of Albert Einstein.

Minutes later, alone, I'm off to the lot with the mower, a pitted sickle over my shoulder.

At the lot, I face a wall of thistle as tall as my father.

Bees squiggle in the sultry air. Above the bees, fighter planes split the blue sky, and bombers roar so low I can see the shield insignia of the Strategic Air Command. I love drawing insignias and logos and will later sketch the SAC shield.

I take a whack. The first stalk is stubborn. I strike again. The stalk is severed, tipping over. A screech of victory comes from my throat and I yell, "Tim-ber!" I give my mouth permission to stretch wide. Something inside me explodes. I swing the sickle, slicing through this jungle. If I topple enough weeds, if I make our lot pretty, it will make my father proud and happy. This will be our promised land before we get to the real one.

I chop long after the sun drifts from our neighborhood, leaving me in yellow-green murkiness; in the distance a June thunderstorm rumbles. Mosquitoes hector my legs. I chop until the sprinkles come.

It takes me three days to finish. Most of the lot is flat. It's the two steep hills that are especially difficult to manage. When I'm through, I have before me a field of my own, a place to run, a small farm filled with mice and snakes, where I inhale the smells of freshly cut greenery, even if it's weeds. This winter, when it snows, I will come here in my bulky snowsuit and space helmet and "walk on the moon." For now, I go to the tops of the hills and fall to the ground, rolling downward, clippings gathering in my clothes. Here, I'm alone but not afraid.

As soon as I finish, the weeds retaliate, and I must begin again.

All I do, it seems, is mow and chop, keeping the weeds at bay, but the constant drone of the mower allows my mind to drift. I sing, too, confident that my voice is drowned out by the mower. I also draw with the mower, creating scenes in the weeds. Every so often I stop and run up the hill to look upon what I'm drawing. I attempt landscapes of mountains and trees. And also downtown buildings. If I make a mistake, I mow over my efforts and wait a few days to try again. The lot is a giant Etch A Sketch.

For my hard work, my father announces he has a reward. He's home early from the U.P., having taken a half day's vacation.

"We're going to build Jeffrey a covered wagon," he tells my mother as she pins a pair of my wet jeans to the clothesline. "Do you have a spare sheet?"

"Will I get it back?"

"Yes, goddamn it."

He takes me to the new garage. Only a few feet of dirt lie between the back of the old white garage and the more modern, redwood version. He says one day we'll tear down the old "piece of crap."

The new garage seemed to fill up instantly. One day I was bouncing a basketball on the pristine cement, marveling at the echo of my laughter in all that hollowness. The next day, junk piled high.

"First we need to find Hula-Hoops," he explains, unfastening the top button of his shirt, loosening his wide, colorful tie.

We proceed to empty the contents of the garage onto the lawn in an orderly manner, as if we'll be required to put everything back exactly the way we found it. We transport ladders, cans of paint, boxes of anonymous trinkets.

"My lawn!" my mother protests, flagging us with a pair of my father's red polka-dot boxers.

"Shhh," he scolds, his index finger to his pursed lips.

All we have is the yard. After the patio long ago overflowed with lamps, bikes, pedal toys, TVs, and lawn mowers, the driveway joined in.

I follow him inside, stepping past the record player, its arm clawing at my ankle. Rolls of old carpet stand as tall as trees. The pathway meanders like an ancient riverbed, the walls of the canyon made up of objects other people stopped wanting. The riverbed will change slowly over time as items are removed and added, a work in progress, my father the unintentional grand designer. There is no overhead light, so we're left to manage by the glow seeping in through a bamboo shade over the only window. I'm submerged in this tomb of sepia, even on a bright summer day such as this.

"Daddy, are you sure the Hula-Hoops aren't in the other garage?"

"Hell if I know. I hate how disorganized everything is." He wipes his brow with his sleeve. "Take that out," he says, pointing to a box.

On the lid, in Magic Marker: "$1." I doubt my father paid full price. Peeking inside, I come across souvenirs of places we've never visited. In the muted light: a decorative plate with a painting of Mount Rushmore, a stained coffee mug explaining that Yellowstone is a national treasure, a sickly green porcelain bust of Abraham Lincoln that doubles as a coin bank (a quick shake, empty), with the inscription "Illinois. Land of Lincoln." Someone else's vacations, someone else's memories. I run my fingers over Lincoln's nose, his eyes, his beard.

"Get going!" my father yells.

I make my way with the box toward the door, toward a sliver of promising light.

The door is open a crack. I hold on to the box, balancing it with one knee, attempting to open the door all the way with my elbow. I can't do it. I place the box on top of other boxes, a stack towering and precarious, something out of *The Cat in the Hat*.

I manage to open the door. The box comes down, tipping over, glass shattering against the concrete path.

"Shit!" I say.

"What the hell was that?" my father calls from the back of the garage. "Did you swear?"

"No," I yell.

"Well, what was that crash? You'd better not be lying."

"Everything's okay!"

"Are you positive?" his voice echoes. "It sure's hell better not've been President goddamned Lincoln. That souvenir's probably an antique — might be worth something someday!"

At my feet is the president's skull, fractured and greenish, aglow in a crevice of light. I clean the mess the best I can, hiding the remains in a garbage can.

My father stays put, rooting around. "If you want a covered wagon, you sure as shit better get off your ass and get working, kid!"

Here's a blender without a lid, two radios, a table fan missing its safety cover, a single lonely shoe in nice shape, another pair of old shoes, one of which appears to have been inhabited by a spider. On and on we excavate. Vacuum cleaners, some missing parts, resemble dismembered robots.

From my front pocket I grab my prism. Lately I carry it everywhere, bulky as it is. Through the glass I watch as Artie attempts to lift the heavy watering can for my mother. He can't. They're both upside down, in the sky, in dreamy color, she tending her flowers. It's all she has in the backyard, and now our stacks encroach further into her territory. Every spring she kneels in the dirt where she plants annuals and tends to her perennials. Marigolds, black-eyed Susans, tulips, snapdragons. But in the end her flowers cannot beat out my father's collectibles.

"Jeffrey! Hurry!" my father calls, appearing at the garage door.

Excitedly, I go to him. "Hula-Hoops?"

"Goddamn it, kid, get some patience."

"But you said—"

"If you can't shut up, I'm going to forget I ever promised you anything."

I stomp off.

"Spoiled brat. Do you want to build the covered wagon or not?"

I run from him, and he follows.

"That's okay, Artie will help me," he shouts from the doorway. "He loves his daddy. Don't you, Artie?"

Artie races to my father. I sink my bare knees into the dirt next to my mother.

"Aren't they beautiful, Cynthia?" She extracts a brown leaf from a stem in the middle of a cluster of bright purple flowers waiting to be planted. She doesn't take her eyes from her bare hands, kneading the dirt.

"Daddy's not going to build my covered wagon," I say.

"He's just in a bad mood right now. I'm sure he'll make it for you. Which reminds me, I have to find that sheet." She pats the ground. "Why don't you take over for Mommy. I need you to soften the earth. You can be like a farmer."

My fingers sink deep into the ground. Although worms make me squeamish, I enjoy the way the moist earth surrounds my flesh, enveloping it. I very much want to keep reaching in, downward, up to my elbow, my shoulder. I want to dive into the ground with my entire body, as if this dirt that brings life to trees, grass, and flowers can protect me.

. . .

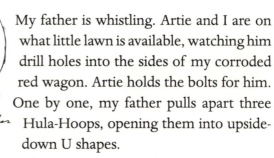

My father is whistling. Artie and I are on what little lawn is available, watching him drill holes into the sides of my corroded red wagon. Artie holds the bolts for him. One by one, my father pulls apart three Hula-Hoops, opening them into upside-down U shapes.

"Jeffrey," he says, "go find Mommy. See if she ever found a sheet."

I run inside, calling for her. No answer.

From my closet, among an army helmet, a space helmet, baseball caps, and my old dress, I dig up a straw cowboy hat.

My mother comes from the attic. Her face flushed from the heat upstairs, she tosses me a purple and green floral sheet. "It's all I could find," she says.

Disappointed, I take the sheet to my father. The ribbed skeleton of the covered wagon is in place.

"What the hell's that?" he asks. "No son of mine is going to go riding around the neighborhood in some flowery covered wagon."

He strides into the house, and from outside Artie and I can hear the argument. My mother says she has only one nice white sheet. It takes some loud negotiating, but a few minutes later, she concedes. As my father fastens the sheet to the framework of Hula-Hoops, I can't help but dwell on how my mother sacrifices, how she has few nice things.

My red wagon becomes a *covered* wagon.

"Climb in," my father tells me.

As was the case with the Batmobile, my body is too lanky to fit comfortably inside. Still, my father pulls me through the bumpy yard, making horse sounds. Artie chases after us, pretending to shoot me. "Bang, bang!"

I ask permission to pull the wagon to the lot.

"Of course! Have fun! We should all have fun! We work too damn hard! Just remember, we have to put all this crap back into the garage." He nudges a box with his foot. It'll be weeks before the yard is empty again.

Artie begs to tag along, but my father says, "No. That's Jeffrey's covered wagon. Come on," he tells him. "I'm going to make you a Viking ship!"

I pull the wagon over the imperfect sidewalk of 14th Street, over crevices, imagining these jagged lines are gulches, to the rugged world of the lot. I park in the shade of the mulberry tree. The wind must be from the west—the smell of the stockyards is in the air, making me gag. "The smell of money," my father calls it. I'm inside now, stretching, my legs and feet dangling in the summer air. My father is the perfect father. He loves me by building covered wagons. And my mother is the perfect mother, sacrificing her nicest bedding for her son's toy. I cover my face with my hat, inhaling the smell of the hat's warm straw, blocking out the smell of money. Pinpoints of light come through the hat's crown—a personal planetarium. I hear myself breathing. Slowly, calmly breathing.

Gone Shopping

I FIGHT AGAINST the warmth of the July air. The windows of the city bus are open, the fumes working on me. Today my father took the Plymouth to work; the Buick waits to be emptied. My mother and I rarely take the bus anymore, so I want to stay awake the best I can to see — *everything*. Other neighborhoods, the buildings downtown. Artie is with us, content to look at one of my old Golden Books. In the whiteness of sunshine, downtown appears unclean. Darkness, like snow, covers mistakes, cracks, flaws, dirt. Charcoal clouds chug from trains and factories along the river, coating the world in grime. The Wow Building doesn't seem as tall. Even the twelve-story U.P. Building, where my father clacks on his comptometer this very moment, appears shorter. Maybe the vast blue sky makes everything smaller in comparison.

What lifts my spirits is the appearance of a large crane and the steel skeleton of a new building.

I tap my mother and point out the window.

"Paper says it's going to be Omaha's tallest," she says. "It's an insurance building."

"How tall?"

"Thirty stories."

I lick the window. The bitter taste makes my face pucker.

She's unfazed.

I lick the window again. Same outcome.

She nudges me to stop.

The bus turns a corner and I lose sight of the building under construction. I love the word "construction." "Construction!" I say. "Construction!" I lick the window yet again.

"Stop that," she says. "We're going to hit a bump and you're going to lose your tongue."

"Stop that!" Artie mimics. A trickle of sweat meanders from his curly hair down the side of his face.

"Stop that!" I say to him.

He sticks out his tongue at me and plugs his thumbs in his ears, wriggling his fingers. He never shows signs of the nervous habits I have in common with my father. I hold my tongue in. I don't want to see it flopping around in my lap.

My grandmother sells dresses at Virginia Dare's, and as we venture in off the busy street, she greets us as if we've traveled cross-country. I love pretending we've been on the road for days to visit her shop. She hugs us and introduces the other salesladies. All of the women are roughly my grandmother's age, but none is as attractive as the name of the store, Virginia Dare, might suggest. Virginia Dare sounds *sexy,* a word I learned from *Laugh-In,* a show my father calls "filthy," but in the same breath he laughs at it. The store is humming with air conditioning. We don't have air conditioning at home; I want to stay here all day. Racks of clothing surround us; Artie and I slip in between dresses, disappearing, chasing each other.

My mother takes Artie's hand and is off to the dressing room to try on blouses. As she walks off, my grandmother says something to her about the farm. I can't tell what. Before disappearing behind a curtain, my mother's face becomes sad.

I keep myself occupied in the storefront, watching for pretty women on the sidewalk. My mother's dressing me as a girl hasn't caused me to want to *be* a girl. Rather, it deepens my interest in women. As I gaze out the window, most of the women could be mistaken for my mother, my grandmother, the women in the store. One woman, however, pads by in go-go boots. I imagine the woman is a secretary, her legs showing above the knee as she sits on her boss's lap.

After half an hour, we say our goodbyes. My grandmother slips Artie and me a dollar each, "for a treat," and we leave the store with a bag containing a blouse that, my mother explains, "Grandma bought me." I'm happy for my mother that she has something new to carry. Now we belong downtown with the other people carrying their bags.

"Will you carry this for Mommy?"

I say that I will.

I assume we will immediately catch the next bus, return to South Omaha, but my mother takes Artie by one hand, me by the other, and at Douglas Street we cross 16th. It embarrasses me to have her take my hand — what if the woman in the go-go boots sees me? Yet the farther we walk along Douglas, among the anonymous people, the freer I become. This is almost Anywhere. I've driven downtown often, but have never before walked along this particular street.

"Where're we going?" I ask.

"Kilpatrick's. I want to do a little window-shopping."

Kilpatrick's is a multistory department store, and as we make our way through the perfume counters, I'm engulfed in strong flowery smells, reminding me of my mother's dresser. We take the elevator, and as we rise to the fourth floor, I pretend we're taking it to the top of a Saturn rocket. The doors open. I miss gazing from the Wow Building. All I have now are the pretend bird's-eye visions of Puffy. I wish I could find a window to see downtown from here.

Artie runs ahead. My mother goes after him. The toy department comes into full view. I step forward, stopping, faced with a display of Snoopy dolls. Snoopy-as-an-astronaut dolls. A sign reads SNOOPY — FIRST DOG ON THE MOON!

The air goes out of me; I squeak. *Dogie is supposed to be the first dog on the moon!*

"Shit!"

"What'd you say?" my mother asks, having retrieved Artie. "We're in public!"

"Goddamned Snoopy!"

My mother grabs my hand. "Jeffrey Arthur, we're in a store. You can't talk that way." She pulls me to the elevator. "Think of Jesus."

"But Mommy, look. Snoopy!" Does she not remember my first issue of the *Dogie the Doggie News*? Before the doors close, I see in the distance the woman in the go-go boots. She's behind a cash register. I'm relieved when I realize it's a different woman.

On the way home, I watch the distorted reflection of the bus, my face, going by in store windows. There's my tongue. Going crazy, a snake, slithering in and out. The stores soon disappear and we pass boring buildings and factories, small wooden houses, houses with windows too small to capture our wavy, funhouse images.

Tonight I come across the dollar from my grandmother, still damp and folded in my pants pocket. When my father is distracted by Johnny Carson, I place the dollar in an envelope and put the envelope on his snare with a note. The note contains a drawing of a woman who looks like Goldie Hawn, and the words "Go shopping, Daddy."

Giant Steps

IN HONOR OF TODAY'S moon landing, my father took the day off and slept until noon. He was cheerful the moment he awoke, whistling while scrambling eggs, well after Artie and I had eaten lunch.

"What should we do to celebrate?" he asks me.

"Throw a party?"

"Sure!" he says.

"Have you looked around this place?" my mother asks him, standing in the kitchen with a laundry basket full of our dirty clothes.

"Oh, it won't take anything to make order," he says, winking at Artie and me.

She gives a quick shake of the head and goes to the basement.

"Of course you boys will have to do your part to clean your room."

"We will," Artie and I promise.

"Good," he says.

"Can I go to the lot first?" I ask. "I'll even take Artie."

"Sure you can."

"What are you doing?" my mother says, returning to the kitchen. "I thought you told them to clean their room."

"Oh, what's the harm," he says. "We're celebrating! They can clean later. The astronauts don't walk on the moon until tonight."

I pull the covered wagon into the shade of the mulberry tree, where we munch on the peanut butter and jelly sandwiches I packed. We swig water from an army canteen. Afterward, I pull Artie in figure eights around the lot.

95

"I'm a horse," I say, trying to make horse sounds. Artie giggles.

"Now me!" he says, getting out, grabbing the wagon handle.

"You're too little."

"Am not."

I let him try. I get in and he manages to move the covered wagon a foot or two.

"Let's go up!" Artie says, pointing to the steepest hill, straining as he pulls.

"We could tip over."

"I want to go up!"

Artie gets in, and as we make the slow climb, I hear my father's voice.

"Jeffrey! Artie!"

He's running toward us, arms waving, a human pinwheel. He calls for us with urgency, "Jeffrey, Artie! Come home. Now! Hurry!"

The moonwalk isn't supposed to happen until later. A few weeks ago, Granny had a stroke. Maybe she's died. Or perhaps my mother's choked to death. She sometimes has trouble swallowing while eating—because she's stressed, my father warns.

I hoist Artie to the ground, grabbing him by the hand, sprinting, nearly stumbling down the hill. "What is it?" I call. My father doesn't hear me. He's halfway home. My mother's turning blue. I'm sure of it. Soon the rescue squad will arrive. Behind us, the covered wagon rattles downhill toward the mulberry tree. Now my father is calling us home with his whippoorwill bird whistle. We race to the end of our driveway.

"Bastard, don't cut across my lawn!" It's Frank's disembodied voice coming from his enclosed front porch.

My father's already inside. My mother holds open the door. I'm relieved to see her pink, smiling face. "The moon!" she says. "They're going to land any minute!"

Once inside, beyond our porch and living room, I enter someone else's house. It takes a moment for my eyes to adjust. It's our family room, but it's not our family room. On the wall is Aunt Jean's seascape painting, the water and foam frozen in midwave as I've always known it. Above me is our ceiling, our chandelier, Saturn. Our hi-fi is here, and so is Times Square. But a large patch of floor has been cleared; I take in the carpet's swirls of muted rose as I might gaze from the Wow Building. I am tall. This is the largest section of clean carpet I've known in our house. Yes, there are reminders of worn pathways. But who cares? Artie plops onto the floor, as he might into a swimming pool. He spanks at it playfully. My mother takes snapshots of us.

Everything is vibrating, changing. The dining table is pushed to the corner of the room, and a Hoover — our latest vacuum — rests against a chair, satisfied and full. Particles of stirred-up dust sparkle, a snow flurry in a beam of radiant light from the window; even the old radios and typewriters, stacked in the corner, seem alive and happy; at any moment the pieces might assemble themselves into something larger and join us for the special report.

The reassuring voice of Walter Cronkite comes from an unfamiliar TV. The set works effortlessly. Does cleaning improve reception?

"I fixed it for the landing," my father says proudly, readjusting the rabbit ears. He can't make the picture more perfect. "No scratches," he says, caressing the brown cabinet. I know better than to get attached to this set, but for now it's a member of our family.

I'm trying to take in this new world, explain it to myself. The four of us squish onto an aqua vinyl davenport my mother calls a loveseat.

"Surprise!" my father says about the loveseat. "It's brand-new!" Which means it's new to us. My legs stick to the vinyl — I'm in cutoffs. This is the first time I can recall all of us sitting together.

"Do you know who Neil Armstrong is?" he asks me.

Of course I know. I've seen his name in the *Omaha World-Herald* and in *My Weekly Reader* at school. He's all I hear about lately on the news. That is, besides the war.

"Yes, Daddy," I say.

I don't know when it became awkward to call my parents Mommy and Daddy. The embarrassment snuck up on me. I want to be older, more mature. Yet I worry that if I call them Mom and Dad they will cease to exist.

We're told the lunar module has landed. We cheer, and my father offers everyone cans of ginger ale as he downs a glass of Gallo. I leap up, walk in big circles, chanting, "We landed on the moon! We landed on the moon!" The fizz of the soda gets in my nose.

While we wait for the moonwalk, my mother makes Chef Boyardee pizza. Finally, it happens. And when Walter Cronkite repeats Neil Armstrong's first words from the lunar surface, I join Artie on the floor, and together we splay out.

"Can we keep this room clean forever?" I ask. From here, peering under the loveseat, I witness where floor meets wall. It thrills me to see the floor meeting the wall.

"Of course!" my father says, downing another glass of wine, his lips purple, the color of mulberry stains.

The moon landing is good for business. To celebrate, my father transforms pegboard, toggle switches, lights, gauges, and knobs into a rocket ship's control panel. My mother paints the panel in bright colors, adding ON and OFF next to the switches. She smiles, calls me her "little astronaut." But when I hug her, when she sighs, I sense that *Apollo 11* hasn't brought her the joy that has come to my father and me.

Artie and I coordinate our efforts as we pitch a pup tent in the backyard, pretending this is our space capsule. Even Artie is old enough to understand that the world is changing. It's warm inside the tent; the musty odor of canvas is exactly how all space capsules must smell, I convince myself.

"I'm glad you two have been getting along lately," my mother says, peeking inside the tent.

If this, my getting along with Artie, can bring her joy, even joy I can't see, I will close my eyes and imagine she has come here in a space suit in a rocket of her own.

The Farm

ARTIE AND I COLLAPSE onto the floor of the family room, exhausted and sweaty. Already there are fateful signs the room will again become packed; we must enjoy it while we can. All afternoon we've been racing up and down our sidewalk in the late-July heat, to the lot and back, arms outstretched, imagining we are "space planes." On the carpet, we stretch our limbs, waving them, making snow angels in the dustiness of summer. My father stands over us. We can see up his nose from here, and above him, beyond him, the white ceiling. Somehow, if we can keep this room clean, maybe I can live down here peacefully after all.

"I have something to tell you boys," he says in a serious tone, causing us to sit up. I swallow hard, fearing something awful. "I won't be running an ad this Sunday."

I glance at Artie, not sure if he grasps the significance of this news.

"We'll have to miss church, too," he says. "And I was really hoping to go this time. But the farm is very important to your mother. That's when I put my foot down and said, 'No ad! No siree!'"

We drive in silence. I read a *Batman* comic, an issue I know by heart, not sure how long it will take to travel sixty miles. I've always imagined that the farm, which is between Dwight and David City, would exist hours—maybe a day—to the west of Omaha, yet somehow close enough for me to view from the Wow Building.

What I know of the farm, I know from my mother's stories. No one lives there. Since moving the family to the city, my grandfather has rented the fields to his brother, Milo, and to neighboring farmers. When the farm was in full swing, my grandmother killed chickens in the kitchen, the bloody headless birds fluttering without aim, smacking into the stove, the cabinets. Cleaning of any kind was a chore; the farm had no running water. The outhouse was an outpost, making the trek across the yard treacherous during blizzards. Because of the farm, my mother fears thunderstorms. When spring and summer skies are low and heavy over our South Omaha home, she recalls how her family huddled in a dugout under the house, her father wiring shut the cellar door to keep tornadoes from ripping it away. Once, a cyclone dropped a cow's head near the silo. The words "cyclone" and "silo" become entwined. I can't think of one without the other, in the same way she can't speak of the farm without mentioning bad weather. She also calls to mind a distant relative, also a farmer, who survived a lightning strike. He'd been playing polkas on an accordion in his living room next to an open window. The bolt reached in, striking the accordion, shocking him, destroying the instrument.

We make our way up the gravel driveway and crunch to a stop. On the road behind us, our Buick's trail of dust lingers, forming swirling apparitions, fissures.

"This is where I was born," she announces. She turns toward my father. "Remember the last time we were here, when Jeffrey ran around the yard?"

The way he squints into the rearview mirror, I can tell he's struggling to retrieve the memory.

I don't remember.

"He ran around," she says excitedly, "like I used to when I was three." She stops herself. "But look at the yard now."

She often regrets not having brought along a camera that day, though she did bring one today, and through the front window takes a snapshot of Artie, the first to climb out of the car, scrambling up the remaining section of road toward the house. My father's out, too, stretching, taking deep breaths. I wait in the back seat, behind my mother. I will not move until she does.

We get out and stand at the front of the Buick. The wind flutters steadily, our clothes like flags. I count exactly one cloud, lost in the endless sky. Together we watch my father and Artie gliding, cutting a path across the overgrown yard, perhaps where a sidewalk once existed. We remain here, the car's engine cooling, ticking, counting. The exterior of the Buick is clicking, too, as grasshoppers ricochet off the car's metal shell.

"Ever tasted grasshopper?" she asks, surely knowing I haven't.

I make a gagging face to amuse her, but her eyes are elsewhere.

"Taste like peanuts," she says.

I do not want grasshoppers bouncing off my stomach or landing in my hair. I fear one will fly into my mouth, so I squeeze my lips tight.

The last time we'd been here, she tells me, the front door had been padlocked. The lock had surprised her; she hadn't anticipated the need for keys. When she was growing up, the front door was always open.

"Smile," she says, taking my picture.

As we walk, she rummages in her purse. "This time," she says, "I saw Grandpa, so we won't have to sneak around, peeking into windows like prowlers." She retrieves what she's looking for, dangling the key in the bright sun, a tarnished fish on a tarnished hook.

I'm pleased to walk at my mother's side, alone.

"It's a funeral," she tells me. "I never imagined Grandpa would sell this place, would allow for the house to be torn down."

Her key leads the way as we venture toward the house, a two-story structure covered in neither gray nor brown. Yet without the presence of either color, the house wouldn't exist. Still, it's not merely the paint, worn and cracked, that provides the glue that keeps it from collapsing, but something more, perhaps its own innate stubbornness, an unwillingness to give in. I imagine long-abandoned spiders' webs in corners and doorways, in the event the spiders' descendants might someday return. Artie is rattling the door; my father makes no effort to stop him.

"Wait," she calls to Artie. Her voice is slapped away in this wind. She rushes forward; something holds me back. Slowly, I turn and run in the opposite direction, through the swaying prairie grasses and weeds, avoiding the occasional thistle. I'm weightless, floating. Where chickens once pecked, where a cow head fell to earth, where my mother's dog scampered, now only grasshoppers engage in flight training. Farther up the hill, next to the barn, the silo I have always believed would appear as a metal tornado or a lighthouse or a Saturn rocket is nothing more than what it is: a silo, askew and dented from years of weather.

But there is life here. Beyond the unkempt yard, past the dilapidated barn, orderly rows of corn and soybeans thrive. And beyond the fields, more fields, on and on into the haze. Here on the farm, the horizon has been smudged. There are no vanishing points. This is infinity.

I stand at the edge of a cornfield. In between the rows, the earth is rich and black, moist chocolate cake ready for the eating. My grandfather calls this fertile ground "dirth," which sets off my father. My mother defends my grandfather, spelling "D-I-R-T-H." I am convinced this is one of my grandfather's quiet jokes. This is cleverness, not the rural ignorance my father professes it to be.

I screech so loud and long it makes my throat sore. Here, no one can call me names. I turn; above the corn, the sagging peak of the house. I have gone too far. My freedom is replaced by an unnamed fear. I think of Jethro and Starkweather, but what scares me is the belief that I can never be free, or safe, for any great length of time. I must always remain tethered to my parents, to my home, to my drawings. Anything to keep me grounded.

My heart races as I sprint toward them, toward my family, already inside the house, the house leaning like the silo. I'm almost there, my eyes flickering, winking back at palsied windows. Up three steps. They're milling around in the first room, past the side porch and the kitchen. The kitchen smells stale, sour. How can anything this suffocating exist in the freshness of "out in the country"? I watch as my mother's eyes examine the decaying room. She opens empty cabinets, stares a moment, carefully returning the cabinet doors to their closed position, keeping order. There is no chicken blood. There are no spiders' webs. She takes no photographs.

"You were lucky," my father says to her. "Your kitchen was much bigger than the one we had growing up."

She says nothing as we move through the house in quiet procession. A table and chairs in the dining room surprise me. I hadn't counted on furniture. Certainly not a nice dining set, ready for a family gathering.

Artie climbs up on one of the chairs. "No," I whisper, but he does not listen. His pants, the front of his shirt, instantly become covered in dust. I make him climb down, and gently swipe away the chalky film from his clothes.

My parents have moved on to the next room, and my mother's strange, wistful voice draws me to her. I rush to get there, to hear what she is telling my father.

"I can't believe it," she says.

"What, Mommy?" I ask.

"This," she says, "is where I almost died." These are new words for my mother, unlike my father's constant retelling of his near-death experiences. "This is where Jethro's gun accidentally discharged."

We study the black dot in the wall, a hole no bigger than the end of a pencil. It takes me a moment to comprehend what she is explaining.

"My dad told him not to clean his rifle in the house," she says, practically in the voice of a little girl. "He promised it wasn't loaded." She retraces her steps. "I was walking by, right here, when the gun went off." She pauses. "I thought I'd been shot. It was that close."

The hole, in its tiny blackness, frightens me. If I were to stick my finger inside, I might never get it back; the hole might take my hand, might pull me in and swallow me. I avert my eyes to a floral davenport, nicer than ours. There, in the middle of it, the *Butler County Press,* dated December 9, 1959, waits to be read. I want to pick it up, to see if there are comics. I can't bring myself to reach for it.

Everyone else moves from the room and I hear them make their way upstairs. One more glance at the hole as I bring up the rear, the creaky steps narrow and dark. We find ourselves on the second floor, in a bedroom awash in sunlight. Curtains are pulled open. Two beds appear freshly made. If not for glaring omissions — no bureau, no dresses hanging in the closet — someone might dwell here. My mother slowly shakes her head from side to side. Is she denying something? A memory? She exhales, breathing life into the room. I try to imagine her younger self, her thinner self, before she became pregnant with me, but I see her only as she is, her breasts heaving with deliberation in this mustiness.

"Was this your room?" I ask, knowing the answer.

"Yes, sweetie. It was."

"Mommy's room?" says Artie.

"That's right." She strokes his soft hair, more golden than brown. "I shared it with two of my sisters."

My father investigates the inside of the closet. From where I stand, I see no clothes, no boxes. I do not know closets this empty.

He moves, and wire hangers jangle, wind chimes in a windless room. "What the hell?" he says, disappearing around the corner.

"What, Daddy?" Artie asks.

"What is it?" I say. I fear a dead animal, maybe a raccoon.

From the closet, the metallic rattling of distant thunder. He removes a dollhouse as big as a TV.

My mother's face lights up at the same time as she says, "You're kidding. I never thought I'd see it again." She reaches for the dollhouse, placing her hand affectionately on its metal roof. "They told me there wasn't room for it in the truck. That we'd come back for it."

"It's filthy but in good condition," my father says. "And I'll bet it's worth something." He gives it a shake. Tiny pieces of furniture slide around inside. A blue plastic chair. Matching davenport. A red plastic TV. All wall hangings are painted on, like something from *The Twilight Zone*.

"Can we take it home?" I ask. I want this dollhouse more than anything.

"Of course we can," my father says.

My mother hesitates. I whisper the word "no," in anticipation of her saying it. "Maybe it belongs here," she says, brushing the dust from her hand.

A look of confusion flashes across my father's face. "After they tear down the house it'll be too late," he says.

"I know." Her words are barely audible.

"I want to play," Artie says, pulling at the dollhouse.

"No, honey." My mother gently guides Artie away.

We stand here in this near-empty bedroom, watching what will happen, my father holding the dollhouse, but not too close to his chest, to keep himself clean.

A gust of wind makes the bedroom shudder; I close my eyes. When I open them again, we are all here in this room.

"What do you think they got for it?" he asks my mother, breaking the silence.

"Got for what?" she says, almost groggy.

"The farm. How much?"

"Why must you always —" She stops herself, her shoulders slump.

"Well, I just think if they're going to be rich," he continues, "they sure as hell could help their children. We all know your mother gambles too much. Bingo. The racetrack."

"Jean goes to the racetrack," she says.

"That's different. She studies the horses, the jockeys, the trainers. But Grandma? It's all about the money, money, money."

"You're not even making sense."

"All I know is, *my* mother would help if she weren't in her condition. And poor. Yet we hardly see her."

"Is that my fault?"

He grumbles.

"I'm constantly telling you to go see her. Don't blame me."

I do not want them to fight, but I do not know how to stop them, here in this alien place. I leave the room, race down the steps, and run outside to the driveway. I will run from them, beyond the farm. I will run forever. But I am too afraid and move toward the Buick. I settle into its familiar back seat, waiting, watching for them to emerge from the house, for my mother to lock the door behind her forever.

My father loads the dollhouse into the trunk, and in my hands, for the drive home, I hold the miniature furnishings that came with it. I also cradle a pink rubber baby that fell out of the dollhouse, one that is too large — "out of proportion," as my father says. My hand sweats as I hold this baby, not wanting anything to happen to it. When we get home, I will make tiny paintings for the walls, but I won't clutter the rooms. I will leave them spare, not quite lived in, a museum. My father will grimace at me for playing with it, complaining that he could make good money on it. When no one is watching, I will live there, squeezing my face into the rooms, the metal edges of the partitions pressing against my forehead and temples. I'll run my fingers along the corners of the rooms, where wall meets floor.

An Unexpected Visitor

THE RADIO'S CRANKED, and the drive to Eppley Airfield is filled with reports from Vietnam and Woodstock, a rock concert my father says is "nothing but filth." It's a month after the moon landing, and the images from the landing mix in with my dreams, mix in with visions of women in go-go boots dancing in mud, listening to what my father calls "not real music." There is a wildness to the world right now. Men are dying in remote jungles and everything is expanding, stretching, buzzing. In the middle of all this chaos my father vows that one day his "music will make a comeback. You'll see."

We travel along Abbott Drive, and as we near the airport, I expect the sky to be filled with the commotion of airplanes taking off and landing. But there is no commotion. We drive closer and I catch glimpses of planes on the tarmac. Here and there, gleaming rudders peek above the terminal, shark fins above the water. The planes, the rudders, even from this distance, appear larger than I could have imagined. Except for TV, I've only seen the planes that cruise above our South Omaha home, some so high they appear as tiny silver crosses. This is my first trip to an airport. We're here to say goodbye to Cousin Eddie, to "see him off," as my Aunt Jean says.

Jean phoned last week to say that Eddie had come to town. The call was a surprise; we'd had no warning he was coming. After the call, my father again dredged up his disgust for a boy who would abandon his father's name. "I want nothing to do with him," my father said as we drove the next day for lunch at Ross' Steakhouse, where I met Eddie for the first time. Jean was there, as was Uncle Len and Aunt Ann and cousins I barely knew. My father was grateful Frank and Mary were away on vacation. Granny remained in the hospital. Still, as far as I could recall, never before had so many of my father's relatives gathered in one place. And besides, I'd long hoped to eat dinner at Ross', the steakhouse with a giant steer head for a sign.

My father was cordial that day as he shook Eddie's hand. My mother hugged him. Eddie shook my hand. I belonged to the grown-up world until he also shook Artie's hand.

There was chatter about Granny, the full paralysis, how she would never recover, how Jean was looking into buying a hospital bed, converting her dining room into a sickroom. At lunch my father complained to my mother about the "ungodly prices" of eating out. We kept mostly to ourselves, at our end of the table. It was strange to watch the relatives engage in conversation, particularly those with whom we didn't get along, like Len and Ann, in their Hawaiian shirts, fresh from their trip to the islands. We didn't speak much to Eddie during dinner, but I snuck glances at him. Nineteen years old and handsome, he laughed with confidence. I strained to hear as he blushingly answered questions about girls. He worked part-time at a toy store, he said, during school vacations. "To save up for a set of wheels," he explained. He uttered something about piano and jazz — that he "loved jazz."

No one mentioned his father.

This made me sad, because I'd grown up listening to stories about his father that he, Eddie, possibly didn't know. Stories perhaps his mother didn't know, and if she did, possibly didn't speak them in an effort to forge ahead with a new husband, a new last name. It is not my right, my *privilege*, to know things about Eddie's father that Eddie himself does not. While growing up, did he know that his father had attended the first-ever televised presidential press conference? Or that his parents once lived next to the NBC anchorman David Brinkley, who now reports about the war? Had he heard that his father once befriended a young photographer, Jacqueline Bouvier, before Jack Kennedy met her?

• • •

We left the restaurant en masse, heading into the white heat of early afternoon. In the parking lot I walked at his side, in his shadow. This was Eddie. *Uncle Ed's* Eddie. Right here. Next to me. I couldn't speak. I wanted to say something, anything, but a lump formed in the part of my throat that makes the strange sounds.

"My daddy invented a toy," I said, practically choking on my words, grateful no squawking came out.

"What's that?" Eddie said, stopping, giving me his attention. "A toy?"

Everyone kept walking in the haze. The gooey pavement sweated.

I swallowed. "My daddy invented the Dizzy Wizzy."

He chuckled, getting on his haunches. "The Dizzy Wizzy?"

"Yes, sir."

"Call me Eddie."

"Okay."

"Anyway, this all sounds interesting. Anything else?"

"You spin it around and it makes noise."

"That so? What else?"

I shrugged with nervousness. He waited in case I had anything more to say and laughed as we caught up with the others.

"Uncle Art," Eddie said, "tell me about the Dizzy Wizzy."

"That?" he said in a low voice. "Oh," he stumbled. "Well, that's nothing. Hey, sure is hot today!"

Eddie seemed perplexed but took my father's answer in stride, giving me a smile.

And to ensure the subject had indeed been changed, my father addressed Jean. "Say, maybe we could find a good used hospital bed for Mom."

Jean considered my father's suggestion. "I think Mom deserves a *new* hospital bed."

"Of course," my father said. "Certainly."

I saw my father's scowl, the look directed at me, the face that condemned me for revealing his secret toy. There was no doubt he was angry.

Before we get out of the car, my mother primps her fake hair in the rearview mirror. "Remember," she says to my father, keeping her eyes on her reflection, "Eddie can't help that he was so young when his father was killed."

"He's not a child now," my father shoots back. "Nothing's stopping him from changing his name back."

"He's *still* a boy," she says, making sure every strand of her wig is in place.

"Why does everyone in this car hate me?" my father growls.

"No one's against you!" I say, unable to imagine my last name as "Gnagy."

"Everyone's against me except Artie." He smacks the steering wheel. "Who helps with TVs? Who wants to learn about them? Who wants to be a drummer like me? Artie, that's who the hell who. If I died, Artie sure as hell would never change his name." He clears his throat, attempts to catch his breath.

"What's the matter?" my mother asks him.

"Nothing. Probably just a heart attack."

"It's stuffy in here," she says, opening her door.

We are the last to arrive at the gate. Eddie boards in ten minutes. My father again shakes Eddie's hand. I am surprised my father gives him a pat to the back, calls him nephew, tells him not to be such a stranger.

"Come out to West Virginia sometime," Eddie says.

"Sure thing," my father says.

My mother embraces him, calls him Eddie, says his mother must be "quite proud."

Eddie tousles my hair, tells me that in the past few days he's heard I'm a good artist.

This must make me blush. I glance around. Here in the airport, strangers gather in a blur of reunions, farewell parties. It's a Sunday. This is better than church. I want to believe that everyone here, everyone on Earth, is loved by someone. There is loud laughter like a sitcom audience. There are tears in the eyes of these people whose faces I will never see again, people revealing their hearts at the gate, in front of tall rectangles of glass, embracing, never letting go. I hope, I pray, that it appears to those people, to the shoeshine man, the janitor, the attractive woman at the airline counter, that we, too, are a loving family.

After Eddie boards his plane, I look at the gleaming expanse of aircraft. The nose, as big as I imagine a rocket's, faces me straight on. The engines roar, whistle. As the plane begins to pull away from the gate, I think I see Eddie in one of the plane's windows, waving. Maybe not. I wave anyway. Artie stands next to me, waves too. My father calls for Artie and me, telling us it's time to go. I lean my forehead against the warm glass of the terminal window, squinting against a stinging beam of reflected sunlight coming from the plane's wing.

"Jeffrey," my father says.

Artie tugs at my shirt. "Mommy and Daddy said we have to go!" When did he get to be so strong?

"I'll be there in a minute, Dad."

Dad.

I don't say the rest of his name. Not finishing, not saying "Daddy," puts my stomach in a free fall, on a roller coaster. I glance around and my father is laughing it up with Len, as if everything is okay between them. I don't know if he heard what I said. Or what I didn't say. I press my forehead into the glass, pushing harder.

I watch as the plane lifts itself from the runway, almost in slow motion. I can't take my eyes—refuse to take my eyes—from the plane as it moves farther away. I watch until it dissolves into the sky.

PART TWO

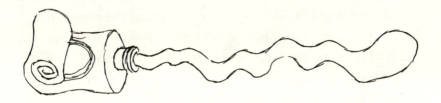

Our Happy Landscape

TURN THAT CRAP DOWN," my father growls at me, shielding his eyes from the June sun. "Think I want to listen to dope fiends in my own backyard?" He's on the filthy driveway, tinkering with a bike for my six-year-old sister, Jennifer. Artie's at his side, awaiting any chance to get his hands greasy. "Why doesn't anyone play Benny Goodman anymore?" I endure my father's complaints whenever I play Led Zeppelin, Three Dog Night, Grand Funk Railroad, or the Grateful Dead. I have countless records, but only these four eight-track tapes. At the moment, the Grateful Dead's "Truckin'" blares from the tape player that sits atop an upside-down garbage can.

I let the music play on, not moving from my garage sale easel, from my almost-finished painting of an imagined mountain scene.

My mother's in her own world, smiling as Little Eddie helps her hang laundry on the clothesline. He was born a year after Jennifer came along. We call him Little Eddie to keep clear who's who, even though we have no contact with Cousin Eddie and haven't seen him since the day we said goodbye at the airport. Besides, my father reminds us that my baby brother is named for my uncle.

Little Eddie reaches into the basket and patiently holds up a pair of my father's plaid boxers for my mother. Without his help she struggles, her big stomach pressing into her chest. "You would have thought my fifth pregnancy would be my easiest," she says lately, gasping.

Despite her difficulties, it pleases her that her family is able to spend time together like this, "everyone doing their own thing." Inside the house it's stifling; at least outside we can spread out, catch a breeze in the shade of our garages and storage sheds.

"And get your hair cut." My father is shouting at me again. "You look like a hippie. Do you hear me?"

I take my time responding. From paint tubes, I squeeze out the last of my titanium white, a fresh splotch of ultramarine blue. My mother likes my hair. She calls me Keith, from *The Partridge Family*, which makes me happy because I'm in love with David Cassidy's costar, Susan Dey.

"Jesus had long hair," I say back to my father, not yelling, not caring if he hears me. The Grateful Dead tape cycles through, starts again at the beginning. I need to concentrate. I'm about to add snow to a rocky peak. I shake my head, flipping my stringy hair from my eyes as I focus. I again jerk my head, hair landing in my eyes. Even my father knows I'm not disrespecting him with my shaking head. This is simply one of my latest habits, part of an explosion of new cravings that comes from within and must be expressed *somehow*. To ignore the desire only makes me want to twitch more. It's a craving that can never be sated, a longing that can never be fulfilled. When my father cares to comment on my new habits, he says it's just my raging hormones. When I'm around others my age, however, it seems that their hormones only change their voices, give them acne. I have that problem, too, but those things are nothing compared to the unnatural way my body wants to move.

Painting calms me, but not entirely. Finally, I sweep my hair aside with my forearm and apply the coated bristles to the canvas. I love the smooth firmness of the brush, the wet paint, the pink, glistening mountain.

I've never seen an actual mountain. The nearest one is five hundred miles west of Omaha, in Colorado. The farthest west

I've been is the farm. What I know about painting mountains, I know from TV. I never miss William Alexander's *The Magic of Oil Painting*, which comes on every Saturday afternoon on PBS. In his German accent, he explains how "ve vill paint zis happee mountain like zis," "zat happee tree like zat." Everything—a cloud, a sunset, a rock—is happy. He is the polar opposite of stress. Nothing bothers him.

For my fifteenth birthday I'd asked for a set of the William Alexander brand of oil paints. Instead I received a five-dollar bill Scotch-taped to a package of Fruit of the Loom men's briefs. They weren't even the right size. The only allowance I receive is when I help my father with TVs, so this summer I plan to mow neighborhood lawns to save up for paint—besides, the loudness of the mower allows me to make all the throat sounds I want. Meanwhile, I work from a limited spectrum of secondhand Grumbacher tubes my father brought home one Saturday. For whatever reason, burnt umber, raw umber, burnt sienna—nearly all of the earth tones—were either missing or dried up. Now all of my mountain scenes are in pastels—pinks, blues, lavenders—even more happy than the happy paintings on TV.

I dab on more paint, covering the mountaintop like frosting. My mountaintop ice *is* icing. I am tempted to lick it.

Out of nowhere, Jennifer is sobbing, sitting in the dirt. She's fallen off our swing set. I look around; my mother must be in the house with Little Eddie, putting away the clothes. My father has turned Jennifer's bike upside down, spinning the front tire like a roulette wheel.

"Are you okay?" I call to Jennifer, putting down my brush. While rushing to her, I stumble over a lamp. Now Jennifer and I are both on the ground. Lately, everything about me—not just the twitches—feels awkward and clumsy. I'm all limbs and feet, tripping over myself, banging into our junk, grunting, shaking my head so hard I worry that it'll fly off across the yard.

I'm not hurt from the fall. "Whoopsie," I say, even though she's probably too old for me to talk to her like that. But because she didn't get to be the baby of the family very long, I feel sorry for her. Plus, she has nervous habits, too. I smile, hoping to stop her tears, hoping to show her that everyone falls sometime.

I don't look forward to having my father home every day during my vacation. This will be our first summer since he had his breakdown at the Union Pacific. I'd come home from school one day last winter to find my mother, head in hands at the kitchen table, my father in bed, sobbing. He cried through the night. From what little my mother told me, he had simply fallen to the floor near his desk at work and curled into the fetal position. None of us had seen it coming, yet it had come as no surprise. In some ways, it made sense that my father would leave the U.P. the way he did.

He hated his job from the start. The monotony. The "asshole" bosses who didn't appreciate that he was a drummer. The cold air blowing on his head, giving him the flu. He said he didn't need any priest preaching about hell—he'd been there, every day he went to his job. He blamed his sisters Jean and Ann, who had worked there long before he started his job, in the wake of my birth. The proper way for a man to provide for his family was to "put his nose to the grindstone," they insisted. But, as he often reminded us, he was meant to play music, to sing. And to invent toys that would bring happiness to others, gadgets that would cure the sick.

He'd received retirement benefits, which, he said later, "I'd sure as hell better get after giving that shithole the best years of my life. But we're still going to have to tighten our belts around here." If there had been any question before about our family's financial picture, all doubt was erased: without my father's full-time job, we were destined for "the poorhouse."

Over the years, my mother had raised the possibility of getting a job, and now, when she again mentions it to my father, he shuts her down in predictable fashion. "I need you here," he says, stretching his mouth so completely I can count his cavities.

"What if something happens to me? What if I keel over? Besides, I know what goes on when women work outside the home. Affairs. The whole world has gotten so goddamned immoral."

During those first weeks after his "medical" retirement he seemed instantly relaxed; even his twitches seemed to lessen briefly. He also hummed and sang more than I could recall, giving me hope that he might again get serious about music. Maybe even travel with a band. And didn't he still talk about reviving the Dizzy Wizzy, applying for a patent? Maybe this was his chance — *our* chance — for the fame and fortune he so often dreamed of. But for some time his drums have been sitting unused in the basement, his cymbals tossed like Frisbees; his Dizzy Wizzys remain jumbled in a box in the old garage.

Artie

W HEN IT COMES to the movement and placement of his junk, there appears to be no logic to the chores my father assigns to Artie. This TV goes to the patio. That record player belongs in the basement. Those rain-filled tires? Into the new garage. No, wait. The *old* garage. On and on. Dutifully, Artie follows my father around the yard, in and out of the house, up and down the basement steps, anticipating my father's every need, his every desire. In our family, objects *are* family. We must care for them, consider where best they should dwell. For this reason, no job is too daunting for Artie, and at eleven, he has the "strength of twenty men," my father tells him, bolstering him, making him grin. It's one more way my father pits Artie against me, the one he calls "lazy" and "worthless."

Artie taunts me, smug that he is able to please our father. But no matter how hard Artie tries to get on my nerves, I cannot resent him. Instead I flash the peace sign at him. He retaliates with his own peace sign, followed by his shoving both fingers up his nostrils.

He knows how this irritates me, but I don't come back at him because I know that Artie fears what I fear. He hears the way our father complains that we are now "broker than broke," completely dependent on TV sales to put food on the table. He sees the way our father gasps when his heart "skips a beat." He sees what follows: our father pounding on his chest as if thumping away at the side of a flipping TV, attempting to set it right.

I know I should do more to help. And occasionally I offer my services, standing around like Artie, jerking my head, awaiting my father's instructions, following him, straining to lift heavy objects, running when he calls for me. I'd rather stay in my humid bedroom upstairs, with my guitar and old *Playboy* magazines I'd once discovered in a box from a garage sale, sketching the centerfolds, studying the cartoons, and skimming the interviews. Besides wanting to be held by big-breasted bunnies, I long to one day become one of the smartly dressed men in the cartoons. Men with skinny ties and trim suits who are always surrounded by pouty-lipped women barely covered in sheer negligees. These men make me think of Cousin Eddie.

Sometimes the rattling hum of my window fan makes me drowsy, and I sleep, a *Playboy* opened to the centerfold, spread on my stomach.

I rely on the fan, and my records, tapes, and guitar, to dampen the noise of the house. I choose not to have a TV. In the eyes of my father, I'm blasphemous: I could pick from any number of sets, but I defy him.

• • •

I can hear my parents below me in the hallway, fighting. Their voices rise through the floor, to my room, with the afternoon heat. My first instinct is to race downstairs and around the house, closing windows. Then I remember we are running our newly acquired air conditioner, a wheezing window unit; certainly the windows on the main floor are closed. I turn off my fan to better hear what's being said, in case I need to intervene.

"He's too young to carry that ox of a TV," my mother screams. "He might get a rupture!" She's always expressing concern for Artie, how he works "like a horse" despite his age.

"What do you know about health?" he shouts. "You should see what *I* had to do at that age."

"He's not you. He's going to hurt himself."

My father dismisses her worries. "This is the only way he's going to grow into a *man!*" he shouts. "Unlike that other thing upstairs!"

It takes me a moment to understand that I'm the "other thing." I imagine myself as a character in a Dr. Seuss book. Maybe I *am* just a thing, a creature whose face is covered in hair, a creature who gets strange looks from neighbors when he rides his ten-speed down the street, his voice screeching, hoping people will think the sound is coming from his brakes and not his throat.

"You're awful!" she shouts.

I rub my fingertips together, yet another new tic, exploring the texture of my calluses. The calluses are the result of practicing the guitar.

Artie usually contributes to the fight, but his voice is oddly absent. He must be working out back. Someone slams a door. The other kids won't stop shrieking.

"Do you want me to have this baby right now?" My mother can barely breathe, she's pushing her voice so hard. I picture her face turning crimson, like fresh oil paint.

For once, I will resist them. Perhaps my absence, my nonresponse, will make them wonder where I am. Maybe I've died in this heat. Maybe I've plummeted to the baked concrete of the driveway, the thud of my body drowned out by their screaming.

I've tried this tactic before. It never works, and for the sake of the kids, I will give in, leaping from my bed with our Catholic Bible. And although I don't read it with any regularity, I do read it more than anyone else in the house, so I keep it with me. I love the heft of it, and the soft leather feels so smooth against my fingers. When I can't take it anymore, I open to a random page and begin preaching, even if I don't fully understand what I'm saying, or believe in it.

"'And in return for their senseless, wicked thoughts,'" I shout, clomping down the steps, the music still blaring, "'which misled them into worshiping dumb serpents and worthless insects, you sent upon them swarms of dumb creatures for vengeance!'" I'm grateful I've chosen a passage that doesn't contain any difficult-to-pronounce words.

We circle through the house. *Oh, my God, the windows are open.* I cradle the Bible, trying not to lose my page, slamming shut the windows.

"You're trying to kill me," my father growls at her in the living room. "You're all goddamned trying to kill me," he says, pointing a bottle of Jack Daniel's at my forehead.

"'My soul pines for your salvation'!" I shout. "'I hope in your word'!"

"Grandma has always hated me," he complains. "It's all about the money."

"'My eyes strain after your promise; when will you comfort me'!"

"But I'll be dead soon," he says, "so what does it matter?"

"Why are you doing this?" my mother asks my father, her eyes red and watery.

His eyes are white with rage; he does not hear her.

I wish I had an answer for her. But the seeds of my parents' fights were planted long ago.

They don't stop fighting. Not even when I was Artie's age and began reading the Bible aloud, standing on the davenport, did they pay attention. The kids keep screaming, too. Artie dashes into the house, hugging my father, glaring at me. He could hurt me if he wanted to. He's stout, brimming with strength. Already he can beat me at arm wrestling.

When I see my father like this, I worry that what happened between him and his brother Frank will happen to Artie and me. Maybe I didn't do enough to protect him.

My mother, her face swollen, slowly makes her way to our new couch. She's defeated, resting, sinking into the deep cushions. This "new" couch, with foam squeezing from torn seams, isn't much better than the davenport we tossed into the ravine.

"C'mon," I tell Jennifer and Eddie, taking each of them by the hand to their room, my old room. "Let's play a game."

We dig through the toy box, searching for missing Candy Land pieces. Out the back window I watch as my father crosses the yard, Artie marching behind, a little soldier in my father's army. I know in my heart I will never follow my father like that.

My Friend

I CAREFULLY PLACE my guitar in the trunk. Everyone except my father and Artie piles into the Oldsmobile Cutlass Supreme; we're headed to my grandparents'. My mother tried to get Artie to come along, but he threw a fit and begged to stay behind. Lately, my grandmother cleans houses as a way to make "gambling money," as my father calls it. My grandfather won't give her an allowance to blow on bingo and at the track, but he can't stop her from making her own money, my mother explains to me. So she's not always at home, and besides, whenever we visit, it causes my parents to fight.

I sit up front, frequently turning around and asking the kids to "keep it down back there, please." I use a softer voice than my father does. It pleases my mother when I help with my siblings, especially now that she's in such discomfort, her stomach bulging against the steering wheel.

My grandparents' driveway is off a back alley, shaded by a single tree. This tree makes me sad; one tree can't begin to compare to what they had on the farm. As we pull in, Jethro is under his Chevy, the car's body jacked up on one corner. Spread across the cement are shiny wrenches—silver bones. He's clanking on something, and his blue jean legs, white socks, and worn black shoes are all we see.

We get out of the car and the kids scramble toward the house, my mother following.

"Hello, Jethro," she says.

He keeps up his racket.

I retrieve my guitar, slamming the trunk to get his attention. I move slowly, hoping he will slide out from under his car and notice the curvy black case I carry. Inside, the guitar I adore, a blond Fender twelve-string my father "picked up" recently for $25. I begged him not to resell it for more money; I received it in exchange for $25 worth of chores.

I yearn for Jethro to ask what kind of music I like. All my father ever talks about, all he ever cares about, is his kind of music.

If Jethro asks, I will tell him that although we can't afford lessons, I'm teaching myself the guitar by listening to my LPs. Everything from Cream to José Feliciano. I'll admit I can't begin to figure out Jimi Hendrix. A bug makes its way toward Jethro's legs, pauses, considering whether to crawl inside his pants.

As long as I can remember, he has never spoken to me directly. No matter how hard I think it, *will it* to happen, Jethro refuses to acknowledge me.

If he only knew I stopped fearing him years ago.

When I was thirteen, I gave in to my desire, running my index finger along the seam under his door. Jethro was not home, but my finger under the door gave me courage. Later, I began to sit on my grandparents' basement steps, listening as Jethro sang and played in his room Johnny Cash's "Folsom Prison Blues" and "Ring of Fire."

Lately, when I listen, I think of Jethro, how his high school football career was cut short. He once kicked the winning field goal in a close game, and afterward the opposing team trampled him, breaking his leg in three places. I'm old enough to understand disappointment's lasting effects. And when I think of the bullet hole in the farmhouse that no longer exists, I know it truly was an accident. That's the Christian thing to do. To forgive.

My grandmother removes her flour-dusted apron so she can hug us.

"How would everyone like to help Grandma bake cookies?" she whispers.

The kids cheer.

My grandmother holds her index finger to her lips.

"We need to be quiet," I tell the kids. "For Grandpa."

"So how *is* Dad?" my mother asks in a low voice.

"He's okay today," my grandmother says, retying her apron. "The humidity is hard on him, though."

I stay in the kitchen to help with the kids while my mother slips off to see my grandfather in the next room. We go in one at a time so as not to overwhelm him. My grandmother flattens a lump of dough, giving the kids scraps they form into balls. I'm put in charge of an upside-down glass to stamp out circles in the dough, making cookie cutouts. There's freedom in making a mess in a clean kitchen. Clean counters, floors, stove, are blank canvases. When my mother returns from the next room, I know I'll have to go to my grandfather. I love him, but I hesitate. I want him to be how I remember him, before he became sick from tobacco. Every time I visit, I hope somehow he will be his old self.

My mother senses my hesitation. "Grandpa really wants to see you," she says, massaging my shoulder.

I finish my job and brush flour from my T-shirt and hands. I grab my guitar. In case he wants to see it.

The first thing I hear is the hum of his machine. The way he's hooked up to an oxygen tank and mask, he appears ready for a deep-sea adventure. Even the tank's metal surface is a mix of blue, brown, and iridescent green — colors that might have accumulated from a deep ocean. Sunk into his big chair, he sits, his Bible open on his lap. I stand in the entry of the dining room with my guitar. Is he sleeping?

I'm here, Grandpa.

His chest rises, falls, with measured deliberateness. I count his breaths. Finally, he peers above his glasses, above the fogged-over mask. He winks.

"Hi, Grandpa," I whisper. I gently put down the guitar case, moving carefully to my grandmother's rocking chair as if furniture, floor, and man are interconnected in their frailty. Just now I become aware of music — a record spins on the turntable, the volume knob barely above three, a polka boom-chucking, providing the room with a soft pulse. My grandfather is religious, but not fire and brimstone; he reads the Bible, prays the rosary, but also enjoys beer-drinking music.

It makes me claustrophobic to see his face covered in this way. As he returns to his reading, I imagine him smiling under the mask. I am grateful to be with him like this, teetering slowly in my grandmother's rocking chair. Even if my grandfather and I don't speak a single word, I will wait, I won't disturb him. Every family needs someone to read the Bible. "We Catholics don't study the Bible enough," he often says. I am comforted simply by sitting here with my grandfather. Sitting, rocking. I find myself relaxing, my breathing calm and natural. Nodding my head to the distant accordion of a new song, I count to myself. *One*-two-three, *one*-two-three — a waltz.

The house begins to fill with the smell of cookies. Over the hum of the machine, over my grandfather's wheezing, I can hear my grandmother ask my mother about baby names. I can't tell what my mother says in response. Across the room from me, my grandfather pulls at straps, removing his mask.

The mask has left a red oval on his wrinkled face. His thin gray mustache arcs over his frown. He reaches for a switch, his machine sputtering to a halt. A tuba oom-pah-pahs from a speaker.

"This is my friend," he says, patting the machine. "Does your friend have a name?" He struggles for air.

I shake my head, not sure what he means. I don't ask. He's capable of saying "Storm's coming" with the same straight face as "I once had a cat who could talk." My father believes my grandfather's poker face allows him to keep great secrets. Secrets like how much money was made on the sale of the farm. My father believes millions. But I love that my grandfather isn't over the top like my father. He doesn't make a show of it when he prays, reads, or kids around. If not for his noisy machine and lungs, he might not ever make a sound.

He closes the Bible and coughs. I don't move. I'm afraid moving will appear disrespectful. I must listen to every thick, watery sound from his lungs. I must listen to every cough.

The record crackles to the next song. A clarinet wails.

"Are you two going to give us a concert?" he asks.

I can't help but laugh. Now I get it: "friend" meant guitar. It was obvious, but I don't feel stupid for not understanding right away.

"I'm still learning how to play," I say.

He inhales. I know there is no pressure to play the guitar for him. Not now. Not ever. Playing music is on my terms.

"Big plans this summer?"

"Not especially," I say, glancing at my guitar case. I almost ask about Jethro, Jethro's guitar playing, but all my grandfather ever says about Jethro is "That son of mine. What can you do?"

He grins. I wait for him to say something, to make a joke. But he simply, yet utterly, smiles at me.

What did I do to deserve this smile?

His face changes as he prepares to stand, untangling his tube. "Well," he says, "it's about that time." He struggles to rise and I help him to his room so he can take his nap. He can handle the machine himself, but I come to his aid, wheeling it behind him.

With my grandfather in bed, I return to the rocking chair, to let the record finish playing.

The kids bring cookies. "Where's Grandpa?" they ask.

"Shhh," I tell them. "He's sleeping."

I guide them to the front porch, to the old glider from the farm, the glider squeaking as we move with the undulating rhythm of a boat on a lake. I draw pictures, making them squeal with excitement. "Draw a bear!" they shout. "Draw a kitty!" After we have our fill of cookies, I occupy them with my grandmother's supply of coloring books. When I'm assured they're content, I slip inside the house. Removing my "friend" from its case, I go to my mother, asking if I may have a break. I know the answer.

"He's so good with the kids," she tells my grandmother, reaching to me. "Come here. You're never too old to hug your mother," she says, pulling me against her, getting flour on my T-shirt. I let myself, the guitar, get hugged, mildly embarrassed by this display of affection in front of my grandmother.

"Is Jethro still out back?" I ask.

"Sorry, Jeffrey," my grandmother says. "He went to his room."

"Oh," I say.

"I think," my mother says, "Jeffrey was hoping to talk to Jethro about guitars."

"Isn't it terrible the way he is?" my grandmother says. "He only plays in his room. He's such a hermit."

"If only he'd found a wife," my mother offers, in the way she might speak of a dead person.

"And a job," my grandmother adds.

They go on like this as I slip past them, to the door leading to the basement.

· · ·

The familiar scent of sawdust and tobacco. There is no light coming from beneath his door. I sit on the steps, somewhere between the top and bottom, wedging my gangly self, my guitar, between railing and wall. While tuning, I rest my head, my ear, against the body of the guitar. This allows me to hear each string in the vibration of the wood without strumming hard. I gently pluck the low E string. Flat. I twist its tuning knob. I repeat this ritual until I believe all twelve strings are at home. I meekly run my thumb across the wide expanse of all the strings. Something is still off. Even one sour string can make all the others sound not quite right. But all it takes is patience, and a slight adjustment to one of the parts, to make perfect the whole. I return my ear to the cool wood of the guitar. One last tweaking. I take a deep breath, softly making a C-major chord. The chord makes sense; the sounds are aligned.

I strum again, with slightly more force. The chord rings out, cutting through the musty air.

Now an F.

Back to C, then G. It could be a country song. Or a song from grade school, like "This Land Is Your Land."

Is Jethro napping, too? Does he listen as he dreams?

I have no lyrics, but if I did, I'd be too timid to let the words filter from brain to lips. It's easier to sing at school, in a group, but even then, I usually just mouth the words. How can I sing when I can't look people in the eye? I hold my head down, my hair in my face to help hide me, even in the darkness of the basement.

All I Do Around Here

WHAT SHALL WE HAVE for dinner?" my mother asks me. It's late morning, when I should be in algebra. She called South High, told them I was sick. Although the bullying dissipated a couple of years ago—now I mostly get ignored—I can't stand school. Never mind that it's not even a month into my sophomore year. And it's not entirely untrue that I'm sick. I regularly carry around a stomachache. Art class is about the only reason why I make it to school when I do.

We're on the edge of her bed, folding towels. I hate folding towels. I can never make them into perfect squares. Always, a thread hangs loose, a corner sticks out. None of our towels match; the ones at Aunt Jean's or my grandparents' always do. These towels are ragged, worn. Some are spotted with oil and grease.

"Hmm," I say. "We just had fried chicken last night. Meatloaf?"

"That does sound good!"

Jeanie lies on the bed. My mother glances at her often to make sure she doesn't fall off and hit her "soft spot." When it comes to her babies, my mother hasn't given up her worrying.

She bends, reaching for another laundry basket, cringing from the occasional pain that lingers from the C-section. "Here," I say. "Let me." I lift it, emptying the basket's contents, the kids' shirts and shorts.

"All I do around here is work, work, work," she says. She never used to talk like my father.

"I know what you mean." We're like two lonely mothers, comparing our sad lives. I wish my mother had a girlfriend to confide in. I wish that I, too, had a girlfriend. But I'm too afraid to call a store to ask them how late they are open, so the thought of ever asking a girl on a date is beyond my comprehension.

My mother sighs. Now that several months have passed since having the baby, her face is thinner. I even detect a wrinkle in her forehead.

Like her face, her room is familiar, but enough has changed so that I no longer feel at home there. Same dresser, though the wigs have long since disappeared. Same paint on the walls, but longer cracks. Same bed, but it sags even more, making it uncomfortable for sitting; I fear I will fall inward, causing the stack of towels to collapse. The old crib remains butted against the bed.

She catches me staring at the crib. "Where will we put the little one?" she asks. "She can't stay in our room forever."

I can't imagine. We're full up. Eddie and Jennifer share my old room. We couldn't possibly squeeze a third bed in there. There's no space in my room upstairs — because of the slant of the roof, I can barely stand up straight. And at the top of the steps Artie has his makeshift sleeping area — essentially a hallway with a curtain.

"Maybe," I say, "we can put up another curtain where Artie is? For Eddie? And Jeanie can move in with Jen?" It's not an ideal solution. There are no ideal solutions.

"What a good idea!" she says, squeezing me. "Artie and Eddie get along pretty well." It's true, which makes me feel somewhat better for my suggestion.

I love making her proud, but I don't want her hugging me like this. I want to pull away.

I am not your girlfriend.

I am not your daughter.

I am not your husband.

I am your protector. The kids' protector. That is the only job I am sure of, and yet I don't know how to do it.

Leap of Faith

IT'S A MELLOW OCTOBER Saturday. The family is away at garage sales, and I'm just drunk enough to get the idea I'd like to bang on my father's drum set. From my room I grab LPs, stacking them on one of the stereos in the living room; first comes Black Sabbath, then Cream, then John Mayall.

I play along to *Paranoid,* smack the drums to "Crossroads." I don't notice my nervous habits as I pound on the toms. Maybe the music makes my twitches go away. Or maybe I don't notice them when I'm consumed with the music, drunk but focused. I'm louder than the music. Something comes over me. I'm not concerned if the neighbors can hear me playing. It must be the alcohol. I hook up bigger speakers. I bang harder. Between songs I listen quickly, to make sure no one's come home. It's not even noon. My guess is they'll be gone all day.

I play until the sunlight through the blinds begins to wane, and in perfect stillness I take inventory at Times Square, to double-check that I put all of my father's bottles back the way I found them. Although my father has so much booze I'm certain he won't notice any missing, I'm overcome with guilt.

Sunday, I will be too ashamed to confess my drinking. Besides, I fear that Father Kleffman will recognize my voice. I'm kneeling in the pew in the near-empty church, going over which sins are safe to mention. Disrespecting my parents is at the top. Also not helping around the house — that's what I'll call it, though it really means not helping my father carry his junk. I could do a better job with the kids. I can't imagine mentioning the drinking. Or lust. Or the sketches based on *Playboy* centerfolds stuffed under my bed. Certainly I won't tell him what I've done to my father's chair.

As I ponder the month since my last confession, my mind drifts. I compete in drowsy staring contests with statues that surround me. The faces on the statues at St. Agnes are downtrodden, like the people who attend this church. When I am here, alone with my thoughts, I think of Granny, whose name was Agnes. I think about her funeral, how my father pressed his hands upon the casket, convinced a jolt of electricity surged through his fingers, up his arms — evidence that his mother was contacting him. It was in the aftermath of Granny's death that Jean purchased a new car and gave us her Oldsmobile. Anyone else buying a car in the wake of a loved one's death would raise eyebrows, but not in Jean's case. Jean fed Granny, bathed her, kept watch over her, never once asking for help or complaining.

It's Jean's generosity I ruminate on. It felt as if we were winners on a game show when she handed my father the keys in her driveway. And since my father lost his job, she brings us groceries, fresh fruit and vegetables, roasts. It's her face I imagine in place of all the sad statue faces. Once, while I was staying with her, she made me watch the Watergate hearings on TV. She encouraged me to draw a cartoon about Richard Nixon. Years from now, my father will touch Jean's casket in the way he touched his mother's. His body will jerk back from the "shock." He will weep and call her "Saint Jean."

The confession with Father Kleffman leaves me cold. There is nothing in his voice that sounds like love or forgiveness. He simply goes through the motions of hearing my sins, dictating my penance, granting me absolution, the smell of his minty cologne drifting to my side of the partition. Why would I expect anything more? After all, his uninviting demeanor from the altar, his bland sermons, do little but inspire me to daydream about other things. I imagine bringing statues to life, making them smile. I float in and out of the scenes depicted in the stained-glass windows.

A strange new voice booms, echoes without warning throughout the sanctuary, jolting me from my drowsy mind-drifting. It's Sunday, 9 A.M. Mass, and an unfamiliar priest with a bulbous head is welcoming us. Together we recite the Apostles' Creed; never before have I listened so closely to the words of this prayer. I listen intently to the readings also, and to the Gospel. I am fully engaged in every movement, every ritual made and followed by this priest. Before the homily, he introduces himself as Father Scott, explains he is a Jesuit from Creighton University, here to help Father Kleffman for the "foreseeable future."

Father Scott bends down—he's tall—and when he straightens again, he holds above him a full-color poster of Saturn. The print is as large as any of Jean's paintings. He stands like this, arms outstretched over his head, robes draped from his arms. When he has the full attention of the congregation, he speaks. "This," he says, "is Saturn. The most beautiful planet in our solar system."

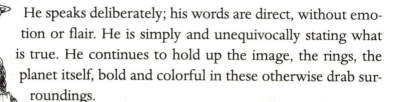

He speaks deliberately; his words are direct, without emotion or flair. He is simply and unequivocally stating what is true. He continues to hold up the image, the rings, the planet itself, bold and colorful in these otherwise drab surroundings.

I am mesmerized.

He puts down the poster and reads a poem about space. I wait for him to refer to today's Gospel. He gives us facts about the other planets, how far they are from the sun, how large they are. He speaks about Earth, tells us how beautiful it is, and also how the astronauts have given us striking images of it, taken from the surface of the moon.

"These things I tell you regarding our solar system," he says, "are examples of the boundless beauty of the Creator." He makes the sign of the cross, indicating the end of his sermon. How can this be? This was not a "real" sermon.

Now I attend every Sunday 9 A.M. Mass, not out of obligation but because I thrill to Father Scott's homilies. Although none has been as surprising as the first, his sermons are brief, always interesting, often referencing movies, great paintings, physics, and atoms.

One Sunday, after returning home, my mother asks about church.

"It was fine." I don't fully express to her my excitement.

"How is the new priest? I read about him in the bulletin."

"He sounds like God."

She's racing around, getting the kids ready for 11:30 Mass. I help put on their jackets, tie their shoes.

"Don't be blasphemous," she cautions.

"I'm not!" I say defensively. "Just forget it." I retreat to my room.

She comes upstairs to my door. "I'm sorry," she says. "It's just that I was always taught only God looks like God, only God speaks like God." She sits next to me on my bed, where I am curled up. I don't want her this close. I hope my *Playboys* aren't sticking out anywhere. "You know, I've always thought of you as someone who might become a priest."

My mother has always believed it's every Catholic boy's duty to pray for a religious vocation. I'd never taken an interest in becoming an altar boy, and only vaguely prayed for a vocation, as my mother suggested. Mostly I'd prayed for my family to remain alive, for my parents not to fight, and for my sketches of Catwoman to come to life, but rarely did I pray to become a priest. It is Artie who is attracted to the priesthood. He dreams of becoming a cardinal. He likes to wear shiny red vestments. My mother sews him a "cardinal's robe" from my father's old red robe. She calls him Father Butterball.

I once saw a photograph in a book about journalism in the Hawthorn library. A woman had jumped from the Empire State Building and landed on the roof of a car. She didn't appear dead, though surely she was. Her body was pressed into the metal, which appeared soft and cushiony. She seemed at peace and might have been a woman asleep in her bed. I used to wonder what it felt like for her the moment she stepped from the ledge. And if a priest gave her last rites. Now I press my forehead against the screen of my open window. Below, my mother is running late for Mass, scrambling to get the kids into the Oldsmobile. Artie holds the baby in his lap on the front seat. The other two are in back. She rumbles down the driveway faster than she should.

Head in the Clouds

AS I PAINT CLOUDS on the wall of the "room for drunks," I'm constantly sweeping my hair from my eyes. I dab my brush into the acrylic glob of titanium white, stirring it with a jab of cerulean blue, a flick of cadmium red. More white. I smush my hair back with my forearm. A bit more blue. I'm sure I have paint in my hair, which today is dry and wispy, full of static—I've been sneaking early-morning hair washings. I scrub the end of the brush onto the cold cinderblock wall.

It's winter, and seven other art students and I are making a mural in the Alcoholics Anonymous meeting room at the main post office downtown. For three days after school we've come here—those of us too young to drive get a ride with our art teacher. Miss Turnquist—we call her Miss T—had asked for volunteers last week, and I raised my hand even before I knew the details. I would do anything she asks. I love the way she brings alive not only the art but the artists themselves. She tells jokes that are understandable only if you have studied art. I laugh the loudest, to let her know how much I love her classes. In art history, I'm drawn to Michelangelo, who, despite his human faults, his sinful ways, was sought after by the pope. When I paint a crucifix scene in the manner of Michelangelo, she praises me, especially for the dark skies that loom over Jesus' body. But she explains that the world already had its Michelangelo. She also encourages me to draw and paint abstractly. I love the real, but also the abstract, because it's *not* real. On the days I get up for school, she alone is the reason. I wear tattered garage sale and thrift store clothes and shoes from the half-price store. But in the same way she seems to ignore my tics, Miss T doesn't mention my tattered corduroys and my ill-fitting fluorescent-green flannel cowboy shirt.

Although we're only painting a mountain scene, as far as I'm concerned the post office A.A. room might as well be the Sistine Chapel. I could paint here forever. My job is clouds. I've always favored sketching clouds, painting clouds. Maybe I love clouds because they're real, yet abstract. In clouds you can see almost anything you want. Clouds calm me down, make my nervous habits subside. Miss T calls me her Cloud Man.

When she isn't around, the students joke about drinking, making fun of alcoholics. Some plan their evenings, how they will score *their* booze. I don't join in. I keep to myself because I don't party. My drinking is *my* business. I keep working. I want Miss T to be proud of me. I don't ever want to lose the title of Cloud Man.

During spring break I ask to stay with my grandparents for the week. My father agrees to a couple of days only, and only after I promise to help him around the house for the rest of the week. I take everything—my guitar, paints, easel, sketchbooks. I plan on spending much of my time in their backyard, in the shade of their one tree.

The first day is rainy, so I stay indoors, going back and forth between helping my grandmother bake and listening to records with my grandfather. I wish I could ask my grandfather about weather. He's always known about weather because he's a farmer. He senses storms coming in his bones. But now is not the time. He heaves, gasps. His eyes close. He's in his chair, sleeping. I watch each rise and fall of his chest to make sure the pattern in repeated, over and over, ensuring that he's alive. My grandmother seems less concerned about my grandfather's breathing. It's something she's used to. Back in the kitchen, I gulp down poppy-seed kolaches while she looks at my sketchbook.

"Your mother always says what a good artist you are."

"Thanks, Grandma."

"Is that what you're going to be someday?"

"Maybe a guitar player."

"A musician? That's a tough life," she says. "Musicians have it very hard."

"My father made a living at it until he married my mother."

She makes a very deliberate *tsk* sound. "Well," she says with an air of superiority I've never heard come out of her, "everyone knows the drums aren't that difficult to play. You're just hitting two sticks against a bunch of kettles. I can do that in my kitchen."

For the first time I can recall, my grandmother upsets me. I become protective of my father. I don't know why she is doing this.

137

Doesn't she understand that my father could have been famous? That he made a sacrifice by working for the railroad to take care of his family?

She offers me another kolache.

I'm starting to feel sick, probably from eating too many. But I can't say no.

"You know, Jethro was quite an artist when growing up. He'd draw scenes of the farm. I've been thinking. Maybe you *should* talk to him. Maybe you could show him your drawings."

I run my tongue over my teeth, removing the granular seeds. Going cross-eyed, I thrust out my tongue to take stock of all those black specks. Since I'm always sticking it out, I'm familiar with the blurry image of my tongue. But now it appears to be covered in microscopic bugs.

Handing me a napkin, my grandmother gives a quick shake of the head, as if she's impatient. Though she never says anything about my habits. I remove the specks from my tongue.

"That boy needs to get out of his shell," she says pensively, referring to Jethro.

I can't imagine asking him to look at my drawings. Would I tear the drawings from my sketchbook, slide each one under his door? No, I will go to watch my grandfather sleep. But now my grandmother is pushing me, physically pushing me in the small of my back, with her strong arms that once beheaded chickens, urging me through the door to the basement. "Go on," she says. "It might do him some good."

With my sketchbook I hesitantly go down each step, shaking the hair from my eyes, accidentally smacking my head on the wall. I shake again, though I can see my way in the darkness. I smack my head again. Hard enough that my grandmother comes to the top of the steps.

"Everything all right?" she asks, sounding irritated.

"Yes." My head pounds.

The steps, the workshop, the distance across the basement to Jethro's room has grown small. As if my grandmother is still pushing me, I go to his door and knock three times. Three times feels right against my knuckles. It feels like good luck. There is an absence of sound for several seconds, then a rustling from inside the room.

The door squeaks open. I'm met with a waft of stale cigarettes. I cannot scan his face. I catch only a glimpse; he is bearded and scruffy. Perched atop his head like a dollop of frosting, a red stocking cap; his lanky frame is shrouded in a plaid flannel shirt. Pencils, pens, cigarettes in his shirt pocket. My eyes dart everywhere but his face.

"What do you want?" His voice is not as gruff as I expect it to be, as I believe I've heard it to be, the rare times I've heard him speak.

I swallow. All I can do is swallow. I run my hand over the silver coils that hold my drawings together.

A moment ago I was holding out my sketchbook. Now it's gone. I didn't offer it, or at least I don't think I did. Everything is spinning, everything is a blur. I am disappearing. I glance around in snippets. Anything to ground me. I hear him turning the pages of the sketchbook. He's saying, "You do these?"

Am I nodding? I can't look at him. My throat clicks. He will choke me, he is choking me. But that's just me, grunting in my throat.

"Not bad," he says.

With my drawings he settles low into a gold chair, the only thing of real color in his room. I remain standing. I can look at his face only in flashes. He has a face of brown wire. From an ashtray, a trail of smoke rises in a vertical contrail. There is nothing else here. No paintings, no decorations except a lone crucifix over his bed. In a corner, near a dresser, his acoustic guitar, small and lonely. He reaches for what remains in the ashtray. There is no cigarette, not a stub; the smoke comes from his fingers.

"You mind?" he asks, removing a pencil from his shirt pocket with his free hand. I realize how boyish he sounds in spite of his appearance.

139

I don't know what I'm agreeing to, but I nod vigorously, leaving no question I am giving permission. Is this when he begins to kill me?

He's turned to a blank page; he's sketching. His eyes burn with intent as he moves the pencil around, shyly laughing along the way. This fierceness with a pencil is how I imagined Bobby Thompson, the boy in my class at Hawthorn, sketched. The tiniest flake of ash, black snow, floats onto the sketchbook. Maybe I am that ash, maybe I am that small, floating away. He pauses, tilts his head, examining his work.

"Here you go," he says, suddenly, utterly uninterested, giving back my sketchbook. With the sketchbook in my hands, I am me again.

He's drawn a man's head. A man with a nose so large, a tinier man crawls up a ladder into the nostril. All of this created from nothing, right in front of me. It's practically a magic trick, his taking this blank page and transforming it into this cartoon so quickly. I can't take my eyes off his drawing. Finally, I look to him, but his mind is elsewhere, as though gazing toward a horizon, despite his being cooped up in this basement cell.

"It's funny," I say.

He lights a fresh cigarette. Takes his time answering. "It's just a stupid drawing." He motions for the sketchbook, but I step back, out of reach. I will not let him rip it out, crumple it, if that is his intention. Rejected, he drops into his chair, again detached. The drawing *is* funny, but not in a way that resonates in my belly. I'm more interested in *how* he drew it. I search it for clues. He's already on to something else, retrieving his guitar. The chord he strums is dissonant, minor. I study his fingers. I do not know the chord.

"Cool," I say.

"I've had her a long time," he says, oblivious to my response, caressing the wooden face of the guitar, rubbing at a small scar on it. "A *long* time." Without introduction he plays a lamenting chord progression. The vibrating strings fill the room. His fingers are long and rugged, crawling upon the fretboard like a fleshy bug.

"Yeah, I don't mind playing the guitar," he says, as if I've asked him a question. Maybe this is the only way he knows how to communicate. Always answering to imagined questions; even when someone else is near, he knows no other way.

"Here," he says, holding up his guitar by the neck, a strangled goose.

I cautiously accept the guitar and sit on a small rug that covers the concrete floor, taking the instrument into my lap. The strings. Tarnished and blackened wires, rough and dead to the touch. I make a D chord, the prettiest chord I know. The chord is sour because of the strings. Even so, the sound fills the smoky air, moves the air around, reassembles the atoms that make up his existence. Maybe he's never played a pretty chord in this room. Maybe that's what this room needs. I look for his approval, but his face is shrouded in a white burst of smoke.

"Thank you," I say, finished.

He nods, exhaling, says nothing. As he leans the guitar in its corner, I somehow know this is my cue to leave. I don't know how I know. I move toward the doorway, not taking my eyes from his feet.

"Thanks for the drawing," I say, quickly glancing at his face.

He nods, his eyes slits. Everything else is beard and smoke.

On Top of the World

THE DAY I TURN SIXTEEN, I ask to take my driving test, but my father says, "Hell no, you're too young." He doesn't know my secret, that my mother lets me drive on dirt roads across the bridge in Iowa.

I don't argue my position; I don't beg. Driving would serve me little, since I know so few girls at South High.

• • •

141

The only time I visit the high school guidance office is to look at the "career opportunities" postings. I apply and get hired for two jobs. One is a daytime summer job as a custodian at my school. It gives me great pleasure to scrub floors, even when they're not dirty. I love that cleaning doesn't always mean picking up trash and bones and scraps of food, and moving junk. Cleaning can mean dusting or washing surfaces that don't appear to need it. This kind of cleaning is almost easy, *fun*.

My other job: part-time tearsheet clerk at the *Omaha World-Herald*. My father isn't as excited as I expect he'll be. This is the paper that gave Uncle Ed his start, that has published countless want ads for my father. They have an art staff and a political cartoonist. This isn't the first time I've worked for the newspaper. In eighth grade I delivered the afternoon edition. I loved rolling up the papers, putting rubber bands around them. I loved the smoothness of the newsprint, the way my hands would get inky. I loved reading the news before anyone else. But after a year, my father insisted I quit the route. He said it was too hard on me in winter. Especially on Sundays, when the paper was so heavy. Reluctantly, I turned in my *World-Herald* carrier bag.

My *World-Herald* job is not glamorous. As a tearsheet clerk, I hand-tear pages from the newspaper that will be delivered to businesses as proof their advertisements ran. Many of the department stores and supermarkets require extra copies to display in their store windows. Each evening at 7:30, I wait in the mailroom for the early edition. The smell of ink and paper, the rolling of the presses like a locomotive, and the rush of the conveyor belts carrying the newspapers make me happy. After the newspaper has been marked up, determining how many total papers I will need, I wheel as many as three hundred to Dispatch. Next, I tear out the pages in full, even if the ad is tiny, scanning news stories on those pages. New York City's blackout. Led Zeppelin's last concert. The space shuttle's first test flight. Over and over, stack after stack, I tear, glimpsing these stories as I go, my hands and my forehead the color of sludge. I fold and place the tearsheets in large envelopes, marking the address on each, careful to print as clearly and artistically as I can.

Afterward, it's off to the pressmen's bathroom, where I let soap and warm water run over my hands, black inky rivulets swirling from skin to sink. I work every night except Saturday. There is no messenger delivery Sunday morning, so I'm allowed to come in Sunday after Mass to tackle the hefty Sunday edition, then I go back later that evening to start the week over again with Monday's paper. This routine gives my week rhythm and meaning. I take the bus downtown and back home, except when I work late and my mother comes for me.

Eventually, I'm asked to work Saturday mornings as a messenger. Since I don't have a driver's license, I walk the downtown route, dropping off tearsheets at businesses and picking up ad copy and layouts. I walk among what few shoppers remain, moving fast, as I imagine New Yorkers move, darting in and out of traffic. Virginia Dare has since closed, as has Kilpatrick's; a handful of stores cling to life.

Sometimes I arrive at my job early, to allow time to wander the second floor, past the large windows of the newsroom, which is filled with desks, typewriters, stacks of newspapers, reams of typing paper. I watch the serious faces of the reporters and editors, their fingers darting across typewriter keys or scribbling in notebooks while clamping telephones to their ears with their shoulders. Off in one corner: arms of drawing-table lamps peek above the horizon like construction cranes—the art department. I am too timid to ever step inside the newsroom. I can only watch the commotion from out here, several steps from the glass.

The pastry from the vending machine is stale and chewy. I lick the frosting from my fingers, down to the ink that coats my skin. It's a Sunday morning during my junior year of high school. Normally, I wouldn't make it to the *World-Herald* until after Mass. But this morning at eight, explosives will bring an end to the Wow Building. I took the day's first bus. It's only 7:15 and I work, sipping coffee, not wanting to miss the big event.

While I'm wiping frosting from my mouth, the newspaper's bearded cartoonist breezes by, portfolio under his arm. I recognize him from his promotional ads. I catch only a glimpse, but my heart races. This is my first sighting of a real cartoonist. Moments later, a janitor I always greet pops in, asks if I'm going to watch the big explosion.

I say that I am.

"Where, man?"

"I dunno. I guess out front, on Dodge Street."

"Like hell you are." He flashes a sly grin, motioning for me to follow. He smells of cleaning solution and cigarettes.

We take the elevator to the top of the building. As we exit onto the roof, the crisp blue morning explodes above me. The sky, the unencumbered view of downtown, make my head spin; I fear I might lose my balance and fall. A small crowd has gathered on the roof, clusters of spectators anticipating the blast that will shatter the calm of a Sunday morning. The Wow Building stands in plain view, awaiting its doom. I glance around, hoping to see the cartoonist again. No sight of him. I wonder if he's watching from his office window, sketchbook in hand.

Moments later a voice crackles over a loudspeaker and gives a spaceship countdown. I twitch with each count. "Three . . . two . . . one" is followed by a disappointing nothingness. Not a sound. It's as though all of Omaha is holding its breath.

The dynamite exhales and the Wow Building begins to topple in slow motion. Next, a blast rumbles to where we stand, thundering through muscle and bone. The Wow Building continues to slump into itself, disintegrating into a heap, plumes rising like escaping ghosts. There is cheering. But I feel punched in the gut. I've known this building all my life.

I shift my gaze west several blocks, toward the Woodmen

Tower. It has no interesting angles or details like the buildings Miss T shows us when we study architecture. The Woodmen can't ease the sadness I feel for the Wow Building, although I tingle at the memory the Woodmen provided earlier this year. One Saturday, Artie and I took the bus downtown. Our mission: to view Omaha from the Top of the World, the Woodmen Tower's restaurant on the thirtieth floor. Artie loves tall buildings almost as much as I do, so I asked him along. Having him with me gave me the courage I lacked when I'd been tempted to ride to the top alone. We raced from the bus stop up Douglas Street, entering the building's marble lobby. Inside the elevator I hesitated to press 30. I somehow wanted to preserve the moment. But before I could reach, Artie had already pushed the button, sending us skyward, our ears popping.

After we eased to a stop and the doors slid open, a bright and hazy landscape came into view. After the dimness of the elevator my eyes felt fuzzy. As we moved toward the tall windows of the restaurant, a man in a suit stopped us.

"We are not open for lunch," he said.

But. All I could do was screech, deep in my throat.

"Excuse me, sir," Artie said. "We just want to look."

"Customers only."

Artie downplayed the tension. "C'mon," he said to the man. "It's not like we're going to break anything. Right, Jeff?"

I shook my head, but it was too late.

"You must leave," the man demanded, moving toward us. "Now."

Artie laughed and steered me toward the elevator.

I stood on tiptoe, one last chance to catch a glimpse of the city. I could see the tops of other buildings, and in the distance, far to the south, where our house was, nothing but trees. Artie stuck his tongue out at the man, and with that the elevator doors squeezed shut and we made our descent from the highest point in Omaha.

Out of the Blue

TWO WEEKS LEFT of eleventh grade, and Miss T announces the school art show. She invites her students to display their favorite piece from that year. I choose a semiabstract painting that incorporates geometric shapes and the shapes of string beans, kidney beans, and clouds. It's hung in the "gallery"—the hallway of the art room—along with other paintings, drawings, and ceramics.

On the next to last day of the school year a girl I vaguely recognize stops me in front of my locker. "Excuse me," she says, "do you have a second?"

This never happens. I'm invisible here at South High. The between-class frenzy rushes past us.

She does all the talking. "I like your painting."

"Thanks." I'm pleased, even if I'm too scared to look her in the eye.

She explains that she'll be the editor of the school paper next year. "I hear you also draw cartoons. Is that true?"

"Um, I guess."

"Would you like to draw for the *Tooter*? Our current cartoonist is graduating." She's all business.

I admire the cartoons in the *Tooter*. One cartoon this semester left me wishing I'd thought of the idea. *But I'm not that good.* The cartoon depicted a garage sale. The joke: it was the garage itself that was for sale.

"You'd have to draw one cartoon a month," the editor says.

"Um—" My head wants to jerk, but not wanting to scare her off, I tell it, beg it, to wait. Surely I can come up with one cartoon a month. Can't I? After all, isn't that about how long it takes me to complete one painting?

"See you in the fall?"

· · ·

It's the start of summer vacation, and my parents insist I quit my job at the *World-Herald*. "You work eight times a week," my father complains. The Beatles' "Eight Days a Week" goes through my head.

"But I love it," I say.

"Your mother shouldn't have to pick you up every night," my father says.

"But she doesn't."

"Well, most of the time."

"I've told you before. I can take the bus!"

"Too dangerous that late."

"Then let me drive! *Please!*"

"Too dangerous. Too damned expensive. We can't afford the insurance for you."

"But I've told you, *I'll* pay for the insurance."

"Hell no. Think I was allowed to drive at your age?"

"Don't you want to enjoy your summer off?" my mother tells me. "Your last school year?"

"Yeah," my father says, "you're going to be working for the rest of your life." He says "working" as if it's a punishment.

I love everything about the *World-Herald*. The smells, the rush of activity, the sense of urgency that pulsates throughout the building. My paycheck allows me to buy records — *new* records — guitar strings, markers, and sketchbooks. Most of the money I save for a rainy day, as my father likes to say.

In the end, he doesn't give me a choice. "Why the hell would you work someplace else when you should be helping me around here?"

Maybe this is my destiny. In our house there is never talk about college, which my father believes is for other people. Despite his dreams of hitting it big, of instant fame, he also believes one should labor to make an honest living. He reminds me that I must stay close to home, to help my mother take care of the family when he has his heart attack and dies. "Until she marries some rich guy," he quickly adds.

In the solitude that comes to our house after everyone is asleep, every TV screen blank, I lie awake. I worry about how I will draw cartoons for the *Tooter*. I practice, but everything I draw is either too realistic or too abstract, nothing like what I see in the *World-Herald*. I start over, studying comic strips and the cartoons on the editorial pages. My mind races as I fill sheets of paper, practicing my signature. I take a break only to softly strum my guitar or to ponder the depth of space, which seems to begin beyond my bedroom, just past the trees and houses. Not long ago I would attempt to capture the blackness, the brightness of the moon and stars, in my sketchbook. My pens would go dry, I would wear down pencils to stumps, nearly drawing with my fingertips in my futile attempt to re-create the night sky. Now I draw faces with bugged and surprised eyes — a cartooning staple — and also chagrined and worried eyes.

The Weatherman

I T'S ALL FIXED," my father says in disgust, motioning toward the weatherman on TV. "A guy can't get a fair shake."

To my father, everyone, from the holiest of cardinals to government officials to local TV weathermen, is on the take. The weathermen especially. "They know the government is controlling the weather but play dumb." He believes the weathermen deliberately "get it wrong" from time to time, to deflect suspicion.

To prove his point, he has what he calls a weather calendar. It's the appointment calendar we get from church each year. He likes it not because of the Bible quotes but because it's free, and because it comes with large squares that allow him to scrawl his latest prediction for storms. On the calendar, I read passages from the Gospels mixed in with threats of "TORNADOES!" and "HAIL!" Predicting the weather like this, officially and on record, is a practice he began — I'm not sure when, exactly. Years ago. He keeps it in the hallway, where we can't help but see it. A Bic pen dangles by a string, always ready for his latest entry.

His predictions come true often enough that I ask how he does it.

"It's a secret," he says.

Artie grins as if he knows the answer.

I beg him to tell.

"It's in the stars," my father insists.

Artie smiles wider, sticks his tongue out at me.

My father's also wrong enough times to make me doubt everything he tells me about the weather.

When he is caught off-guard, when the rain comes early and he's rushing around outside, covering everything with his tarpaulins and sheets of plastic, he cusses the government. "They're all in this together," he mutters. "Goddamn weather machines. Just so people will shop and spend money. It's all about collecting taxes. The rich get richer . . ."

Artie fears storms more than I. Three years ago, on May 6, 1975, the day I turned fourteen, a massive tornado cut a path across Omaha. We spent that afternoon in the basement with my father's junk. Our house was spared. That night, in the cool air after the storm, my mother attempted to restore a sense of normalcy, inviting me to blow out the candles of my cake. But I was engrossed in the TV coverage. We all were. Artie fell into complete silence. My mother held him in her lap like a baby. I took turns holding the other kids. My father focused on his conspiracy theories. "If they'd just let that storm hit a few days earlier, it wouldn't have been so strong." The next day, we piled into the car and defied National Guard barricades so we could gawk at the twisted wreckage.

Despite the devastation we witnessed after the tornado, I enjoy storms. My stomach goes topsy-turvy anytime the skies flicker. Some kids love roller coasters; I love "Mother Nature's light show." Watching the weather is an activity my father endorses; I help him keep an eye on the skies on the outside chance he won't get his prediction right.

"Aha!" my father proclaims from the floor below. "Do you see, Mother? We're in a thunderstorm watch. I *was* right after all!"

It's early evening and my bedroom is sticky with late-summer mugginess; I'm struggling with my guitar, my strings stubborn from the humidity. In my room, if I'm not playing music, the only sound is the noise my throat makes. The only time I regret not having a TV is on a day like today, when I have to head downstairs to keep up with the weather.

From my window, I can see the sky is chopped in two. The eastern half is blue and endless, the western half a ceiling the color of pencil lead. Our storms almost always come from the west.

As I move past Artie and Eddie's makeshift room, Artie is engrossed in taking apart an old radio and putting it back together. Eddie is here, too, having created a small town consisting of model-railroad buildings and my old Hot Wheels cars.

"Might be a storm's coming," I tell Artie.

"I know," he says smugly. "Dad and I already did our work." But behind his smugness I sense fear.

The air downstairs is only slightly cooler than upstairs, but it's enough to make me realize that I've been sweating all afternoon. The door of my old room is open, revealing the same yellow walls I've always known. But the bedspreads are floral and bright. On my old dresser, a pink lamp. Jennifer is on the floor reading to Jeanie, who is playing with blocks in her bed. I'm glad to know this; it's tiring keeping track of everyone.

My father paces in the kitchen, trying to get my mother's attention. She's frying hamburgers. "See how smart I am?" he says. "See how Artie and I covered my TVs outside?"

"Yes, already," she says, "you're smart."

All day the skies had been filled with happy clouds and sunshine. The TV weathermen made no mention of bad weather.

"Look, Mother!" He gestures toward the kitchen TV, shaking his hand at the cartoonish thundercloud, the words WEATHER BULLETIN splashed across the screen in bright yellow.

"I see it," she says, not turning from the stove.

"They should be paying *me* to do the weather," he says, slapping his chest. "But who listens to me?"

A thunderstorm warning has been issued for three counties to our west and south. It appears likely the storm will move in our direction. I still have time for a shower, but I'll have to act quickly, before my father notices. Now, with a family of seven, he believes more than ever that showering or bathing regularly is a waste of money.

I sneak off to find clean underwear in a clothes basket in my mother's room, then slip into the bathroom. As soon as I turn on the water, his voice booms through the bathroom door. "Goddamn it, punk!"

Afterward, with the exception of the fresh underwear, I put on the jeans and T-shirt I had on before. I run through the house, my goal the front yard, ignoring his condemnation for my having "thrown money down the drain."

The sidewalk is warm against my bare feet, and the weedy lawn is cool and comforting. I crane my neck, circle around as water drips from my hair. Our maple trees. The neighbor's trees. The roof, the apex of our house. The sky is completely painted over in a spectrum of gray hues. I concentrate and finally, *finally*, a sheet of light reflects across the sky. The flash is barely noticeable in the early-evening light. I know from my drawing and painting classes that to make something appear brighter, you must have contrast. The lightning doesn't have the contrast of a night sky. The clouds aren't black enough. I haven't counted the seconds, but I know from the slow gurgle that the storm is still miles away. I keep watch, listening as the locusts pulsate, surrounding me, creating a dome of sound. I know I have enough time to stand here before the storm arrives in force. And because I've studied art, and the existentialists in my world-lit class, I come to believe that what I see above is a work of art, unique to me, as I am the only one in the whole world standing in this very spot.

I'm several yards from the front of the house but can hear my father thud across the porch, flinging open the front door.

"Better get in here, kid. Storm's coming fast."

"I will," I say. "I will."

He stands there, attempting to wait for me, but soon gives up. "Suit yourself." The door smacks shut.

On our silent street, a few porch lights fend off the darkening skies. Our tree branches are unmoving, the clouds low and promising, but nothing, nothing at all is happening. I am perfectly still.

. . .

The shotgun explosion in my head, the jolt my body takes, the screaming light, all happen in an instant. Lightning and thunder are no longer separate entities. Nor is my body separate from the weather. The lightning and thunder, my eyes and muscles, are unified as the electricity burns through me, killing me. Wild colors that don't exist in the universe stream out like fireworks before my eyes. I am inside the lightning, it is inside me, the electricity rewiring my brain's circuitry in some way that doesn't make sense, yet does make sense. There is no time. I have all the time in the world to die. I will die here, in my parents' front yard. I've been here forever, in this yard, the electricity running through me like this, making me die. My eyes tell me I'm on the ground, on my knees, paralyzed. I've been here forever, waiting for the lightning to do its job, to completely circulate through my veins.

I am not afraid.

I have a wish. A simple wish. To die inside my parents' house. This wish is all I can think of, all I can hope for. I desire nothing else. To crawl inside, to lie on the floor, curled up anywhere there is space for this body that is no longer me, to die, die, die in peace. I can't move. It's like dreaming someone is chasing me, but I can't operate these long, fleshy things. These legs. All I can think, all I know, is *get inside, get inside. Get inside* becomes my prayer. It's so simple. I do not want the rain to soak my body. I see myself moving slowly, so slowly a month passes before I can take one step. Another month, another step. My body is hunched over, not fully evolved. Somehow I get there, to the door that minutes, days, a lifetime earlier seemed an unreachable destination. This is a door handle, but I do not understand how it works. I have a foggy memory that I must wrap my hand in such a way that will open it, but I cannot make my hand do what it's supposed to do. Like my wish, a knowingness begins to rise to the surface — I begin to understand I've been struck by lightning. I will never know how, exactly. The bolt might have struck one of our trees and followed its roots, shooting up from the ground. The lightning might have covered me in a sheet of electricity. Or a ball of electricity might

153

have shot toward my head — a great cannonball of power. I will not have burn marks on my body.

It's been forever since I was hit, and only now a man's face appears on the other side of the door. His face grows large as he approaches. There are actually two faces: the man's and the reflection of a teenage boy's. The door is opening. I am pulled inside. I am floating. I do not know where my feet are. Maybe I've left my legs outside.

What is the man shouting?

Is he asking if I'm in shock?

There is a lively discussion between the man and a woman. They both seem familiar. The woman more so.

"He must have gotten scared," the man says. "That lightning was damned close."

He is now slapping my face, I can hear him slapping, his hand a blurry thing at the end of his wrist, smacking my cheek. But I feel nothing; I am numb.

"He needs to go to the hospital," the woman cries. "I think the lightning got him!"

"Goddamn it," the man tells her, "I told everyone we were going to have bad storms! Doesn't anyone listen?"

"But look at him!"

"He'll be all right," he says. "Won't you, Jeffrey? You're going to be just fine!"

I cannot answer. I have lost my voice.

"Dad!" the woman cries. The woman is my mother.

"Jeffrey," my father shouts. "Jeffrey, Jeffrey, Jeffrey! Did . . . you . . . get . . . hit . . . by . . . lightning?"

"The hospital!" she cries.

I am led to the sofa by my father. My mother places the palm of her hand on my forehead. I know this because I watch her hand get close, disappearing as it lands on my skin. Slowly, I begin to *feel* her skin, the pressure of her palm bringing me back to life.

Everything goes dark; I've squeezed tight my eyes to counter the burning in my throat. "It's medicine," he says. The burning won't stop; I can't breathe. I squint open my eyes. My father is hovering over me, forcing me to drink. The fire taste is familiar. It makes me gasp. I cannot breathe, I cannot tell him to stop. My father is forcing whiskey down my throat. I watch as he tilts the bottle of Jack Daniel's, refilling the glass. I can't tell him I don't want it, because I have no mouth. My face is just these eyes, watching helplessly as he moves toward me. It is the sting of the booze that makes me understand I *do* have a mouth, and the gasping, the gagging, that tells me I'm alive.

He backs off. "That ought to do the trick," he tells my mother. She is next to me, running her hands through my hair. My body is calm. The kids encircle me, gawking. Artie's lips are moving. His mouth forms the words "God" and "please." He is praying for me, keeping me alive.

Every TV in the room flickers. Thunder crashes, pounds on the windows. My mother's arm is around my shoulder. My father is drinking from the bottle. Artie keeps praying and all I can do is listen.

Reincarnation

IT'S TAKEN NEARLY two weeks, but I'm just beginning to feel normal. My muscles regain strength — all along, I've felt as though I've been wading through water. Even my nervous habits return, somehow reassuring me that I'm going to live. Sleep is the biggest struggle. My dreams are filled with lightning. Plus, it doesn't help that wicked storms roll through Omaha almost nightly, sending me to the floor of the living room — I want to get as low to the ground as possible. Sometimes I take my pillow into the basement and huddle among the boxes.

My senior year of high school begins, and when I tell what few friends I have about the lightning, they tease me. "Is that why your hair turned so curly?" In fact, a few days before, I'd gotten a perm and also bought myself new clothes at Brandeis, the last big department store downtown. My father ridiculed me when he saw me come into the house with my shopping bags. My hair, my clothes, can't fix my fear and shame.

On the days I'm hungry, I sit alone in the lunchroom or on the periphery of my friends. Often, my stomach churns so I don't eat. All of my clothes, even my new clothes, hang loosely on my frame, I've lost so much weight. I cut my hair short, to make it straight again. With my bangs, my mother says I remind her of John Boy from *The Waltons*.

I throw myself into my artwork. Last spring, I registered for as many art classes as possible, and now Miss T encourages me to apply for a scholarship at the University of Nebraska at Omaha. "I think you'll have a good shot," she says. She doesn't understand that in our family, college is for everyone else.

One morning before the first bell, I stop by the journalism classroom, where the *Tooter* is assembled. The editor, the girl who suggested I submit cartoons, is here; she immediately asks if I have a submission for the first issue.

"No," I say, panicked.

"That's okay," she says. "You have another week. You're still interested, right?"

I say that I am. "What should it be about?"

"Anything you want. You're the cartoonist."

"Oh." All along I'd assumed I would be assigned a topic. I have no idea what I'll draw.

Every morning before school, I read the *World-Herald*. We also get the evening edition, and I take in as much information as I can. In the news are stories of Firestone tires coming apart, Ford Pintos exploding when rear-ended. A neighbor of ours drives a Pinto. One evening after dinner, I stand at the edge of his driveway, attempting to capture in my sketchbook what a Pinto looks like. Somehow this task allows me to believe it's okay to be here. I'm with the *Tooter*. My sketchbook is my shield. At home, I redraw the Pinto with Firestone tires. Something's missing. I add a high school student lamenting that it's not bad enough his tires have come apart; now his car might blow up, too. I admire the student in my drawing. Not for how I've drawn him—he doesn't look the way cartoon people should look—but rather because he represents what I am not: a teenager, his hair feathered, who is good-looking and is allowed to drive. I'm sure he has a girlfriend.

Copies of the *Tooter* are delivered to each homeroom. Viewing my drawing in print like this makes it official—a *real* cartoon. Glancing around the classroom, it's strange to see my name, the signature I've practiced, repeated the same in every copy. I bring home an extra *Tooter,* and my mother promises to save every issue in her scrapbook. Though I expect my father to mention Uncle Ed, who worked on the *Tooter* when he attended South, he just says, "That's nice."

I begin hovering around the journalism room before and after school. Eventually, I switch a study hall to Journalism 101. In the morning and after school, I help put together the *Tooter.* I write, edit, and draw. Every so often, Uncle Ed pops into my mind. I can't help but think it's more than a coincidence that Uncle Ed's death and my birth occurred in such close proximity. *Maybe I am reincarnated.*

Joni's not sure what she believes about reincarnation. "I suppose it's possible," she says, contemplating my question. Joni is on the staff of the *Tooter,* but she also writes poetry and enjoys talking about art. I don't mention Uncle Ed; I only ask "in theory." She remembers my painting from the student show last year and is the nicest girl I've met at South. I come to believe she's a kindred spirit, but I am too shy to ask her on a date. I can't imagine that any girl would want to be with me. Besides, I worry that if I were to date someone, it would be a painful reminder to my parents that I'm growing up and they're growing old.

The Patient

TAP LIGHTLY on my mother's door. "I can't go to school," I tell her. "My stomach."

She pulls on her robe, comes into the hallway so as not to wake my father. "You can't miss any more school," she tells me. "You won't graduate."

It's true. My parents received a pink letter from South High that I'm already at my limit of missed days.

"But I can't," I say, holding my stomach. "I'm *really* sick. Honest."

She scrunches her brow, worried. "Okay, I'll call. But we should get you to the doctor."

She's suggested this before; this time I relent. "Okay."

"Maybe the lightning caused your stomach problems," my father says, joining us in the living room. His voice is rich and low in the morning—he's usually not up this early. He whistles, unconcerned about anything.

"No, Dad," my mother reminds him. "His stomach started hurting way before the lightning."

"There's nothing wrong with the kid, goddamn it."

"Yes, there is. I've been telling you for months."

He clutches his chest and coughs. I can't tell if this is an episode of nervous habits or if it's something more serious. Then again, he's been known to feign a heart attack, like Fred Sanford. When he does, he might as well shout, "Here comes the big one!"

He plops into his recliner. We bring him hot water and I massage his shoulders. After we determine that he's okay, my mother takes me to Dr. Z, the same doctor I've had my whole life.

I feel silly here at the pediatrician's office, considering I'm nearly eighteen. I haven't seen him since starting high school, when I was required to get a physical. Even then, I felt lanky and too old.

Dr. Z examines me but finds nothing wrong. "We'll have to run some tests," he says. "I'll set things up with your mother."

It's not until we're riding home that my mother explains that the testing will be done at Children's Hospital, requiring a stay of three days and two nights.

While I'm in the hospital, my mother visits once and my father doesn't come at all. He hates hospitals, because as a kid he hallucinated while hospitalized with diphtheria. Besides, it shouldn't surprise me, as he's never taken me to the doctor and never goes to open house at school. My tests are unpleasant. I sleep a lot and watch TV. I am in a room with two beds, and the other bed is empty. Outside, the January weather presses against my window, frosting the glass, thickening it.

Something wakes me. Someone has changed the channel on the TV. I've gained a roommate, but I'm hesitant to look. I fear someone critically ill or severely injured. Out of the corner of my eye: jeans, boots, a dark blue parka. I crane my neck.

A beard. A red stocking cap.

Jethro.

He's watching *Match Game '79*. "Hey," he says without looking at me.

"Hi!" I haven't seen Jethro in months.

"How's it going?"

"Okay." I don't elaborate on my tests, the enema, the pink barium I was required to swallow. "Thanks for coming."

He gives a quick nod and turns off the TV. Neither of us speaks for a considerable length of time.

"Been playing guitar?" I ask.

"Some."

Again, we lie in our beds, not making conversation. I'm glad for the company, though I'm having trouble staying awake.

• • •

Maybe I'm dreaming when "bastard" breaks the silence. "Bastard" is contained among other words, but it is the only one I hear, even though he says it nonchalantly, not angrily, as if it's any regular sort of word.

"What?" I say groggily, sitting up.

"I said, You do know why you're a bastard, don't you?"

Why is Jethro saying this? I haven't been called this since before Uncle Frank died.

He lies there in silence in the other bed, stretched out, still in his coat and hat, his dirty black boots on the clean white sheets. Everything is so white. The beds, the walls, the scene outdoors, everything except my hairy, bundled uncle.

"Don't you know why you lived with us when you were a baby?"

I lived with you?

"Your mother, too. Grandma took care of you. So did Grandpa. We all did."

I search my memory, but my brain works sluggishly. I can't think. I can't make sense of his words. I don't want him to say any more, yet I secretly beg him to keep going.

He smirks behind his beard. I can sense it. He's remembering something. "Grandpa had your dad arrested, but the charges didn't stick. Ask your father about it sometime." He *is* grinning. "It's time you knew the truth."

I feel sick.

I do not know you, Jethro.

I am invisible.

Leave, leave, leave. I cannot speak. I don't move. I'm staring at the blank TV screen. I turn in time to make sure he's left my room.

I go to the bathroom and throw up.

When my nurse comes, I fall apart, crying.

She holds me against her. I'm sure she doesn't understand what I'm attempting to explain through my tears. I know she thinks

160

I'm crazy. My head flails against her chest. I worry I'll be thrown in the mental ward.

Later, when I can't sleep, I replay a particular story of my father's. The Mills Brothers were playing at Ross' Steakhouse for the week, and my father was hired to play drums. One snowy night my mother came to the show, and afterward my father gave the singing trio a ride to their hotel. My mother sat in the back seat between two of the singers. I can picture the sleet hitting the windows, the wipers trying to keep up, the car's heater not able to take the chill out of the air. Maybe the Mills Brothers and my father were singing as a quartet, their breath filling the inside of the cold, dark car.

"Can you imagine?" my father would ask me. "Your mother, just off the farm, sitting in between the most famous colored trio in the world?" His voice would lower on "colored." "And," he would continue, "you were there also, even though you weren't born yet."

"How?" I would ask.

He might chuckle but would not elaborate, would not use the word "pregnant." Other than this story, other than his few cryptic hints, he never mentioned my mother's pregnancy with me, my birth, or what ensued.

The following morning, Dr. Z explains that my stomach is perfectly fine but that I have a jaundiced liver. *But I don't drink that much.* This information doesn't jibe. I'm given a prescription. Whenever my stomach hurts, he tells me, I am to take one of the pills. That afternoon, my mother drives me home, making small talk on the way.

"Everyone missed you. The kids haven't stopped asking when you were coming home."

"Oh."

"Aren't you glad you now have medication?"

"I suppose. Dad's not angry?"

"Of course not. Why would he be angry?"

"About the money. For the hospital. For the pills."

"Of course not."

When we arrive, the kids cheer. Even Artie hugs me. My father pauses long enough from his work to say, "Long time no see."

In bed, I shake my bottle of pills. The bottle is labeled DIAZE-PAM. I've already had two today. I'm not in the mood for my guitar. Or for drawing. My *Playboys* are missing, and I suspect Artie. My mother comes to check on me, sitting at the edge of my bed. I turn away from her.

"How's my John Boy?"

"Stop it."

"Oh, don't be such a crabby cakes. Isn't it nice to be home in your own bed?"

"I guess."

"You poor thing."

"Jethro came to visit."

"Oh? That was nice of him. I'm so glad you two get along. Grandma goes on and on about how proud she is you helped bring him out of his shell."

"He told me."

"What's that, sweetie?"

"About *me.*"

"Oh?"

I want her to know what I know. But she doesn't understand. She doesn't read my mind, after all.

"He told me how you got pregnant with me and how Dad was arrested and everything." The words slip out with ease.

"I didn't know what to do," she says without hesitation, not surprised by what I tell her. "They wanted me to give you away. Some even wanted me not to *have* you." A dam breaks. Everything spills out; she's been waiting for this moment. She keeps going, telling me things I can't comprehend. "Grandpa wouldn't

162

let me see your father for two years. They kept us apart for *two years*."

"Why?"

"Because he was so much older."

"How much older?"

She shakes her head, drifting back. "I was eighteen when I got pregnant." She hesitates. "Your father was twenty years older."

"Did we all live with Grandma and Grandpa?"

She's sobbing, barely able to speak. "Yes."

"I don't understand." I refuse to cry.

"Your grandparents loved you *so* much. Do you understand? They loved you like their own son. I loved you. Your father loved you."

I see her as a young girl, innocent and scared, gazing out my window, beyond the snowy rooftop of Mary's house.

It never occurred to me that there might be truth to some of the accusations my father made over the years.

"Leave me alone," I say, falling to my bed, turning from her.

"But, Jeffrey . . ."

"Please. Please leave me alone."

Deadlines

IT'S A CRISP SATURDAY evening in March, and my heart is racing. "The Ed Fischer Cartoon Contest," reads a headline in tomorrow's newspaper. The *World-Herald*'s cartoonist invites any and all cartoonists to submit work. The deadline is a week away; winners will be announced the week after that. Like a younger version of me, I scamper with the editorial page to my room, reading, rereading the contest rules. The winner will receive a fifty-dollar U.S. savings bond. What interests me more: the top winners and runners-up will be published on the Sunday op-ed page. Immediately I begin sketching, in hopes of coming up with an idea that will win the contest. The contest is all I can think about. Finally, I settle on a drawing of Uncle Sam, Sam juggling eggs labeled with various concerns: POLLUTION, SOVIET UNION, ECONOMY, THE MIDDLE EAST. I recently purchased a new drawing pen and am meticulous with my lines. To make sure my entry doesn't get lost or bent in the mail, I take the bus downtown and drop off the envelope in the lobby. The guard recognizes me, asks how I've been. The scent of ink fills me with melancholy.

Two Saturday nights later, I happily tag along with my father downtown. He doesn't know anything about the contest but is pleased I've joined him. Downtown has become even more desolate. In place of the toothless man who used to sell my father his paper, a woman of equal weariness comes to my window. I place fifty cents into her palm, our skin touching—hers rough and cold. "Keep the change," I say shyly, proud we are well off enough to allow for a fifteen-cent tip, yet embarrassed we didn't give her more.

We drive on, and in the rhythmic flicker of the streetlamps along 13th Street, I riffle through the newspaper in search of the opinion section, hoping my father will ask what is so important. I drift in and out of a story he's telling about how he once delivered typewriters downtown. I come to the first-place winner, a cartoon that is not mine. Neither is second or third place. Below the winners, in smaller format, several honorable mentions, none of which are my juggling Uncle Sam. I am devastated but say nothing to my father, who is whistling, finished with his story.

It's just after 7:30 in the morning and I'm running late for school, arguing with my father because I've just washed my hair. When the phone rings, my father answers in his usual professional voice.

"Certainly," he says. "Here he is."

He hands me the phone. I'm dripping wet but take the receiver from him, stretching the cord around the corner into the hallway.

"Jeff Koterba?" says the man. "This is Ed Fischer."

"Hello, Ed Fischer." Nervously I blurt his full name. A cartoonist. I am speaking to a real cartoonist.

"I just wanted to let you know I really liked your cartoon for the contest. I had chosen you for an honorable mention. But when the cameramen tried to reproduce it, all the lines didn't show up. I tried to thicken up the lines myself, but . . ."

Ed Fischer tried to thicken my lines! This is better than winning. He tells me to keep practicing. And to get a thicker pen.

I'm jolted awake. The bus lurches again. Drowsily, I survey my surroundings. I can barely keep my eyes open. I was told the pills might make me sleepy. At least my stomach, which must mean my liver, feels better. The other seats are empty. It's a June Sunday, and I'm en route to a meeting with the editor of the *Gateway*, the University of Nebraska's student newspaper.

Upon receiving the news, this past spring, of my acceptance to college, my parents' reaction was one of neither disappointment nor joy. Because I'd waited until the last minute, I missed the opportunity to apply for an art scholarship. My mother helped me fill out the financial aid forms, and when my journalism teacher learned I would be attending the local college, he suggested I get in touch with the editor of the student paper. I watch the buildings go by as we head up Dodge Street, Omaha's main artery that divides the city into north and south. In my lap is a brown Hinky Dinky grocery bag filled with South High *Tooters* and recent sketches. Although I'm eighteen and have a driver's license and am now included on my parents' insurance — after my mother's prodding — I'm allowed to drive only in the event of a family emergency. If my father keels over, for example, or if my mother is turning blue. "Besides," my father says, "you're not supposed to drive while on that medication."

I cross wide and busy Dodge Street and make my way across campus, admiring the trees, the manicured lawns, the brick Arts and Sciences Building topped by a cupola. It's beyond the brick building, in its shadow, that I find the *Gateway*, housed in a Quonset hut. The summer semester hasn't yet begun; the newspaper has been on hiatus. Typewriters wait quietly against the backdrop of a window air conditioner's hum. In one corner, an out-of-place acoustic guitar.

Behind me the door swings open.

"Koterba?"

"Uh-huh."

I'd imagined the editor would appear older somehow, like a professor. Instead, Kevin Quinn, tall and lanky, is boyish, topped by an explosion of red hair. I'll learn later that he'd been an up-and-coming quarterback here at UNO until a back injury ended his career. My palm is sweaty but he doesn't seem to mind as he grips my hand firmly.

"Welcome to our humble abode." He laughs, waving his big hands around the office.

I scan the room. Full ashtrays populate every desk. Wilting posters of the Ramones and Blondie hang askew on the walls. My eyes land on a winter coat draped on a hook.

"Ah, the sex coat." He laughs. "It's what everyone throws on the floor of the darkroom."

"Oh."

He smacks his desk. "Let's have a look."

Nervously, I place the bag on his desk, retrieving first the stack of *Tooters*, then my sketches. I expect he'll want to look through everything. I've brought maybe forty sketches—a few on President Carter, the Middle East. Maybe I haven't brought enough. My hands are shaking, but not in a nervous habit sort of way. I hand him the *Tooters*. I prefer my sketches because they're more recent, but I assume it's better to start with work that has been published.

He opens the first thin newspaper. "Three Mile Island, eh?

166

Let's see," he says, reading the caption. He doesn't laugh. On to the next issue. Nothing.

I regret not having shown my sketches first. Looking into my bag, I can see Carter's big cartoon teeth.

Kevin's finished with the *Tooters*. He's examined only two cartoons.

I hold out my paper bag but he waves me off. "Your stuff's damn good, man," he says. "Our first deadline is Wednesday. Nine P.M. Sound good?"

I stammer. "But I don't start school until fall."

"So?"

Such a simple thing. Such a simple rule I was convinced I must follow: *You can't draw for the student paper until you're a student.* Gone, with his shrug.

"Okay," I say.

"Great." As I turn to leave, he slaps me on the back as if I'm already one of *them*. As if I, too, will be having sex on the darkroom floor. My interview lasted all of five minutes. As I make my way across campus, I can't stop grinning.

Because it's a Sunday, the buses run only on the hour. I wait in the heat with my paper bag. I laugh. It never occurred to me to ask what I will get paid, if anything. I laugh because I don't care. My father will ask, of course; he will care. But for once I don't worry about money.

I transfer twice to get to Joni's house. I'm sleepy and nearly miss my stop. I tell her about my interview at the *Gateway*. She tells me how proud she is. She plans on attending the same school after her graduation next year. "Maybe we'll both work for the *Gateway*," she says. I don't know if we are dating. We'd promised to keep in touch after my graduation, and to my surprise, we do. Sometimes we play tennis, or take walks. In the park, as we lean against a tree or lie on a blanket in the grass, she reads me poetry. I always have my sketchbook, so I draw her face. But I am too shy

167

to kiss her. Her mother makes us grilled cheese sandwiches. Joni's house isn't as old as ours, but it's smaller. When we pass by her parents' bedroom, the door is open and I see that her mother and father sleep on separate beds. When her parents watch sitcoms on their only TV, they chuckle politely. Everything about their house is reserved and in line. There is nothing fancy about their home, yet it is spotless. When we eat, I am aware of every crumb that drops into my lap. I retrieve each speck, carefully placing it on my paper plate. I wipe my mouth after each bite. I want Joni and her parents to know I come from a good family, from good parents who have raised a well-behaved young man.

Off and on all week I squirm in my chair, at a small desk in my bedroom, sweat dripping on typing paper, sketching, napping, sketching again, ultimately completing drawings in pen and ink. When my liver acts up, I pop a pill. Through it all, I fight off sleep. It's nearly impossible to burn the midnight oil. A small mountain of crumpled paper forms at my feet. Nothing is good enough, but I'm not as worried as I usually am. I don't twitch as much. By Tuesday, I settle on a cartoon showing two men making observations about all the downtown stores closing. The two men stand atop the Woodmen Tower. Drawing my characters leaning over, looking down from thirty stories, makes me lightheaded, the same way I feel when I stand someplace high up, fighting the urge to jump.

The next day, cartoon in hand, I take the bus to the *Gateway*.

The door is locked. It's almost noon. I sit against the hot metal of the building, drifting in and out of sleep. I have a hole in the knee of my jeans that I can't stop playing with, making it worse. It's over an hour later when I squint toward the form of Kevin Quinn striding toward me. "Hey," he says on approach, "hope I didn't keep you waiting."

"No." I pick myself up off the hot concrete. I run my hand through my hair, over my damp scalp.

"We didn't get out of here until seven this morning," he says, fishing for his keys.

"Oh." I love that people were here until earlier this morning. Maybe they finished their deadline, then had an orgy.

"Let's see what you've got!" He takes the drawing, holding it in one hand, unlocking the office door with the other. He reads carefully, chuckling. "Nice job," he says.

"Thanks."

"Just one thing," he says casually. "You misspelled 'Woodmen.' It's 'Wood*men*' with an 'e,' not 'Wood*man*' with an 'a.'"

"Oh, man," I say. *Damn it.* It's all I can do not to smack my forehead. How could I be so stupid? How many times have I gazed at that building, fantasizing about it, longing to eat at the restaurant that closed not long after Artie and I visited?

"We have whiteout all over the place. Just look around."

I dab on the white goop, blowing on it, waiting for it to dry. I twitch a little, watching Kevin Quinn. Everything about him says *confidence.* The way he picks up and dials the phone, the way he slips a clean sheet of paper into the typewriter. Here is a man who was up all night but isn't complaining about it. Here is a man who pointed out an error I've made, but it's not an *emergency* that I've made a mistake. No one is screaming at me, telling me how dumb I am. I did not run away. I stayed here, dabbed on the whiteout, making an "e" with a Bic pen.

I return the corrected cartoon.

"Great," he says.

I am grateful for his easy forgiveness.

Meekly, I ask to use the phone.

"No problem."

I let Joni know I'm running behind. From this angle, I notice a guitar case next to Kevin's desk. "Do you play?" I ask.

"Hmm? Oh, the guitar. Yeah, I keep it here for those late nights when things get crazy. Helps me work through the stress to do a little picking."

169

"Cool."

When I start to leave, he stops me. "Oh, hey," he says, "I'll need you to fill out a form to get paid. You know, bookkeeping stuff. I'm sorry we can only get you three dollars a cartoon."

"Sure." Three dollars? I'm ecstatic. I would draw for free.

"Anyway, see you next week?"

"Yes. Next week."

I nod off on the bus, waking every time someone pulls the cord, buzzing the driver to stop. Once I get to Joni's, and after her mother makes us a late-afternoon snack, we walk to a nearby park. We lie in the grass, daydreaming into the sky. She reads me a poem she's written that contains the word "constancy." We fall asleep, then walk back to her house in twilight. Joni is concerned we've been gone too long; we've missed dinner.

There is no yelling, no obvious signs of anger. Yet Joni pulls me aside, tells me her parents are upset with her, with us. She relays a message from her mother that my parents called, asking for me. Although my parents know about Joni, I reassure them we are only friends. If I were to admit to them — if I were to admit to myself — that I have a girlfriend, it might destroy them. I will not worry them in that way. Yet I *have* worried them. I call and my father answers. His voice is polite, musical. Maybe he answers this way to encourage his customers.

"It's me," I say.

"Your mother was worried." He sounds genuinely concerned. I'm grateful he doesn't yell. I tell him I'm sorry.

"Here's your mother," he says.

"You've been gone all day," she says. "You didn't call."

"Sorry, Mom."

"I'm just glad you're okay. We thought something bad happened."

"Mom, I think I missed the last bus."

While I wait for my mother, Joni and I eat cold leftovers in silence. Her parents don't speak to either of us, don't say good night. It's just before ten when they simply disappear behind their bedroom door. In this house, I don't feel shame, but guilt. I miss my house. Joni and I go out to the driveway, and when my mother arrives, Joni takes me around the corner of her house, out of sight of my mother, pecking me on the cheek. I don't want to leave Joni, but I also fear that my mother might honk, disturbing Joni's parents, making them more upset. I jog to the car; the headlights are bright and I can't see inside. It's not until I get to the passenger side that I discover my mother is sitting in my seat; the driver's side is empty.

"Thought you might like to drive home," she says through the open window. I get in and she rubs my shoulder. "Thank God you're safe."

Our family may not have the nicest house on the block, or the tidiest, but at least my parents don't sleep in separate beds. When we are sad, we show it. And when we are laughing at the TV, we laugh loudly, so everyone on our street can hear how much fun we are having. We worry about one another more than other people, too, I'm convinced; there's not a better way to show love.

Moving Forward

MY MOTHER REMINDS ME I have a six-month follow-up appointment with my pediatrician. Aren't I too old, now that I'm eighteen? Yes and no. She still wants me to see Dr. Z because he was the one who ran the tests in the hospital. I don't resist.

"Can't I go by myself?" I ask my mother.

"I'd like to be there," she says. "In case he has anything to say to me."

I'm in the examination room, alone, waiting in my underwear, sitting on the table, the white paper beneath. I'm tempted to grab a pen and start drawing.

There's a knock. "How we doin'?" Dr. Z asks, coming into the room, reading over my chart. "How's the gut?"

"Fine."

"Glad to hear it. And besides the stomach?"

"Fine. Well, besides feeling tired all the time."

"That's just the Valium."

I grip the sides of the table, crunching the paper. Something doesn't sound right. Valium? Kids at school joke about their mothers getting hooked on the stuff. And for a jaundiced liver?

He glances over his wire-frame glasses, away from my medical history. I can't look at him. "Let's see what we have," he says, sticking a tongue depressor in my mouth, making me gag. He beams his penlight into my eyes, my nose. "And your nervous habits? They seem to be better?"

Nervous habits? I give a quick shake of my head, no, shifting to a quick nod, yes. *Yes, they're better, I think. Wait, I don't know. We've never talked about this.*

He taps on my back, asks me to take deep breaths. He listens to my heart. He has me stand, says to "drop your drawers, turn your head, and cough," checking under my testicles for a rupture. I'm always relieved when I pass this test. I worry he'll find a rupture in Artie one day.

I get dressed as he stands at a counter, writing in my chart.

"What about my liver?" I ask. "Will my liver be okay?"

He keeps writing.

"Your liver?" He sounds confused, doesn't turn around. "Your liver is fine."

But aren't I on the pills for my liver? I'm screaming, but nothing is coming out. "So my liver is okay?"

"Hmm?" he says, finishing what he's writing. "Oh, yes, just fine." For a moment he stares at me over his shoulder. His body follows. Recognition comes to his face. "That's right," he says, leaning casually against the counter. "Now I remember."

I'm standing, tucking in my shirt.

"Your father said you'd be paranoid about taking pills for your anxiety. Considering your stomachaches are caused by a bad case of nerves."

My father said that?

"Do you have enough, by the way? Of the pills?"

"I think so," I say meekly. Nothing makes sense. *Where's my mother? Aren't you going to talk with my mother?*

"Well," he says, making his exit, "don't hesitate to let us know when you need a refill."

I say nothing to my mother when I meet her in the waiting room. The receptionist offers us sticks of Dentyne. They've been offering Dentyne as long as I can remember. And even though I don't enjoy it, I always take the Dentyne — my father taught me never to turn down anything that's cheap or free. But today I decline. My mother accepts two sticks, in case I change my mind. She asks if I'd like to drive, but I answer by slipping into the passenger seat. Like a dog, I stick my head out the open window, trying not to think about anything, my hair not quite long enough to blow into my eyes.

"The doctor didn't want to see me?" she asks, smacking on her stick of gum. I am put off by the spicy, almost antiseptic scent of the Dentyne.

I shake my head, still facing away from her, counting the passing houses.

"So everything's okay? *You're* okay?"

I keep counting houses.

When we get home, I do my best to avoid my father. I flush the pills down the toilet, watching them spiral away like a school of tiny fish.

I need an apartment. Worse than anything I need this. I need a car, too, and a job. First things first. I start to ride my rusty tenspeed — a bike I bought with my own money, a bike ruined by the rain because there was no room for it in either garage. I also scrounge for bus fare in our couch. I apply for any part-time job that will allow me the flexibility to remain a full-time student. I search the want ads. There's not much to choose from; because school's out, most of the part-time jobs are taken. I apply at Kilpatrick's at the Center Mall, in the men's department. As I sit in the personnel office, completing my application, I feel the glares of the coming-and-going employees. They stare at my too short and outdated burgundy bell bottoms, my worn athletic socks, my old shoes. Nothing about me matches, nothing about me makes sense. *I am unfinished.* I hand the receptionist my application, relieved knowing I won't receive a follow-up call. I hop on the bus and head downtown to the *World-Herald*. My old job isn't available, and anyway, it wouldn't pay enough. I ask, but there aren't any other jobs I'm qualified for at the newspaper.

One day, I'm heading home on a bus that takes me past my grandparents' home. I watch their turquoise house on the hill go by. A block passes. Two blocks later I pull the cord and jog back.

"What a nice surprise," my grandmother says, letting me in.

"I was on the bus," I say, out of breath.

"Wouldn't it be easier if you drove?"

"Yes," I say. "But first I have to find a job."

"It's time for you to get out from under your father," she says. "Making you carry TVs like that."

I always believed the TVs were a secret.

"Why don't you stay for dinner. We're having fried chicken."

I call home to say I'm okay. I'm grateful my mother answers.

When it's time to eat, my grandmother calls to Jethro. "Jeffrey's here," she says from the top of the steps. "He's joining us for dinner."

We wait, but Jethro doesn't come. The mere *idea* of him makes me nervous. I haven't seen him since he visited me in the hospital. I don't know if my mother told my grandparents about what he said. It's not that I hate him for telling me. I'm glad I know. Just the same, it's a great relief when my grandmother gives up on Jethro for dinner.

As we eat, my grandfather finds it difficult to breathe, let alone chew. My grandmother does most of the talking.

"Jeffrey's looking for a job," she says to him, "aren't you, Jeffrey?"

My grandfather swallows. I wish I had known him before he got this way, when he was full of energy and tanned from riding his tractor, before he moved his family to Omaha and took a job at the meatpacking plant. I cannot recall when he helped raise me until I was two years old. I want to ask them both what I was like at that age.

"He needs a car," she tells him.

He stops eating, covering his face with the mask.

My grandmother smiles at me, acting as if everything is okay. "You know, we feel bad we didn't do more for you when you graduated high school."

"That's okay, Grandma, I loved the card and the ten dollars."

"Well, we were talking the other day, weren't we, Grandpa? That we needed to give Jeffrey a little gift."

My grandfather can't nod, he's too focused on getting air, heaving in, taking in more than he exhales. He can never get enough air. My grandmother nods for him.

That night, my grandfather hands me a check for $200. My grandmother encourages me to ask for Jethro's help. "He does know a lot about cars. I want him to give you a ride home. Maybe you can talk about buying a car on the way."

This door I've always known. I knock. He greets me as he always has, shyly, childlike. Not a single thing in his room is ever moved or replaced. Somehow I miss this place. This place, for all its plainness, spareness, is solid.

"Grandma wants you to take me home."

He grunts, stares at the floor.

During the drive we are quiet until we pull up in front of my house.

"Can you help me find a car?" I ask.

He grunts again, but this time his grunt sounds like yes.

Two days later, Jethro takes me to investigate a 1971 Chevy Impala I found in a car lot's ad. The ad read, "$225, needs work." I imagine a Chevy Impala as classic as his '57, but instead find a dull blue body in mid-deterioration, its metal skin flaking. We look under the hood, though I'm not sure what for.

"The engine looks okay." He squats, peers underneath. "No oil leaks that I can see."

We take it for a spin, only to discover it's missing reverse.

"That's no good," he says.

But I'm in a hurry.

"The tranny will need fixing. That's expensive."

I can't wait.

"Can you fix it?" I ask, my tics in full throttle.

"That's a big project."

"Please?" I realize how childish I must sound, begging him like this.

"That's out of my league," he says. "Sorry."

It's clear that Jethro isn't in favor of me buying the car. Still, he stands in the shadows of the car lot and doesn't stop me from offering the salesman $200, which he readily accepts.

Until I can save up to get the transmission fixed, I'm careful where and how I park. Late one night, on Joni's street, I get blocked in and have no choice but to drive across the lawn of Joni's neighbors. Twice I have to push the car out of a jam. I have to remind myself, over and over, I can never go backward. I can only move forward.

Forward, forward, forward.

All summer I draw my weekly cartoon, and in the fall I begin school. From the start, one of my art professors ridicules me.

"You the same Koterba in the *Gateway*?" he says.

I answer proudly that I am.

"Well, I'll have none of that in here. This is art. Not cartooning. Just remember that."

I'm deflated by his comments but throw myself into my work. There is so much more time for art in college, so much more opportunity for experimentation. Maybe my professor is right. Maybe what I want is to be a serious artist.

I see Joni in the evenings. She's a senior at South High and has more homework than I. Maybe because the only classes I take seriously are art classes. It's almost too easy. All I have to do is draw, paint, sculpt. Eventually she takes a part-time job as a leasing agent for a suburban apartment complex. I often wait for her after work, driving her home.

My father never asks about my car, never asks about school. When I tell him I've been hired by an insurance company to work in customer service, he seems pleased, if only briefly. "Great," he says. "There's good money in insurance. They keep getting richer as we get poorer. 'Bout damn time somebody in this family got rich."

"Dad, I'll only be working part-time. Because of school."

"What the hell do you mean, part-time?" He's fiddling with a Sony TV. Empty beer bottles are lined up on the set. He's one empty away from finishing off a six-pack.

"Dad. I have school."

"Do you know that the Japanese are putting me out of business?"

I want to scream: Don't blame the Japanese, Dad. They didn't do this to you.

"Everything is components now. How the hell am I supposed to fix a TV with tubes when everything these days are stupid-ass component panels? How?"

"I don't know, Dad. I just thought you might be interested in my school. At least in my art classes."

"Are they teaching you about components?"

"Dad, please . . ."

"All right, goddamn it. Tell me about school. Go on!"

"Forget it."

I inhale, slowly letting out the air.

The lip of the sixth beer bottle disappears under his mustache. I watch, listen as he swallows. Everything he does is loud. It riles my stomach to hear his lips smacking, his throat gurgling.

"I have an assignment to go to a cemetery where my relatives are buried," I explain.

He wipes his mouth with his sleeve.

"So we're supposed to do a rubbing of headstones," I continue. "I was thinking about Granny, and your father, maybe Aunt Jean."

"What the hell do you mean, a rubbing?"

"You take a sheet of paper and place it against the headstone and rub your pencil over the paper. The words — the names, dates, everything — show up. Then you can do other things with it, add other drawings, and —"

"Like hell you'll do that. That's disrespectful."

"But it's not. My professor gives this assignment all the time."

"I'm not going to let some bullshit college nobody have my kid disrespecting my dear mother and father and sister. No goddamned way."

"Yes, I am."

My father is quick; his belt is out of his pants; he's smacking it against the Sony TV. Bottles clank, fall to the floor.

"My God," my mother cries, coming into the room. "What's going on?"

Artie and the kids aren't far behind.

"What did you do?" Artie says angrily, possessively. He slugs me in the spine.

"Damn it," I shout. "That hurt like a sonofabitch!"

My father gets in my face. "What the hell did you call your mother?"

"I didn't call her anything, goddamn it!"

"Hell you didn't. Don't you use that kind of language around my children," he scolds.

"I'll say whatever the *hell* I want."

He smacks the belt again, careful not to hit any of the kids or my mother. "Listen, you little shit. You apologize right now!"

"Fuck you."

"What did you just say?" He scowls so much his face looks like a Halloween mask. "What the hell did you say to me?"

My mother is crying, pleading for us to stop.

I poke my finger in his chest. "Fuck you, fuck you, fuck you. Fuck. You."

When I explain to my instructor why I'm unable to complete the assignment, he raises his eyebrows in disbelief.

"That's a new one," he says, uninterested in my reasons or my father's concerns. I want to please this teacher, make him proud like my high school art teacher.

"I'm sorry," I say.

After class, I go to my car, slapping my forehead over and over. I can't stop. Sometimes I start out doing something like this because I'm mad at myself, but then it turns into a nervous habit. I don't want to be afraid of the world like my father, like Jethro. I'm even too scared to take Life Drawing 101. Me, the boy who has always drawn imaginary naked women, women from magazines. If only my Chevy could take me to Virginia or wherever Uncle Ed is buried, then I could do a rubbing of *his* headstone. I would add drawings of rockets, of Washington, D.C., of JFK.

Joni says she has good news. A small one-bedroom unit has come open at the suburban apartment complex where she works. Sounds great, I tell her, but not all of my school costs were covered by financial aid and my student loan. Plus, I just had my transmission fixed. I don't have enough saved for a deposit, nor do I have credit to qualify, but thank you anyway. No problem, she says. She's spoken with her boss; it's all set if I want the place — no deposit required.

On the day I move, my father offers me anything I might need or want. "TV?" he calls, hobbling, practically chasing me to the car with a dated console.

"No thanks," I say.

Nevertheless, he manages to put the TV in the driveway, behind my car, blocking me in. The TV is as close as he'll come to saying he's sorry.

"Dad, please, I don't want it." I'm not trying to hurt his feelings. I truly do not want a TV. I drag it out of the way, leaving a regretful scar on the cement.

He goes into the house and returns with a beige plastic portable. A Hitachi. "You *sure* you don't want one? Look, it's a newer model."

"No already."

He almost gets angry but stops himself. "Okay, suit yourself. But if you ever change your mind . . ."

My mother takes my moving out personally. "What have I done to deserve this?" She shakes her head in her familiar defeated way, carrying bags of groceries, meat from the freezer, half an apple pie, canned goods.

All I can do is thank her for the groceries. Most likely I won't eat half of what she gives me, but I accept it all.

She presents doodads and ornaments, ceramic fish for my bathroom wall.

"Why in the hell would he want those dust collectors?" my father asks her. "Leave the kid alone!"

My father's right, but I receive her gifts anyway.

The kids — even Artie — come bearing pillows, old newspapers, half a loaf of Wonder bread, two vacuum cleaners, a glass of water. I drink the water. I take one vacuum.

Now my father offers me a stereo.

"I already have one, thanks."

"But you can have two! One for your bedroom, one for your living room."

"Dad, my place is small enough—"

"Is it safe?" my mother interjects. "Maybe it's too small!"

"Just one little stereo?" my father says.

I ignore him, packing my car. It's crammed with sketchbooks, canvases, paints, clothes, blankets, records. I've already made one trip this morning when my parents were still asleep. I tied my twin bed to the roof of the car, squeezed my desk into the trunk, left it sticking out. Artie came along to help.

I hug the kids and my mother goodbye. My father has been inside for several minutes. I can't imagine hugging him; even shaking his hand might be uncomfortable. It's best for me to leave while he's not here.

As I back down the driveway, I hear him calling after me.

I skid to a stop at the bottom of the hill. The hill I once believed was long and steep appears over the wide landscape of my Impala's hood as nothing more than a slight gradation.

He's at my window with—a ukulele? But it has seven strings —it's missing one—and the back of the instrument is round, a gourd.

"Here. I *know* you have room for this."

"What is it?"

"I think it's a lute. Or a mandolin. I'm not sure. But when I picked it up a couple of Saturdays ago, I thought of you." He holds it by the body, and the neck and headstock poke at me through the window. "Here," he says, jabbing it at me.

I take the instrument and place it on the heap of blankets in the passenger seat.

"Thanks" is all I can say.

"Don't mention it," he says. "Don't be a stranger. And when you change your mind about a TV . . ." He gives me a sly wink, our little secret.

"Okay, Dad. When I change my mind about a TV . . ."

Driving like this to the suburbs with my junk hanging out, with my car full again for a second round, fills me with disillusionment. I remind myself that the reason my car is packed full is that I'm moving. That anyone, anywhere might end up with a full, junky car while moving.

I inhale the view from my balcony in the suburbs; my stomach relaxes. My apartment is on the third floor and looks out over the other apartments that resemble mine. When those people look at my apartment, they see what I see. Everyone, *everything* is the same on the outside. There is comfort in this sameness. Here, we are all lined up at the same starting line.

Joni tells me these apartments are where the tornado of 1975 descended and began its path of destruction. Some of the buildings survived the storm; others were rebuilt afterward, in their original likeness. I do not know which category my apartment belongs to. If a storm comes, I can go to the laundry room or the basement. It gives me strength to say to the weather, or to God, or to . . . *I won't let you paralyze me with fear.*

I have no furniture save my bed, desk, and a couple of old chairs. My mother gave me a stack of dishes, a pot, and a pan. I have an ample supply of bedding, curtains, rugs—though I don't need rugs, since everything but the bathroom and kitchen is covered in outdated green shag. I joyfully pace my apartment barefoot, pretending my floor is a lawn of warm grass. When I vacuum, I imagine I'm mowing a perfect yard. I stretch out on the floor, gazing at the white ceiling. In the suburbs, in my apartment, every wall is painted white. I hang nothing on my walls. Not any of my mother's gifts or my paintings or drawings. My walls will remain plain, fresh, a blank canvas, in case I want to paint on them, big landscapes or abstracts or cartoons. Yet I never would. Not ever. These walls must remain pristine always.

PART THREE

Far Away, Close to Home

THE LIGHT OF THE DARKROOM makes everything—my hand, my pen, my drawings—an eerie red. I'm practicing my caricature of Ronald Reagan, waiting for a halftone Velox to develop. I'd hoped by now, at age twenty-five, to be drawing editorial cartoons for a daily newspaper, but I bear down to support Joni, who struggles with her pregnancy. I work for the *Bellevue Times,* a weekly newspaper in a suburb not ten minutes from where I grew up, printing Veloxes and plate negatives with a camera so large it fills the next room. With its gauges and dials and toggle switches, I imagine it's a machine that can shrink humans. I breathe in developer, each night bringing home the liquid odor of my work in my jeans, my unruly hair, my lungs. The darkroom is a cinderblock cocoon. I would be protected here from a tornado. Not even the fighter jets and bombers taking off from nearby SAC can make it vibrate.

Here I twitch to my heart's content, letting my limbs loose, flailing like an octopus. But the desire to twitch is as insatiable as lust. It's exhausting.

Until recently, I was occasionally allowed to draw a cartoon for the *Times,* off the clock. But that ended when the publisher expressed her displeasure at my drawing of two poverty-stricken African-American kids rummaging through a garbage can. One of the kids is telling the other, "President Reagan was right . . . He said if we wanted food bad enough, all we had to do was look."

The *Times* is nothing like the *World-Herald.* Operating on weekly deadlines, the tiny newsroom has none of the commotion of a daily. I try to convince myself that this weekly pace makes sense for me. Maybe I've had enough of the perpetual rush I've always known.

185

I read the *World-Herald* by the darkroom's red light, sketching ideas during my downtime, finishing the cartoons at home. I submit these samples to the *World-Herald,* dreaming that the editor will hire me to fill the void created when Ed Fischer left. But every submission is met with a rejection, or worse, no response. I fight back by practicing, working harder, staying up until all hours.

From the darkroom I can hear my work phone ringing; my eyes struggle to adjust as I open the door to the camera room, reaching for the receiver.

"Camera," I say, always answering by department, never by my name.

"Jeff Koterba, please," a man says.

"Speaking." My eyes adjust to the bright light.

The man introduces himself as Frank Partsch, the *World-Herald*'s new editorial-page editor.

I can barely say "Oh." Plus, I'm nervous that someone walking by will hear my conversation. When I'd listed the *Bellevue Times* on my résumé, I hadn't expected to receive a call here.

"I thought I'd update you on the situation."

"Yes?" My heart races.

"I know you've been submitting to us over the years. But at this time we're in no position to hire a cartoonist."

"I see." I try not to let him hear my disappointment.

"But we'd sure consider buying an occasional freelance cartoon on local topics." He goes on to say the cartoon would have to pertain to a subject of great significance, and there's no guarantee the paper will buy any cartoon, ever. "How does that sound?"

I stammer. *What kind of questions should I ask?* "Um. So, would I send finished cartoons?"

He thinks a moment. "No," he says. "A rough sketch is fine. If I and the editor of the paper and the publisher approve the idea, we'll call and have you finish the drawing."

Getting the approval of three important people sounds like an insurmountable barrier, yet when I get off the phone and return to my darkroom, I feel lighter, filled with hope. I must be beaming.

The next day, I mail ten sketches on a variety of subjects — everything from ideas about Nebraska's governor to sketches about Omaha's mayor. A week later, I receive a rejection letter. Except this rejection letter doesn't *sound* like a rejection. Real rejection is being told I am stupid, ignorant, or that I don't understand perspective. This letter reads: "Good effort! Unfortunately, it's a 'no' this time around. Keep us in mind in the future." *Good effort. The future.*

Every week, I try again. And every batch is returned, the reasons varying from "Not a story we want to comment on" to "The idea isn't working." But always, I am encouraged to keep submitting.

As I sketch in my darkroom and again at home, I begin to say aloud, "I am a full-time editorial cartoonist." I don't know how it happens. It's as though the words form deep inside and bubble forth to the surface. I can't keep from speaking these words.

Too embarrassed for Joni to hear me, I limit this mantra, or obsession, to when I'm showering or in the car, always when alone. I force the words inside, integrating the words into my bloodstream, now silently repeating them while eating, while doing dishes, while drawing and playing music.

I am a full-time editorial cartoonist.

I'm positioning a photograph in the camera's oversized glass frame, attempting to get the settings right, the dials clicked into the exact positions, when I hear a commotion in another part of the *Times*. It's late January, and a reporter is at the back door, stamping the snow from his boots, repeating for the handful of employees who work here what he's heard on his car's radio.

"The *Challenger* blew up," he says matter-of-factly.

"The space shuttle?" comes another voice.

"Yep," he confirms, removing his parka, snow powdering the floor in his wake. "Right after takeoff."

Why isn't he running? Why aren't we all running — someplace? *This is an emergency.*

As the staff somberly gathers around a TV in the break room to watch the replay of the disaster, I imagine the mood at the *World-Herald*. Are editors sorting through wire stories about the shuttle? Are reporters already on the phone, heading to the streets, gathering local reactions for the afternoon edition? We are helpless at this small weekly. We can do nothing. We can do nothing but watch TV. And shake our heads in anguish.

I cannot just stand here. I grab a stack of paper from the copier and hunker in the darkroom. Thankfully, my In basket isn't very full, and as I continue to shoot halftones, I rough out ideas in secret. During lunch hour, I drive to the *World-Herald* and drop off my sketches in the lobby. This disaster isn't a local story, but I keep my fingers crossed that the paper will want a cartoon on the *Challenger* crash right away and not wait for the syndicated cartoons to arrive by mail a few days later.

As the afternoon dwindles away at the *Times,* I make a rare call to my parents to ask if they've been watching the coverage.

"Isn't it so sad?" my mother asks.

"Yes. What about Dad? Has he been watching?"

"Oh, yes. All day." She pauses. "Those poor astronauts . . . ," she says, her voice trailing off. "Do you want to speak to him?"

"That's okay. It's pretty crazy around here today. I'd better get back to work."

It's five — quitting time — when I receive the go-ahead call from the *World-Herald*.

I'm watching coverage of the disaster with Joni. I have no photographs of the launch pad, so I study news footage, sketching quickly. I stay up late, drawing the empty launch pad, the stark sky. Before work, in the bleakness of early morning, I drive to the *World-Herald*. It's too early; Frank, the editorial-page editor, isn't in. I leave the original with the security guard, worried the cartoon won't make it to Frank's office.

Back at the *Times,* I go through the motions, moving in and out of my darkroom, shooting Veloxes that won't see publication for days.

The night can't come fast enough. In the snow I drive to the same downtown corner where my father and I used to pick up the early edition. I buy tomorrow's newspaper and park along Dodge Street. In the hush of a streetlight, the aqua hood of my Ford Escort appears sickly, drained of color. I glance over the front page, the headlines about the tragedy, the photograph of the pretzeled contrail. I'm hesitant to open the paper. What if the cartoon didn't reach the editor? What if the powers that be didn't like the finished drawing? My heater whirs. *I can't sit here forever. What if my car has a leaky tailpipe and they don't find me until morning, dead from asphyxiation?* I crack the window; the cold air breathes life into the car, into me. Carefully I open the newspaper, peeling back to the editorial page. I immediately recognize the black sky of my cartoon, positioned above the letters to the editor. It is published. It is *official*.

I rev the engine. Here is the empty launch pad, the quote from Byron I've scripted in white lettering across the soot-colored sky: "They never fail who die in a great cause." As I read and reread the cartoon, the inexplicable force of the tragedy sinks in; the cartoon no longer belongs to me. The cartoon belongs . . . I'm not sure to what or to whom. It just *belongs*.

When Joni and I married four years earlier, we honeymooned two hundred miles south of Omaha, in Kansas City. It was all we could afford. While there, I asked her if she would mind my contacting Lee Judge, the cartoonist for the *Kansas City Star*. "This may be my only chance," I told her, truly believing I might not ever travel to Kansas City again. Barely older than I, Lee readily took me under his wing. He also welcomed Joni, giving us a tour of the newspaper and his office, which looked very much like Ed Fischer's: ink-stained drawing table, metal drawing lamp, bookshelves stuffed full, newspapers everywhere. He stressed the importance not only of drawing every day but also of reading. He recommended books on economics, national defense, and gun control, and I returned to Omaha with a summer reading list. Lee helped me understand that editorial cartooning isn't merely about drawing. It's about words, and thoughts, and core beliefs.

I write to Lee, and sometimes splurge by calling long-distance, telling him about the sketches I submit to the *World-Herald*. Although it is rare for the newspaper to buy a cartoon, he encourages me to keep at it. But he also warns that they may never make a move to hire me permanently. He suggests I send work to other Nebraska papers, and tells me that if he hears of job openings elsewhere, he'll be sure to let me know. I follow his advice, and occasionally my work gets picked up by small weeklies and dailies in Nebraska towns I've never visited. Dusty, water-tower-sounding places like Benkelman, on the western edge of the state. There is romance in the knowledge that my cartoons — and my name — appear in print hundreds of miles away.

The day Lee calls to ask if I've ever considered drawing sports cartoons, I don't admit the idea scares me. The *Star*, he says, might be looking for a replacement for their previous freelance sports cartoonist. Although I played Little League baseball and have an awareness of sports, I don't pay much attention to the details. When the guys at work discuss standings and statistics, I'm back on the grade school playground, left out. But I won't disappoint Lee.

"To get you started," he says, "I have three ideas — a week's worth — I can't use. Just in case."

"Really?" I say hesitantly. *But isn't that cheating?*

As though to reassure me, he says this is a one-time offer. "After the first week, you're on your own."

When he tells me his ideas, they have nothing to do with batting averages and points scored — rather, they are about athletes who behave badly off the field.

It's two in the morning and I'm dabbing whiteout, attempting to cover a drop of tomato sauce at the edge of my sports cartoon. Eating at this hour allows me to pretend it's only evening, not the dead of night. It doesn't help that my drawing table is wedged into our tiny dining area, off the kitchen, tempting me with frozen pizza and Coca-Cola. Surrounding me: stacks of paper, sketches of baseball players, brushes, pens, pencils, bottles of correction fluid, Rorschach ink blots. A transistor radio defies gravity, perched on one of the stacks of paper, doing its best to cling to the weak signal out of Denver's KOA-AM. Like pizza, talk shows keep me awake and alert, and Omaha's lack of overnight news and sports talk sends me searching for distant nighttime voices that make their way over the Great Plains and into our cramped suburban townhouse.

I blow on the whiteout, my lips so close they practically kiss the Strathmore drawing paper. Watching the whiteout dry, I turn my attention to my fingerprint grooves, how they're filled in with ink.

I've made the transition to the world of sports more easily than I might have imagined. In my drawings I take aim at spoiled athletes, drug-abusing athletes, violent athletes, wealthy team owners who care little for their personnel beyond winning championships. I don't care who wins. I don't care how they play the game. It's how they conduct themselves as human beings that concerns me.

Now, in addition to keeping up with the news, I read the sports coverage in the *World-Herald* and *USA Today* and soak up *Sports Illustrated*s whenever I have a spare moment in the darkroom. I continue to submit to the *World-Herald*, but often I am rejected.

And although the *Kansas City Star* always arrives in our mailbox two days after the fact, I devour every sports section as if it isn't old news. Despite our paycheck-to-paycheck existence, I convince Joni we need cable for ESPN coverage. I justify my TV watching, I allow it, because it's my "job." Our only treat comes when we rent a videotape machine and movie from Captain Video. Otherwise, our one TV remains dormant.

But in order to sketch, I require solitude. The thought of my father's failures inspires me to draw in the middle of the night. While I twitch and work as he does, I will not end up like him. But I will not sacrifice my family, either. My days are filled by my job, and evenings Joni and I spend our time together eating dinner and caring for our baby. I strum my mandolin for him, letting him run his tiny fingers across the strings.

Upstairs, the baby wails.

Quickly, I take the steps. Joni is asleep, exhausted from caring for our sick newborn. Most nights Josh cries out in pain. Maybe tonight it's the stent that protrudes from his kidney and drains into his diaper that causes him discomfort. Maybe a pain shoots deep inside his body that can't be fixed, not now, not tonight — a pain Josh can't describe because he's not yet two months old. The surgery on the kidney, the blocked ureter, will be a success, but until then, Joni and I do our best to love and comfort him.

"Shhh, shhh, shhh," I whisper. "It's going to be okay." I gently lift him from his crib. His room is awash in creamy orange, from the night light in the corner, a gift from my parents.

I take him downstairs, swaying him gently until he settles against my chest, asleep. Josh is my only child, but I've been here before, rocking babies, changing diapers, spooning out baby food. I pace back and forth across the linoleum, rhythmically patting his bottom, reminding him, *I'm here, I'm here.* I strain to keep from twitching. I will wait another few minutes before I take him back to his crib, to make sure he remains sleeping.

Back and forth I move, counting the five steps from the dining area to the living room, glancing at my drawing table. My cartoon is nearly finished; I just need to erase my pencil marks. I begin every cartoon in pencil, tracing over my lines with pen and brush. Inking the lines gives me a second chance to make the cartoon perfect. But at this hour the drawing appears to be getting stale. Maybe I should start over. Or if I get some sleep, perhaps the cartoon will look better in the light of morning. This pattern is repeated every night I'm on deadline, always striving to get my cartoons, myself, perfect: I finish. I second-guess myself. Sometimes I begin again.

After I return Josh to his crib, I watch as his chest rises and falls with soft precision. Peeking in on Joni, I watch her breathe, too, finally pulling myself away to return to my drawing table, tidying my mess, stacking newspaper clippings. When I am sure the ink is completely dry, I erase, brushing the dust into my hand, carefully transporting it outside. The May air is cool and damp from an earlier shower. I swing my arm, opening my fingers, releasing the eraser dust, which dissolves instantly into the night.

One afternoon while I'm holed up in the *Times*'s darkroom, studying the Kansas City Royals roster, the story of outfielder Jim Eisenreich grabs my attention. After he was released by the Minnesota Twins, his contract was picked up by the Royals for one dollar. A bargain, as my father might say. What gives me pause is the mention of his tics. Although Eisenreich was a talented player, his symptoms were so bad that in Minnesota he was often booed off the field. As I read about his vocal tics and strange head and arm movements, I marvel at our similarities.

After Eisenreich's arrival in Kansas City, the story goes on to explain, a doctor diagnosed him with Tourette's syndrome. Although the term looks familiar, I'm not entirely sure I've heard of it—I know I can't pronounce it—but my heart goes out to him. I'm also grateful *my* nervous habits are just that, the result of stress, not a disease or a syndrome.

In my darkroom I have time to think. I mix chemicals and develop halftone prints. I pull apart slimy paper to reveal the faces of local bankers and real estate agents. For days, I can't get my mind off Jim Eisenreich.

I imagine him living in a modern, sprawling house, tootling around Kansas City's boulevards, dining in fancy restaurants, managing his syndrome as best he can. And like Kansas City, this syndrome that plagues him seems remote. My cartoons, my signature, "Koterba," may appear in print in Kansas City, but I exist in Omaha, struggling in my new marriage, taking care of a sick baby, paying hospital bills, making ends meet. Yet on deadline nights, when I climb into bed next to Joni with my smudged fingers, only to wake three hours later, I remind myself there was a time when I believed no woman would ever love me. To have this, at least, is nothing short of a miracle.

Jeff Kaye

'BOUT READY, BOYS?" Kevin Quinn asks Paul and me, with the authority he once commanded on the football field. His newsboy cap brushes the rafters of the low ceiling. Although I am six feet tall, he towers over me. This comforts me. Maybe no one will notice me up here onstage. I turn briefly away from the audience to face the brick wall, to get in one good mouth stretch.

"Ready," I say, facing Kevin, not the crowd, spreading the fingers of my left hand over the frets, pressing the strings, forming a G chord.

Kevin runs his pick across his banjo strings. He starts in, his voice clear, lilting: "Good evening, folks. Welcome to the Dubliner. We're the County Corkers."

The crowd cheers. I can't look any audience member in the eye. Instead I cast my gaze over the smoky room, attempting to take in the entirety of the sight. That is, when my eyes aren't squeezed tight, concentrating on what chord comes next. When I let go, I soar. I am not me. I am the music and the laughter, the cheering, the camaraderie of the Dubliner Pub. My nervous habits ease up, or if they keep going, I'm not aware of them.

What was hatched as a fluke two years ago has evolved into a regular gig at this downtown Irish pub. Kevin had contacted another former *Gateway* staffer about playing bass, who in turn contacted me, knowing I played guitar and owned a mandolin. When asked if I *played* the mandolin, I told Paul I did, not mentioning that I'd taught myself only one song on the instrument, "The Irish Washer Woman." I couldn't have imagined what I was getting myself into. At our first rehearsal, Kevin explained that I was not only to play guitar and mandolin; I was expected to sing, too.

I could barely comprehend the thought of playing an instrument in front of a roomful of people. But Kevin was persistent about me singing, and one night after rehearsal and a few beers, I agreed to give it a try.

The plan was for the group to perform at various pubs on St. Patrick's Day for free beer and corned beef sandwiches, with no expectations of playing music together again. What was the worst that could happen? We needed only a dozen or so songs, Kevin explained. At most twenty, which we could repeat. Maybe playing and singing for one day didn't seem that impossible after all. *Just one day.* We named ourselves the County Corkers after Paul's belief that his ancestors had come from Ireland's County Cork.

At the first bar, without microphones, the Corkers strolled past the booths; nervously, I followed Kevin, hoping to hide in his shadow. I'd never been in a bar on St. Patrick's Day—I might as well have been in Times Square on New Year's Eve. I sang, but I could not detect my voice. It was amid this revelry that I found a sense of safety.

All day, we wandered from bar to bar, from the suburbs of Omaha to downtown. We repeated "Whiskey, You're the Devil," "Danny Boy," and "Johnny, We Hardly Knew Ye," songs I started out unsure of, but before long knew by heart. At the end of it all, my fingertips were blistered, my throat was raw.

I'd never felt so invigorated.

Later, there was a half-serious, drunken discussion of regrouping the following St. Patrick's Day, but when the owner of the Dubliner asked us back a few weeks later, we accepted the offer, scrambling to add songs to our playlist.

Since high school, I've dreamed of one day performing in a rock band. We aren't a rock band—will never be—but maybe *this* is my true calling, to travel the country as an "Irish" musician. From the library, I check out books on Irish history. I purchase cassette tapes and LPs of Irish music. I become swept up in the romance of drinking songs, traditional ballads, and raucous numbers recalling great events in Ireland's history.

I'm not Irish, of course. My father's parents were born in Czechoslovakia, where they got married before coming to the United States. My mother's ancestry is also eastern European, although she recalls a family story about a far-off relative who might have been an "Indian woman taken by a Scottish man." She doesn't know the particulars. She doesn't know if the Indian or the Scotsman belongs to us.

When Kevin introduces the band members to the audience, I am embarrassed by my name, grasping onto the vague notion that perhaps I have at least a little Scottish blood. Kevin, although half Bohemian, is a Quinn. Paul, a Hammel. Everyone at the Dubliner, whether guzzling a black-and-tan or downing shots of Bushmills, I imagine to be of Irish descent. A Koterba playing "From Clare to Here" doesn't sound right to my Czech ears.

My family name was originally spelled "Kotrba," without the "e," and Uncle Ed disliked it enough to add the vowel. The rest of the family followed suit. When my father formed a band, he went a step further, presenting himself as "Artie Kay." But he never considered changing his name legally to Kay. He was still a Koterba, and deep down, a Kotrba. Before the curlicue vowel was added, I don't know if it was difficult for my father and his siblings to contend with teachers and classmates who struggled with that cluster of consonants. I imagine it was. Not necessarily because their last name was difficult to pronounce, the tongue having to roll over the "trb," but because of what those consonants represented to them: *We are poor children of immigrants. Our father, a musician and packing plant worker, drank himself to death. We are the Kotrbas.*

But did the added "e" Americanize them enough to believe they belonged, that they deserved success?

I recently came up with a stage name. I'd started with "Jeff K," but decided against it, fearing its Kafkaesque overtones. I also skipped over "Jeff Kay," settling on "Jeff Kaye," adding an "e" to distance myself from my father's nickname. Besides, I believed it made the name appear more authentic, more like a name one might find in the British Isles. "Koterba" can still sign his cartoons, but maybe as Jeff Kaye I *do* have a right to perform in an Irish bar.

I'd seen my father play in a club only once, three years before he suffered his breakdown. The band was "corny," as he later put it. He was also disgruntled that the bandleader allowed him just one four-bar solo all night. I wish I could go back in time to watch him onstage in his heyday. When I was younger, my idea of heaven was that God allowed you to call up the entire history of the world on a special TV made of clouds. This cloud TV would allow me to watch my father take five-minute drum solos, and listen to him croon while women of all ages sought after the handsome, eligible bachelor. And might I also catch a glimpse of my father gazing beyond the fanfare, past the audience, sensing, anticipating me, a child not yet conceived, a spirit in waiting?

The Toymaker's Family

Jeff, it's the chance of a lifetime." Artie speaks quickly, full of urgency and promise.

"I don't think so," I whisper, awkwardly holding the phone with my left hand, keeping a sheet of paper from slipping away with my left elbow, all the while sketching ideas with my right hand. Not wanting to hurt his feelings, I say nothing about his calling after midnight. I'd grabbed the phone on the second ring, relieved that Joni and the baby hadn't been startled awake.

"We need you," he says.

"I have to get back to my drawing."

"Listen," he says, "he doesn't use Hula-Hoops anymore. He uses a Ping-Pong ball."

"A ball?"

"Yep. Now you're interested, aren't you!"

"No, I just don't understand."

"It's basically the same idea as the old Dizzy Wizzy, but instead of all the rubber bands strung over a hoop, it's the string itself that makes the noise. The ball is the weight at the end of the rubber string."

"Artie, I can't."

"But we're gonna be rich! Don't you need money?"

I glance over my shoulder at the refrigerator, where Josh's hospital bills are stacked. "Listen, Artie, I really appreciate it. But let's talk about this some other time. It's late, and I have work to do." I have no intention of ever discussing the Dizzy Wizzy.

"If you can't do it for yourself, do it for me. Do it for Dad."

"Why can't you sell the Dizzy Wizzy without me?" I can feel my face twist like elastic—my tics get worse when I'm tired or stressed out.

"Because you're a Koterba, and Dad needs you to be part of this. He wants to form a company."

A company? Where's my father going to come up with money to start a toy company?

"We'll all be on the board of directors and everything. You, me, Mom, Dad. He wants you to design the packaging. It's time we had some luck."

"Then why didn't he call me himself?"

"Maybe he's afraid you'll turn him down."

"After all the crap he's put me through?" I pause. "Yeah, I probably would."

"See? You're proving me right! That's why he didn't call!"

"Artie, I'm on deadline." *I am a full-time editorial cartoonist.*

"I'm on a deadline, too. A deadline to get rich. Am I gonna have to come over there and break your nuts?" *He also lives in the suburbs, not far from me. He's capable of showing up unannounced.*

"Why are you up so late, anyway?" I say, attempting to redirect his focus.

"Doing what *you* do. Busting *my* nuts to make a buck. I just got home from a wedding. And I have an ad tomorrow." *He works part-time for Complete Party, a company that sends disc jockeys to weddings and other special events. He supplements his income by fixing and selling TVs and stereos. It scares me that he works on TVs.*

I remember Artie at his South High football games, racing with the ball as a running back. In the last game of the season, we held our breath after one play when he took a lifetime to rise from a dog pile, only to find out later he'd suffered a career-ending broken neck. He'd had hopes for a college football scholarship.

In the end, I couldn't save the kids or my mother. I could not find peace with my father. I could only escape. Still, something gnaws at me, some inkling deep inside my bones, whispering to me, urging me forward into the misty cloud of my unformed life.

Maybe the answer is where I grew up. Maybe the answer is the Dizzy Wizzy.

I come armed with a sketchbook, pens for note taking, and a healthy dose of skepticism. It's September, and I haven't set foot in this house since last Christmas, and even then, I stayed just long enough to exchange gifts. I'd had an excuse: Joni stayed home, under the weather with her pregnancy. If she hadn't been sick, I would have found some other reason to bolt. Now, as I come onto the porch and move into the living room, not much has changed, except everything seems smaller, shorter, more closed in.

Jeanie is thrilled to see me. She's ten, but hangs on me, hugs me as if she's a toddler. My mother's eyes fill with tears; my father treats me like the returning prodigal son. "Hey!" he cheers, acting surprised. "Look who's here!"

I sense a twinge of jealousy rising in Artie. And if so, who can blame him? Isn't he the one who frequently visits, often — no, *always* — helping my father carry his junk from here to there? My father continues to trade in TVs, but not in the same volume he once had. There's no market for tube TVs. Now he buys sets that already work, for as cheaply as he can, cleaning them and reselling them in hopes of making a profit. He's moved on to electric typewriters, and also sells stereos, radios, lawn mowers, and any knickknack or supposed antique.

I look around the living room. An effort has been made. The floor is visible and there are chairs to sit on. I glance into the family room and find it full of boxes of rubber string and large bags of Ping-Pong balls.

"Jennifer's picking Eddie up from football practice," my mother says. That Jennifer is old enough to drive is by itself difficult for me to swallow. That my father allows her to drive at sixteen is impossible to imagine. Even Eddie, at fifteen, has his permit. But then wasn't Artie also allowed to drive the moment he turned sixteen? Didn't my father help him buy a Camaro?

"Sit down, everybody," Artie says, waving his hands, playing the part of big shot. "Let's begin our meeting!" To Jeanie he says, "We'll call you in when we're ready."

"Why can't I stay?"

"Yeah," my father says. "Why can't she stay?"

"Okay," Artie says. "But she has to keep quiet." Artie's voice, although lacking the richness and depth of my father's, fills the room.

It takes several minutes for my parents to take a seat. First my father has to get himself a drink, and when he returns with a can of 7-Up, no one but me seems to notice he's not drinking booze. He sits in what he calls his new recliner. The Naugahyde is torn in only one place.

My mother and I sit on their latest sofa — a puffy, flowery number — as Jeanie sits on the floor near the TV; the sound is off, and *Wheel of Fortune*'s wheel spins silently, eerily.

"Dad and I have been talking," Artie says. "We think the time is right to finally put the Dizzy Wizzy on the market."

My father and mother nod. It's clear they've already decided, the three of them.

"We're going to start a company. Dad will be president, Mom vice president. I'll be treasurer, and Jeff, you can be secretary. Of course, I'll also be sales director and promoter."

"Shouldn't we discuss all this first?" I ask.

"Dad?" Artie says.

"I agree with Artie," my father says, slapping his leg to make it official. "That all sounds good to me!"

"The lawyer says we can be up and running in no time." Artie fingers his mustache. With his wavy hair and his mustache, my mother calls him Burt Reynolds.

"Lawyer?" I say. "When did all this happen?"

My mother gives a weak grin, shakes her head as if also out of the loop.

"And as you know, we have a company name," Artie continues, ignoring me. "The Terby Toy Company."

Admittedly, it's a catchy name. I jot it down in my sketchbook. But we're jumping the gun.

"First," I say, "where will we get the money to finance this?"

"Don't worry," Artie says, grinning, "it's all figured out."

"If I'm going to be part of a company, I'd like to know how we're going to pay for everything." I can't help but grunt.

Something doesn't feel quite right. But maybe I'm wrong. Maybe my father has had a spate of good luck.

My father slides forward in his chair, signaling he will speak. He clears his throat three times, focuses on me. "Do you not understand how I have waited for this moment my entire life? Do you?" He raises his voice defensively, even though I haven't challenged him.

"Yes, Dad, I know it's been your dream."

"That's why I'm cashing in my war bonds," he says.

"War bonds?" I ask. "But —"

"Listen, Jeff," Artie says, "that's Dad's prerogative."

"You're goddamned right," my father says. There it is, his bad-man face, albeit with more wrinkles.

"Do you think I don't want everyone to make a lot of money?" I say, sinking into the couch, not wanting this discussion to escalate into a fight. I know if we keep going, a box will get kicked over. Someone will stomp off, slamming a door. How quickly I am drawn back in.

"Okay already," my mother says. "Let's everyone keep calm. This is a big decision, and everyone has something to say."

"Mom's right," Artie says, regaining control of the meeting. "Now, Jeff, what we're hoping you can do is design the packaging."

"Um, sure," I stammer, hesitantly jumping on the speeding train of the Terby Toy Company.

"Great," my father says.

"I," Artie says, patting his chest, "will handle advertising and promotions. I'm going to go to all the department stores. Set up demonstrations. Best of all, I have an in with a radio station. We're going to buy radio time."

"Radio time?" I ask in the nicest voice I can conjure up. "Isn't that expensive?"

Artie winks. "Not when you have friends like I do."

"How much?" I ask.

"Not much. Believe me, I know how to work these things."

"Artie, how can we all agree on this if we don't know how much?"

"Trust me!" Artie says.

I roll my eyes. What starts as a gesture of frustration turns into a full-blown tic. I can't seem to convince my eyes to stop rotating under my brow. Jennifer and Eddie return, and my father puts his finger to his lips and graying mustache, instructing them to keep quiet. They wave at me as they slip by us and go upstairs to their respective bedrooms. Jennifer is lanky, her hair long and blond. I'd expected Eddie to be in his uniform, sweaty and grass-stained. But he's fresh, his hair still damp from his locker room shower. Everyone is so imposing in this house.

The rest of us go on discussing, but not discussing. The plans have been set for who knows how long—days, weeks? Longer? I'm still not sure why I'm needed here, except to offer my services designing packaging for the toy.

Artie yells for everyone to gather around.

"What is it?" asks Jennifer, coming back downstairs. She's all legs and arms as she flops on the floor near Jeanie, her eyes darting toward the ceiling, her shoulder giving a twitch.

Eddie plods downstairs and hovers in the entrance to the hallway, combing his wet hair.

Jeanie scoots away from Jennifer, across the floor toward me, leaning against my leg. I realize that I haven't spent much time with my baby sister, that I've shirked my duties as her godparent. Out of all the kids, I know her the least.

"Okay," Artie says, "here's the deal. We're going to need you three"—he points to the kids—"to help make Dizzy Wizzys. Isn't that great?" Jennifer and Eddie exchange an annoyed glance; Jeanie stares up at me.

Artie announces he will now demonstrate how the new toy works. "Ladies and gentlemen," he shouts in the voice of a circus barker. "I present to you the new and improved Dizzy Wizzy!"

They've all seen the new version who knows how many times. My father cheers "Yeah-hey!" as though he's surprised, and everyone claps, but not me. I can't. I don't know why, I just can't. I sketch "Terby Toy Co." in my sketchbook to give my brain something to do. My mother smiles to cover a worried look.

Artie tosses the white ball into the air, begins twirling, squats to keep the ball from clipping the cobwebbed chandelier. The ball circles his head, moving faster and faster, a blur. The sound increases, barely. Gone is the depth of tones created by the previous model. This design, with only one rubber string, mimics a squadron of flies. *Bzzzzzzzzzzzz.*

I slip away into the kitchen for a glass of water. My mother follows. I can hear my father cheering in the other room.

"I don't know, Mom," I say. "I mean, can you and Dad really afford to do this?"

"Your father is so excited. Please don't ruin it for him."

"I'm not trying to ruin it," I say, taking a quick gulp. "I'm trying to be realistic."

I down the rest of the water. How is it, in the time I've been away, my mother has become so accepting of my father's quirky schemes? But doesn't she always capitulate?

"I guess it is pretty exciting," I tell her, attempting to cheer her up.

She stares at me blankly.

In the other room, my father and Artie are plotting. My father says, "Hoo-boy! I can't wait!"

"Stay for dinner?" my mother asks.

"Can't," I say. "Gotta get home."

She turns to hug me, tears running from her eyes.

"Please," she whispers, "let him have his dream."

I nod against her shoulder, pulling away as quickly as I can. Looking past her, beyond the kitchen into the family room, I realize what is missing. Where Times Square once stood are boxes marked in my father's writing: RUBBER BANDS.

"The bar," I say.

"You didn't know?"

"Know what?"

"Oh, my word," my mother says. "Of course you didn't know." She gives her head a quick shake, as if receiving unexpected but positive news. Her face brightens. "He stopped. Just like that." She doesn't have to explain what he stopped.

"What? You're kidding. Why didn't someone tell me?"

"Maybe if you . . ." Her voice trails off. "It's good to see you. I'm glad you came."

"But how? There's no way he joined A.A."

"Of course not. You know your father doesn't like belonging to groups."

"So how?"

She shrugs. "I came home one day from the grocery store and the thing was gone. Thrown into the ditch, Artie told me."

"I'll be damned," I say. "I'll be damned."

As predicted, my involvement in Terby Toys is limited. Not that I mind. Although my father formally incorporates the company, we never hold official meetings that require me to take the minutes. I miss other impromptu discussions, like what price to charge for the toy. Somehow, $1.99 is the amount that is settled on. When I tell Artie that I can't understand how charging so little will cover expenses and generate a profit, he reverts to his authoritarian role.

"I've got it handled," he says.

As promised, I come up with the package design: colorful balls, the words "Dizzy Wizzy" in fluorescent colors against a black background. I write ad copy for the radio spot. In the commercial, two space aliens land on Earth, surprised by what they find—the Dizzy Wizzy. Sound effects are added, and Artie and another radio DJ do the voices. I can't imagine how many war bonds Dad cashed in to buy the twenty-two radio spots.

Everywhere in their house—on the dining room table, the kitchen table, on the tops of TVs—are gray rubber strings and plastic balls in primary colors, a strange pasta dish. Despite the new mess in my parents' home, the air is light, bubbling with expectations. Maybe this is what it took for Artie to get things rolling. Maybe I'm wrong about buying radio airtime, about what the price of the toy should be. Maybe I've been wrong about everything. The fact that my father stopped drinking inspires me to believe that our family is capable of sea changes.

"C'mon, everybody!" Artie announces. "Step right up! It's the perfect thing for Christmas!" It's two Saturdays before Christmas, and Josh, Joni, and I visit a JCPenney where Artie is demonstrating the Dizzy Wizzy in the toy department. Wearing a brown three-piece suit, he looks like an insurance salesman. In the pallid light of the store, he works the toy that in this hollow space sounds even weaker than before—like a single fly. Two children, bundled for the weather, shuffle hesitantly to where Artie stands, in an area of the toy department that the store has reluctantly cleared for his demonstration. The children's heads make small ovals as their eyes follow the ball until their mother, weighted down with her shopping, pulls them away without so much as looking at whatever has captured her children's attention. We—the three of us—watch from a distance, finally coming forward. When Artie sees us, he grins widely.

"Hey!" He points at me. "Here he is, the man who designed this beautiful package! Yes, sir, it's the best new thing on the market!" He doesn't let up on his sales act even though no customers are in the vicinity.

"How's it going?" I ask.

"Fantastic!" he says, painfully optimistic. From above, "Rudolph the Red-Nosed Reindeer" chirps from tiny speakers.

"How many have you sold?" Joni asks.

"How many?" Artie seems irritated, as if at a trick question.

"Well, you can't only look at numbers today. Right now, I'm trying to introduce it to people. Let them know it's here. It hasn't taken off yet, but it will. I guarantee it! Then we'll all be sitting pretty."

Josh is grabbing at the toy. Joni juggles him, says, "No, sweetie, you're not old enough."

"Sure he is," Artie insists. "Here, take a new one." His muscles bulge through his suit jacket as he reaches to a card table for a packaged Dizzy Wizzy, handing it to Josh. "For you!" Josh rips open the package.

"Artie," I say, "we can't take it out of the store without paying. They'll think we're stealing it."

"If anyone gives you a hard time, you tell 'em I gave it to you."

A group of teenage boys come into the toy department. "Hold on," Artie says softly, before whooping it up, laughing, making the Dizzy Wizzy soar.

The boys seem unimpressed, taken in by a shelf of electronic football games.

"They don't know what they're missing," Artie says, his arm extended above him, twirling now almost in anger.

"Forget 'em," I say.

Artie's attention is diverted by an older man who stands on the periphery of the toy department. "Hello, sir!" Artie says, now more DJ than barker.

The man doesn't nod. He glares at Artie, not at what spins overhead.

"I'm sure one of your kids would *loooove* a Dizzy Wizzy," Artie says.

"I don't have kids," the man says.

"Then get one for your wife."

"My wife died two years ago this Christmas, you sonofa-bitch."

My adrenaline rushes, my stomach quakes. I expect Artie to up the ante, to get in the man's face, to call him a name. But as he continues his demonstration, he simply says in a low voice, "I'm so sorry, sir."

As the man leaves, Artie again turns on the charm, grins sincerely, almost crazily — a televangelist ready to save the next sinner. As much as he embarrasses me, I admire his gumption.

"Here," he tells me now. "Why don't you try for a while?"

"No thanks," I say. The idea of standing in the middle of a department store, demonstrating a toy, fills me with dread. It's hard enough to stand on a stage behind a guitar.

Although I can't get a straight answer out of Artie or my father, in a subsequent call to my mother, she estimates that Terby Toys has yet to sell three hundred units. I'm supposed to help assemble the toys, but I've kept my distance. I envision the house mired in rubber strands, hundreds of plastic balls — a soup of disappointment — overflowing from anonymous, unmarked boxes. We're there, too, in the boxes. Me. My parents. The kids — especially Artie. How I'd hoped the Dizzy Wizzy would answer our prayers.

My father has the drive to create, to invent. But he's always playing catch-up. Catching up and living in the past. Is the past safer? At least when you dwell in the past, you know how things turn out. You might have suffered, you might have almost died, but you survived; in the world of the past there's no pressure to perform, and you can daydream about what might have been. Maybe if he'd put the Dizzy Wizzy on the market in the 1960s, along with every other gimmicky toy, he might have made it. Maybe if he had truly pursued developing a transistor, or a Wankel engine, or any number of devices to help the deaf, or if he had gone back on the road as a drummer . . . who knows? We all might be on some beach in California right now. Or I might not exist.

Bagged

JONI CRIES WHEN I tell her I want to quit my job at the *Bellevue Times*.

"I won't end up like my father," I explain. "He had dreams but did nothing about them. It was like he expected someone to come to his door and say, 'Excuse me, Mr. Koterba, but you wouldn't happen to have an invention that could revolutionize the world, would you?'"

I find my scenario secretly amusing, hoping that somehow Joni will find the humor in it, too.

"But the hospital bills," she says, not laughing.

"Here's my plan," I tell her. "I mean, it's not like we don't have your income from the day care, and it's not like I'm not bringing in anything with my gigs and freelance. Well, now I'm going to focus even *more* on cartooning and music. And between the two I have a feeling I can find success." Even as I say the words to her, I realize how I must sound like Artie. How utterly irresponsible she must consider me. On the spur of the moment, I add, "I'll give it six months, and if nothing happens, I'll go bag groceries if I have to."

A whirlwind of doubt surrounds me.

"Okay." She sighs, giving in.

"I have to do this." Now I'm trying to convince myself.

"I said, okay."

"I know. I just want to make sure."

I shift my work schedule to the daytime. I begin to believe I am a real cartoonist, getting up in the morning, seeing Joni and Josh off to Joni's job, drinking coffee, reading the morning newspaper. When I'm not drawing, or dredging up other freelance cartooning work, I send résumés and samples to newspapers. I also decide to attempt self-syndication with my sports cartoons. I name my syndicate Time Out Features. Even though it will cost precious money, I have brochures printed.

What little savings we had dwindles away. Collection agencies begin to call. In our living room waits a box full of brochures. All I have to do is put them into envelopes, address them to sports editors around the country, and buy postage. It's on this last point I get stuck. I tell myself that I — we — can't afford stamps. Stamps will cost well over one hundred dollars, and that's one hundred dollars we don't have. By attempting to be responsible to my dreams, I have not done right by my family. Is this what it was like for my father when he learned he was going to be a father? Yet there is something more than money holding me back. By keeping those brochures in a box, there remains hope.

Three months later, I put in my application at Baker's Supermarket. At age twenty-seven, I'm hired as a grocery store clerk—a bag boy. I go through training with a gaggle of teenagers, taught by an instructor nearly ten years my junior on how to keep the ice cream away from the cereal boxes, the bug spray away from the bananas. I stack cereal boxes next to each other, providing a foundation for smaller boxes, or loaves of bread. Cans make for a good foundation, too. I know how to make things fit from helping my father in the garages. I am humiliated by how elementary the training is, but I am frequently praised, held up to the others as an example to follow. A good bag boy, I am told, fills his bag so perfectly you can tear it away without disrupting the contents. I am told to tear my bags, and like a magic trick the cereal boxes and cans remain standing.

The next morning, I hover near the front of the store, sweating in my parka, going from this checkout stand to that, bagging and carrying groceries to customers' cars. "Cold enough for ya?" everyone seems to ask with mind-numbing frequency.

On my way back inside, I run, stopping only to pick up any trash I might see, or to straighten floor mats and mop muddy footprints. My supervisors take notice of my diligence, my "hustle." Two weeks in, I am promoted to stocking the baby food aisle. I still help with bagging, but only when we are very busy. Although I would have preferred the cereal aisle, or produce, I'm thrilled with this promotion — anything to relieve me from constantly going out into the January weather (and, come spring, anything to avoid thunderstorms). My aisle has to be fully stocked and "faced" by the store's opening, at 7 A.M. Some mornings, if I had a gig the night before, or freelanced another cartoon, I struggle to arrive by 5:30. But even when exhausted, I am refreshed after gazing up at the skeletal ceiling, where ductwork and pipes and conduits are intentionally exposed, as though this trendy supermarket were some kind of futuristic church.

The orderliness of the aisles — particularly my aisle, its clean sight lines — brings me joy. When young mothers ask my advice on formula or diapers, I happily offer assistance. And I love helping the mothers who don't wear wedding rings. I can't imagine how they must struggle.

In the mornings as I work, I meditate. I think about baby food and what babies need. There are so many brands and varieties, it's difficult to believe that there isn't enough food in the world to feed everyone. Joni and I hadn't planned on having a child so soon — we had not even discussed children. But when Josh arrived, health problems and all, he brought out in me the belief that I could somehow reverse all I was attempting to escape. This is why I let Josh strum my mandolin and guitar with his soft pink fingers. I never force him. And one day, if he wants to draw, I will gently show him how to hold a pencil, but I will not wedge a pencil into his fingers. I will support and encourage him no matter what he loves. Just as he needs physical nourishment, I will also provide him with emotional nourishment — the ingredient that can't be found in my aisle. I laugh to myself when I imagine baby

211

food jars adorned with labels such as "Kindness. Infants to one year." And "Patience. For Toddlers."

In this expansive grocery store, there is a deli, a bakery, and a floral department, and in each of these departments hang elaborately decorated chalkboards pitching the week's specials. When I inquire about helping with the chalkboards, the store manager gives his okay. He tells me that after the holidays he wants me to start cashier training, and within the year he would like me to consider management training. But for now, yes, I may help with signs—it's good for me to know and understand all the jobs in a grocery store, from the bottom up. Although I make only eighty dollars a week, I am respected by my superiors. And now I'll get to use my artistic talent, drawing on the chalkboards. Maybe *this* is my destiny.

The woman in charge of signs eyes me suspiciously, and at first treats me like a child. I must watch as she decides which themes to develop. "First," she says slowly, "we *study* this piece of paper with all the specials." She peers over her glasses to make sure I'm following her instructions. "Next we *think* about a theme we might want to use. After that . . ."

Since we're in the holiday season, I watch as the sign lady makes chalk drawings of Santas and snowmen surrounded by the words "Fried Chicken" and "Donuts." Hesitantly, she allows me to make my own chalkboard. I am excited about the forgiveness of the board, the ability to erase and start again.

I recognize my father right off by his trademark fedora. No one wears hats like that anymore. In his suit and tie he's straight out of the 1940s, yet he's here at this modern Baker's, pushing a shopping cart. "Nice store you've got here," he says, his smile revealing perfectly aligned teeth. He's always had good teeth. "You running the place yet?"

"Not quite, Dad," I say.

My mother smiles as she takes in the countless options in the baby aisle. "It's beautiful," she says. "Not like our old Hinky Stinky."

My parents could be any couple, anyone's parents or grandparents. No one would know by looking at them that at home they have a compound of overflowing garages and sheds, and piles of unsold Dizzy Wizzys.

"Isn't he cute in his red apron?" my mother says.

"Mom, please." I glance down, brushing off the chalk dust that coats my apron.

It's midmorning, and I've already stocked and faced my aisle. I take them to the deli section, where three of my chalkboards hang. My parents admire them, telling me how professional they appear.

"And you're still drawing cartoons for that paper in Kansas?" my father asks.

"Kansas City, Dad."

"Right, of course. Kansas City."

"And yes. I am."

He sings, "Kansas City, Kansas City here I come . . ."

"How do you find the time?" my mother says over my father's singing.

"And you're still in that Irish band?" he says.

"Uh-huh."

"I'll never understand why you don't have a drummer," he says, making drumming motions. His swinging arms and fluttering hands make me uneasy. He taps his finger on a can of Similac.

"Dad," my mother says, "leave him alone. He's working."

"Yeah," I say. "I'd better get back to it. I have a few more signs."

My parents tell me that maybe they'll see me again before they finish their shopping, but I duck into the stockroom, taking inventory for my aisle. I want my parents' visit to end on a positive note. I don't want my father offering more advice, drumming in the soup aisle, or juggling apples.

• • •

213

"Jeff, may I speak to you a moment?" The manager of the grocery store is in the doorway of the room where we make our chalkboard signs. The sign lady left me here alone. The manager has a serious look on his face, but not too serious. I take it to mean he wants to speak with me about my career, my future with the company. Maybe discuss stock options.

"Yes," I say, putting down a bright pink stub of chalk. I almost reach to shake his hand but stop myself, instead wiping my hands on my apron.

"About the signs," he says, moving toward me.

I glance at the table where I'm working on my chalk drawing—Old Man Winter blowing a gust of wind, along with reduced prices for mashed potatoes. I ready myself for a compliment, preparing to react humbly.

"I'm afraid I'm going to have to remove you from sign duty."

"For the rest of the day?"

"No. Permanently."

It takes a moment. "I don't understand."

"From what your supervisor tells me, you're not a very good artist. And what we need on these signs are people who can draw well enough to get the message across in a clear manner. You know what I'm saying?" Our eyes meet briefly. I glance at my chalk drawing, but all he does is lean toward me, giving me a half-hearted slap on the shoulder. This slap is meant to be encouraging, but it leaves me cold.

I can't imagine having drawn anything better. Frozen icicles double for Old Man Winter's hair. His cheeks are rosy, with highlight marks. Same for his nose. I even tried to make his cloud face look like mashed potatoes. I want to hoist the sign over my head and exclaim, "How can you not call this good?" Before the manager disappears around the corner, he tells me he's going to need me on the "front lines" for the rest of the day, bagging groceries.

My sign never makes it to the deli. Later that morning, I see that someone has erased it and made a new drawing. I can faintly discern my old drawing, now covered with a simpleton snow-man. "Come out of the cold for big savings!" it proclaims.

I am perplexed, disillusioned. After I tell Joni what happened, I struggle with my sports cartoon. I do finish a cartoon — I never miss a deadline — but I draw it in a fog of anger and hurt. *Stupid motherfucker,* I think. But what if the store manager is right? What if I'm not good enough?

After Joni falls asleep, I call my mother. I know she stays up late, always waiting for the kids to come home after they've been out.

"That's awful," she says. "That guy doesn't know what he's talking about. Of course you're a good artist."

"Mom," I say, "I don't think I can go back there."

"You should quit," she says without hesitation.

"I can't," I say, astounded by her suggestion. "I have to have a job."

"You'll see," she says. "You have to have faith."

I'm too tired to have faith.

"Your father and I have been talking. That's not the place for you. I know you thought you would enjoy it, but you have too much talent to work in a grocery store."

"Dad said that?"

"Yes. He says he feels sorry for you."

We hang up and I space out at my drawing table. I'm sketching the Gerber baby with a sad face. Underneath, I write the words "World Hunger."

The clock radio is buzzing. It's nearly five in the morning, and I ponder my next move. The January wind pummels the side of our townhouse. Joni shifts under the covers, but I won't wake her. I'll tell her when she gets up for work.

I drink coffee, read the *World-Herald* help-wanted section.

When Joni comes downstairs she finds me hovering over the kitchen table, circling ads with one of my drawing pens. "What's going on?"

"I can't go back."

215

"Are you sick?"

"I just can't go back."

"But you can't *not* go back."

"I know. I've never done anything like this. I've always given my two weeks. But I can't."

She doesn't have to say anything. I know what's on her mind. I know she's fretting over our mounting debts. I can't blame her. I am also aware of a growing distance between us.

"But I'm going to get another job. Maybe at an insurance company. I promise." Landing a decent job, I tell myself, will fix everything.

That day, I begin making the rounds, completing applications all over Omaha. Even so, as I put on my only suit, my only necktie, I can't help believing I'm dressing for my job as a cartoonist.

When my last paycheck from Baker's arrives in the mail, I immediately cash it, and impulsively I drive to the post office with my box of brochures. More than my belief that something will come of my syndication is my desire, once and for all, to rid our home of these reminders of my big plan. I don't have enough money to send every brochure; I mail eighty-three dollars' worth, discarding the rest.

I again head out across the city, asking for job applications, filled with a sense of . . . resolve? Peace?

California Dreamin'

I CAN'T UNLOCK the door and make it inside the house in time to answer the phone. As I put down my two bags of groceries, the machine is already reciting our outgoing message; I'll wait to answer after I hear who it is. These past few days, every time the phone rings I hope it's one of the insurance companies I've applied to, calling for a second interview. So far, I have three follow-up interviews scheduled.

The woman's voice is professional but friendly. It takes me a moment to sort out what she is saying, to sort out that my life is about to change. "I'm with the *Los Angeles Times*," she says. "We're very much interested in your sports cartoon. Please call with your rate information."

The. *Los. Angeles. Times.*

My heart is racing. I stand by our bed, gazing at the fake-wood plastic of the answering machine, hearing the woman's voice giving her number with a California area code, listening as she hangs up. The answering machine clicks, the tape rewinds and resets itself. A single red light — a beacon — blinks steadily from the machine. *One new message. One new message.* My hand is shaking as I press the replay button, jot down the number. The machine resets, and again I press the button, double-checking the number. A jab of doubt strikes at me that this is a cruel prank. Yet in my gut I know this call to be true. I pace through the house for nearly an hour, working up the courage to call back. Kevin Quinn's voice is in my head: *You're gonna do fine. You're damn good.*

The stage is this telephone.

My senses race as I dial. The warmth of the receiver against my ear, the hum of the dial tone, the numbered plastic squares I press — everything is quivering with life. She picks up on the second ring. All I can do is swallow. I nearly hang up.

"Yes, this is Jeff Koterba with Time Out Features returning your call." I surprise myself with how steady I sound. Surely, though, she will see through me, my "company" name, to realize what a fraud I am. She will somehow know that my company headquarters is a dining room table and will politely end the call, realizing she's made a terrible mistake.

She pleasantly cuts to the chase, telling me what the *Times* is willing to pay a modest fee for my work. "Okay," I squeak.

In the coming days, I begin to receive calls from other sports editors. Not dozens, as I hoped, but still. When they ask where my work appears — besides Kansas City — I can now proudly say, the *Los Angeles Times.* Not the *Bellevue Times.* No, not that *Times.*

• • •

217

The *L.A. Times* is like a password. In a matter of weeks I'm up to sixteen newspapers, some with large circulations, others small.

I must keep promoting, calling editors so I might pick up more newspapers. With each call, my butterflies lessen. I find I *enjoy* calling strangers; my confidence builds. I tell myself in a mantra, *It's only a call.* I write a press release about my new feature, which gets published in *Editor & Publisher,* a trade journal.

The press release generates more calls. Unexpectedly, I receive a call from the *Omaha World-Herald.* Although I'd sent my brochure to the sports department and received a polite rejection, this call is from the editorial department.

As I drive along the interstate toward downtown Omaha, I find myself fixated on the skyline. I have often daydreamed about one day working among these modest skyscrapers. But today not even the art deco architecture of the *World-Herald*'s headquarters is enough to capture my imagination. Today, for the first time, I'm able to say to myself, *I don't need you, downtown.*

On the second floor, executive row, the hallways are lined with famous front pages: the *Hindenburg* disaster, the JFK assassination, Nixon's resignation, the 1975 tornado. Years before, I would sometimes sneak in here to read these front pages, imagining this news *wasn't* old news, imagining reading these stories in the moment. Now I notice a recent addition: the afternoon edition on the day the *Challenger* exploded.

Frank, the editorial-page editor, a seasoned journalist who could double for Dan Aykroyd, invites me into his office and motions for me to sit; I sink into a deep leathery chair.

"Looks like you're having quite a bit of success with your sports cartoons," he says, taking his place behind a slightly cluttered mahogany desk, expansive as a bed.

"Yes, sir." My mouth wants to stretch wildly, but I suppress my tic.

"You have quite a few fans here at the paper, you know." Frank explains how one reporter is continually sending notes to the front office on my behalf. "Then he drew our attention to your story in *E and P.*"

"I see." That there are people rooting for me without my knowing it is an unfathomable thing. It's like a confirmation that I do indeed have a guardian angel.

"We'd sure hate to lose you to another newspaper. That's why we'd like to offer you a full-time position on our editorial page." He's quick to add, "On a trial basis." *Full-time, as in a salary, health insurance, and other benefits.* Tears I didn't know I'd been holding in stream down my face. I'm embarrassed as I attempt to wipe them away.

"Can I go down the hall and grab you a cup of coffee?" he asks.

I readily accept, hoping to compose myself in the few moments he's gone. This simple act of kindness, his asking if I'd like coffee, reassures me that this is where I'm meant to work.

I take a deep breath and gaze blurrily out Frank's — my new editor's — window, at the phone company building on Dodge Street. I can't quite see the Woodmen Tower. I also can't see the Union Pacific headquarters, west of the *World-Herald*'s building. But I imagine all the people going about their workday, riding the elevator, chatting around the copy machine, repeating last night's Johnny Carson monologue. And in this building I can sense the reporters, editors, photographers, artists, the workers in the composing room and platemaking, inky men on the presses, all bustling, hard at work. All of them, all of *us*, creating something together, a newspaper, a real newspaper, like a family.

Frank says it's only a suggestion that I give up my sports cartoons. Even if he hadn't said anything, I can't imagine starting out as a full-time editorial cartoonist, drawing six cartoons per week, all the while drawing three sports cartoons. Yet my self-syndication is something I created from scratch. It's still in its infancy. The self-syndication is what allowed me the freedom to know I didn't need the *World-Herald*. Yet it is this very thing that led to their hiring me. The sports cartooning becomes, in my head, a sacrifice fly, advancing the runner home for the game-winning run.

The nameplate on the door reads LIBRARY, but old-timers at the *World-Herald* call it the morgue. This is where I seek refuge after deadline, in this large, sunny, but somehow gray room where the newspaper stores its photographs and clippings in tall metal filing cabinets. This room is filled with life, with the history of Omaha and Nebraska, the world.

It's here, on an August afternoon after the morgue staff has left for the day, particles of dust lingering in the beams of sun shooting through the windows, that I finally allow myself to look under "K" — under "Koterba." I've been working up to it, savoring it, knowing I will never have this first moment again.

The file is disappointingly slim.

The first photograph: a bespectacled Uncle Ed, caught in a slight grin. He is handsome, posing with his wife in front of an Airstream trailer. How long has this file gone unopened? How long has his face waited to be gazed upon? I search for clues for a resemblance to my father, a resemblance to me. I strain to recall the face of Cousin Eddie. Uncle Ed doesn't look much like my father, or me, but before disappointment sinks in, I remind myself that I don't resemble Artie. In spite of the lack of physical similarities, it is the eagerness in his eyes, his yearning, his hope, that makes this man appear infinitely familiar, alive, as though at any moment this black-and-white face will speak to me.

The clipping glued to the back of the photograph explains that the former *World-Herald* writer, now a syndicated columnist with Scripps-Howard, is shown about to embark on a cross-country trip from Washington, D.C., to California. He is to write about his travels, filing columns along his journey. Uncle Ed. Escaping. Going someplace. Anyplace. There are a handful of other photographs of Uncle Ed. There are none of my father. I come across a photograph of me, a photograph I know that my mother clipped — the story on the back about my having won a college cartooning award seven years earlier. For seven years my image has existed here with these images of Uncle Ed.

It's the yellowed clipping, an orphan without a photograph, that now grabs my attention. A modest story that might have been cut from an inside page, six paragraphs long, topped with the headline "President Sorrowed at Koterba's Death." The story is to the point, explaining that the president announced Koterba's passing during the previous day's press conference.

All I hold on to are these photographs, this slip of newsprint small enough to fit into my palm like a prayer card.

Back to the Drawing Board

I'M AT MY DRAWING TABLE, squeaking, jerking my head, downing my fifth cup of coffee, procrastinating, waiting for an idea. I dread having to submit sketch upon sketch, not only to Frank but also to the editor of the newspaper. Every detail, every word of my sketches, is checked and rechecked. Always, I am challenged by both men to do better, to go beyond the obvious cliché, to take my ideas to the next level. Gags and puns cannot carry an idea. Every cartoon must exude substance, weight.

Occasionally, what one editor likes, the other doesn't. Sometimes the editor of the newspaper writes lengthy rejection notes on my sketches, critiquing my approach on a particular idea. His comments are often harsh and cutting. When I least expect it, this same editor praises me, tells me how much he loves an idea. He even gives me modest bonuses and generous raises. I look beyond his approach to better understand his *journalism*. I want nothing more than to work as I hard as I can to make him proud.

In my first year on the job, I've already created nearly three hundred cartoons. Still, the thought of all the deadlines I will face in the future, all the deadlines of my career, is daunting. I apply the Alcoholics Anonymous motto to what I do: *One cartoon at a time.* Unfortunately, this thinking takes me only so far when it comes to my dual editors. It's difficult enough to invent one workable idea a day. Some days, to please both men, I must present five or more ideas. Too often, I find myself in the composing room, my deadline just minutes away, fixing or correcting my cartoon, cutting and pasting. For this reason I rarely allow myself downtime. I read deep into the night, taking in as much as I can, studying the issues. In a constant state of anxiety, I'm up before dawn to read the sunrise edition. In the evening, after dinner, I routinely drive to a convenience store or return downtown to get a jump on the news with the early edition. Each morning I attend daily editorial board meetings, and as the editorial writers discuss the waning days of the Cold War, gun control, unrest in the Middle East, the pending death of horseracing in Omaha, and the influx of casino gambling across the Missouri River, it becomes blindingly clear that I am not my uncle. How dare I entertain, even for a second, the notion that I might be his reincarnation?

At first I blamed myself, the stress of the job, my obsession with cartooning. Certainly our mounting debt didn't help matters. Perhaps Joni and I were simply married too young, too naïve to understand the difficulties of marriage and raising a child.

It saddens me that my dream job couldn't save us. It nearly destroys me to think I will be away from Josh, even for one night. It helps, however, that my mother is sympathetic and understands that my marriage is unraveling; she reassures me of how important it is to be happy. Not just for myself, but for Josh. Now, on my nightly trips to pick up the early edition, I drive by our old apartment and gaze up at Josh's window, wishing I were tucking him in, telling him a Puffy story.

After the divorce, I dive deeper into the cartooning world, trying to find an easier path to coming up with ideas. Desperate, I reach out to other editorial cartoonists for help. One of my cartooning heroes, Jim Borgman at the *Cincinnati Enquirer,* is generous with his time. He suggests reading Rollo May's *Courage to Create.* In the book, May argues that it takes creative courage to develop new forms, new symbols on which a society can be built. May also discusses the nature of the unconscious mind. From his book I come to believe that if I input information into my brain and let it clunk around for a while, even if I am not actively and constantly thinking about the next cartoon, somehow the brain, with its mystical, electrical, computerlike synapses, will eventually give me that aha! moment. Jim Borgman also suggests that I keep a daily sketchbook, like a diary or a journal. And also that I get myself a mirror.

Now, if I need to see how someone looks when throwing a punch, I pose for myself. Or if I want to better understand how the body appears when dejected, I look in my mirror, a garage sale gift from my father. If the mayor has a shocked look on his face in one of my cartoons, it's usually *my* shocked look that provides the inspiration. If the governor is pensive, rubbing his chin, it's my fingers, my chin I've implanted on the governor.

This morning, I lock my office door and gaze in the mirror as I press my forehead, where my third eye would be, against the warmth of the drawing lamp that hovers over my cluttered table. I think of the lamp as a sun, kept afloat by a robot arm, an earthly extension of something bigger, harder to pin down, like the universe. Is it just my brain giving me ideas? Or is my brain the filter for the universe, God, to come through me? Maybe it's all of these. These ideas that come from the heavens and are called to this metal arm, this lightning rod. I tap at the lamp with my forehead, then my temple, slowly urging the lamp across the table like a sun across the plains, and back again, according to my own rules of astronomy. It is morning on the south side of the table; morning in the north and back again. I push the lamp, casting my table in artificial light, real shadows. I'm out of my chair, the lamp over the floor, over the southern edge, as far as its mechanical arm will allow. The spring on the arm makes a squeak and I imitate it.

I take a break and reread the newspaper, refilling my head with topics. I go down the hall for coffee and return to my office, sipping the whole way. By the time I'm back at my drawing table, my coffee is almost gone. With one hand, I tilt the paper coffee cup to my lips, coaxing out the creek of black water and grounds. With the other hand, I grip a forest-green pencil, a 2H, a slab of typing paper at the ready. This is what I do. This is how I *prepare* for the ideas to filter through me, from wherever they come.

Today I sketch myself rolling my eyes, sticking out my tongue. I've never drawn myself this way before. I've always left out the tics, rendered them invisible. But I know what the world sees. I've gotten better at suppressing my tics for short periods. So if a co-worker comes into my office, I push them away from my head and face and down past my throat. I force them into my chest and stomach and legs. This is my game, my mission to go undercover with the nervous habits.

TV, TS

MY NEW APARTMENT is spare. My guitar, a clock radio, and a portable TV I readily accept from my father keep me company late at night when I'm working on cartoon ideas. I sometimes fall asleep with the TV running, half dreaming, dissecting

Johnny Carson's monologue, trying to figure out what makes his jokes, his timing, work so well.

At Christmas, I can't afford a tree, so Josh and I decorate a tropical plant—my new apartment's only embellishment. We carefully string lights and hang what few decorations I brought with me after the divorce. We dim the lights of the apartment, putting all the attention on the tree, the lights like stars that have been sprinkled into a tiny jungle.

I hope I can show him it is important—vital—to follow one's heart. Not to be swept away by some false sense of what will bring happiness, not simply to follow what must be done. Josh stays with me most weekends and some weekdays. On nights he stays here, I turn off the TV and lightly strum my guitar, singing him to sleep.

Besides *The Tonight Show,* I try not to miss *Star Hustler.* The host, Jack Horkheimer, in his trademark Members Only jacket, paces across the superimposed rings of Saturn, describing what celestial happenings one might find in the night sky of the near future. His slogan, "Keep looking up," stays with me as I fall asleep and pretend that my ceiling is the sky. When the *World-Herald* runs a story on Horkheimer, I learn that his mentor was Father Scott, when the priest taught at Marquette University, before coming to Creighton, in Omaha, and before professing the beauty of the universe from the pulpit at St. Agnes Church. I revel in this connection.

I'm not sure why, but tonight *Star Hustler* doesn't cheer me up as it usually does. Flipping from PBS to regular TV, I hope for a syndicated rerun of *Three's Company* or *Love Boat*—any show that won't require me to think. As I'm drifting off, I'm nudged awake by a public service announcement. I recognize the Kansas City Royals uniform, but only vaguely the face of the player. "I'm Jim Eisenreich of the Kansas City Royals," he says. "And I have Tourette's syndrome." He uses terms like "neurological disorder," "genetic," "treatable."

The next night, I land on the same PSA.

Tourette's.

There is something in the word itself that rings true. Like when I was called "bastard" but didn't yet know I'd been born out of wedlock. My gut had informed me that the word came with baggage. Maybe it's the way it sounds. "Bas" rhymes with "ass." And "tard" — like "retard" — sounds like "turd." Tourette's, on the other hand, possesses an elegant warmth — something sophisticated and serious.

It's late April, days before my thirtieth birthday, and I schedule an appointment with a physician, a general practitioner whom I've seen for nothing more than sore throats. Sarcastically I think, *What a gift to myself, going to the doctor to find out if I have Tourette's!*

I explain my symptoms. "I'm wondering if it's Tourette's."

He shrugs, seems unfazed, as though he has far greater medical concerns. Now I'm embarrassed for having come here. "It might be," he says. "But this isn't something I normally deal with."

When he writes a referral for a psychiatrist, I am sunk with disappointment. *A psychiatrist?* My father has always believed psychologists and psychiatrists are only for crazy people. While I don't believe this, I can't help but feel the weight of the stigma my father has attached to these professions. Rather than calling the psychiatrist, I spend a lunch hour seeking answers at the library. I read that Tourette's is like having an urge to scratch an itch. I think about astronauts, how they're not able to get to itches through their space suits. Some of what I find is more of what I already know, that Tourette's is a neurological disorder that shows itself in tics. When I read for the first time about coprolalia, the rare manifestation of Tourette's in the form of public swearing, it allows me to distance myself from the possibility that I have Tourette's. Because I *can* control my swearing, I fall back on my father's old stance, that what I have are simply nervous habits. Habits, by the way, that I can overcome if I choose. *Not just suppress my tics to hidden parts of me, but also truly rid myself of my nervous habits.*

Like hell.

Each day at my drawing table, in front of the mirror, distorted and grotesque faces haunt me, remind me how much my tics are in control. And at night, I am frequently faced with Jim Eisenreich's PSA.

In Dr. M's office I sink into a deep leather chair — no couch here, like in a *New Yorker* cartoon. Wood-framed diplomas checkerboard his walls, neatly stacked papers and a single pen break up the otherwise spare surface of his oak desk. This place, I tell myself, could replace any regular doctor's office anywhere, which reassures me that perhaps I'm not mentally ill or crazy.

"How may I help you today?" Dr. M asks. With his boyish swoop of hair and strong-chinned good looks, Dr. M appears too young to have earned all those diplomas.

I avert my eyes, gazing into the carpet's speckled pattern. I hold in my twitches as best I can. I think of the irony of doing this. There is a long silence. The stillness surrounds me, but doesn't push. The quiet seems to be a third entity in this room, saying, "We have all the time in the world."

I glance up and Dr. M seems neither impatient nor overly pleasant. He has a nonexpression. Now I'm observing the ceiling, the lines where ceiling meets wall. It's important for me to take note of how things look, in case I someday need to make a cartoon about a psychiatrist's office.

"I think I have Tourette's syndrome," I say, now watching a tree sway in the breeze beyond his window.

He takes a moment. "Why do you think that?"

"Well, I'm always twitching." It embarrasses me to admit this.

"What kind of twitches?"

"I don't know. I squint a lot."

"Uh-huh. And?"

"Um, well," I stammer, "I sort of jerk my head."

"I see."

He has no pad of paper in his hands. Shouldn't he be writing this down?

"What else?" he asks. "Any vocal tics?"

"Sometimes I grunt. Or squeak."

"Any swearing?"

"No more than anyone else."

I anticipate a smile, maybe even a chuckle, but his expression remains flat. "It's just that some people with Tourette's have an element of the syndrome that results in excessive swearing."

I don't mention that I know this information. Instead, I stretch my mouth wide. I imagine my mouth is a rubber band. A barely audible squeak wriggles its way out of my throat. "Sorry about that," I say. "I guess I'm nervous."

"Nothing to apologize for," he reassures me.

My head snaps this way and that. But it puts me at ease, being told I don't have to apologize, that I don't have to say I'm sorry.

He asks me several more questions. Am I easily distracted by ringing telephones? Do I like to count random objects when I enter a room? How about streetlights — do I count them, too, as I drive?

Yes, yes, and yes. How does this stranger know my brain?

"I'm fairly certain you have Tourette's," he says with matter-of-fact candor.

Our eyes meet briefly; I look away and indulge the need to grunt. I hope he doesn't think I'm putting on a show. "Really?" I say. It's almost as though I've won a prize, the way he says "Tourette's." I'd expected this to be far more complicated, involving blood tests, maybe a hospital stay. His simple acknowledgment begins to sink in, makes me tear up.

"Well, there are still a number of questions I'd like to ask, but in the few minutes you've been here, I'd say you've certainly displayed many of the classic tics associated with Tourette's. I see it all the time. Does anyone else in your family have Tourette's?" he asks.

I shake my head no. "I mean, my father and sister twitch. But they've never been diagnosed."

"Although I can't say for certain, there's a good chance your father and sister have Tourette's. It's more commonplace than people think."

"I see."

Dr. M explains that Tourette's stems from abnormalities in the brain. I hear the words "neurotransmitters" and "dopamine." "How do you feel about medications?" he asks.

I shrug. "What kind of medications?"

"Well, we have several options available to us . . ."

"I don't want to take anything that's going to knock me out. Is it like Valium?" I imagine walking around in a daze, sleepy all the time.

"Valium? No, we're talking about an entirely different family of meds — SSRIs. Everyone reacts differently, of course. It's difficult to predict."

"Would I still be able to work?"

"That's an insightful question."

I must beam with pride that he says this. I want to be a good patient.

"Tourette's," he explains, "happens in the same part of the brain as spatial thought."

He sees the confusion on my face.

"Creative thought," he says patiently. "It's the part of the brain where you get the ideas for, say, your cartoons."

"Oh."

"Now, some do fine on meds, others find other ways to lessen their stress levels so their twitches decrease."

"Stress?" I joke. "What's that?"

He forms an obligatory smile. "I might suggest," he says, "starting at a very low dose and seeing how you handle it."

My body presses against the seat. I want to run from here. "Is there anything else I can try first?"

"Cut out sugars and caffeine."

"Coffee?"

"Yes," he says. "How many cups a day do you drink?"

"Maybe three," I lie. I could easily add ten cups to that number.

"Three's pushing it. You also need to get plenty of rest and exercise."

I can't imagine giving up coffee. "But would medications cure me?"

"Cure?" He seems surprised I don't know the answer. He shakes his head no. "There's no cure."

"Gotcha." My head jerks hard to the right.

"Tell you what. I'll write a scrip and you can take it with you and think about how you want to proceed."

What I find most intriguing: Dr. M explains that many, if not all, of those suffering from this syndrome are musicians, artists, photographers, writers.

My father's telephone greeting is melodic, inviting.

One last chance to hang up. "Hi, Dad. It's me."

"Well, hey there. How's my favorite cartoonist?"

"Dad, please."

"You're the only thing in the paper I read, you know." His compliments are always heartfelt, but general. I'd rather we discussed an actual news story — politics, sports, anything — but we never do.

"Thanks" is all I can say.

"Sure thing!"

I tap the receiver against my head. There's so much about me he doesn't know.

"Do you want to talk to your mother?" he says, filling in the awkward silence.

"Maybe later."

"That's fine," he says patiently.

But I don't know that I deserve his patience. Or his compliments. I may live in town, a short drive away, but haven't seen my parents in three months.

"I think we might get a thunderstorm this afternoon." He still talks in a singsongy way, like an old-time radio announcer.

"That so?" I take a breath. "Dad, listen, I saw a psychiatrist the other day."

"A what?" His tone changes. He's suspicious — something I'm used to after thirty years. "What the hell for?"

I swallow. "For the twitches, Dad."

"Twitches?" He acts as if he doesn't know what I'm talking about.

"You know. The *tics?*"

"Rikki-Tikki-Tavi!"

"Dad, it's not a joke. You make jokes of everything. This is serious."

"Can't a guy have a little fun?"

No! I want to scream. *You can't!*

"Oh, hey, we might even see a tornado," he says.

"Dad, I have Tourette's syndrome."

"Tourwhat?"

"Tourette's. You probably have it, too. It's genetic."

"Hell I do." He laughs.

"I *know* you do."

"Damned psychologist."

"*Psychiatrist,* Dad."

"When I was a kid, did my mother have money to send me to a doctor?"

"I know, Dad. I know you were poor."

"You're goddamned right we were poor." Any hint of music has left his voice. "When I was a kid carrying papers," he continues, "a dog bit my finger. I had to go to a veterinarian for stitches."

I've heard the story countless times and I'm truly sorry for him. But I ran out of sympathetic words a long time ago.

I stretch my mouth.

I imagine he's doing the same.

Goodbye, Hello

I SURPRISE MYSELF that I'm able to tell my father about my diagnosis, despite my concern he wouldn't accept the news gracefully. Other than my father, I tell few others. When my coworkers notice with some astonishment that I've switched to decaf coffee, I tell them caffeine keeps me from getting proper sleep. I cut back on sugar, too, and take up jogging—in spite of the headaches that come in the wake of caffeine withdrawal. I begin to notice a slight decrease in the frequency and intensity of my twitches. This encourages me to cut out all sugar. Soon my headaches disappear; my jogging transforms into running. I run harder and faster, in hopes of completely ridding my body of tics, as though my twitches can be left behind in the dust. Yet no matter how hard I push myself, the tics remain, albeit somewhat muted.

On those days when I struggle for an idea, when a deadline is breathing down my neck, my tics return with full force. Stress. I have no idea how anyone can work on a daily deadline and not have stress.

When the entertainer Danny Thomas dies, an idea for a cartoon comes to me with ease. I'm at home, getting ready for work, guzzling Sanka while reading the morning edition. *Good Morning America* is turned low in the background. I sketch the idea on the envelope from my electric bill. The idea references the series in which Danny Thomas once starred, *Make Room for Daddy.* I show Thomas at the gates of heaven, Saint Peter exclaiming,

"Make room for Danny." I head to work, content I already have my idea — the drawing is the fun part. When I have an idea early, it's as if I'm on vacation.

The drawing comes easily, too. Saint Peter, the Pearly Gates, Danny Thomas, and pillows of heavenly clouds. Cartoon clouds are a breeze to draw. I make big loops, over and over. I'm relaxed, even-keeled. My inked lines are less wavy, shaky. A heavenly scene doesn't require a lot of ink — everything is so white. I'm barely twitching. I begin to believe I've tapped into something. Maybe it's because I've accepted my Tourette's. Rather than get angry that Tourette's is incurable, I ponder what Dr. M explained, that many with Tourette's are artists, musicians, writers. Maybe creativity and Tourette's are two sides of the same coin.

Joy soon turns to dread as, over the next few days, I begin to see similar "Make room for Danny" cartoons in other newspapers. I'd drawn the obvious thing. I'd committed "original sin."

I receive a handwritten letter from Marlo Thomas, Danny's daughter. Somehow, she saw my cartoon and requests the original, to be hung at St. Jude Hospital in Memphis, which Danny founded. From her words I get the impression that she hasn't seen all the other similar cartoons. I should be thrilled, but as I send the cartoon, I imagine it is coated in invisible embarrassment.

For several days I beat myself up. Mimicking my thoughts, my body follows, jerking and contorting. My penance is to create the most original cartoons I can. It's not enough that I develop five good ideas. I must push beyond to ten. When I reach ten, I must bring fifteen ideas to life. It's not until weeks later, after I've drawn stacks of cartoons, that I begin to believe I've atoned for my transgression.

The Johnny Carson file from the morgue is open, his many photographs spread across my drawing table. I try to forecast how other cartoonists might capture Carson's retirement. I envision

233

Carson as Carnac the Magnificent, holding an envelope to his forehead, making a joke about playing golf every day. Or perhaps Ed McMahon is crying out, "And theeeeeeeeeeere goes Johnny." I run through a mental list of potential ideas that other cartoonists might draw. He's swinging his imaginary golf club one last time. He's leaping into Ed's arms—Ed is labeled RETIREMENT. On and on. I settle on Carson stepping into the backdrop behind his desk, which for his last show is changed into a sunset. Not earthshattering, I know, but at least it wasn't the first idea that came to me. If others come up with the idea, at least I made the effort to be different. As I draw, I daydream about all the kinescopes of early *Tonight Show* episodes that no longer exist. I imagine his TV signals shooting off into space, intermingling with my father's radio waves. I daydream Carson will see the cartoon and someone from his staff will call, asking for the original. I will send Carson the cartoon and ask if he remembers my father. He'll write a nice note to my father: "Art—I guess it's a good thing I got into television. Between the two of us, you always were the better drummer." I fantasize about what might have been had my father followed Carson first to New York, then Hollywood. I still get frustrated with my father for not having followed his dreams. This, I am convinced, is why he is so miserable. Yet, had he followed his dreams too soon, I wouldn't be here, on deadline, following mine.

When my aunt Ann dies, my cousin Sally visits from Boston. I haven't seen her since Jean's funeral. And like all other funerals, I hope Cousin Eddie will be able to make it out, but he sends a sympathy card instead. Ann's husband, Uncle Len, appears to be the same age he was when he worked on my teeth, when I was five. He is sad at his wife's passing, but not distraught. He almost seems to take her death in stride.

After the cemetery, we gather at Ross' Steakhouse. I make sure to sit across from Sally. I can't remember which of her eyes is the glass eye—I'm not sure how to look at her. Sally is an artist, and

234

it fascinates me that she is able to draw with one eye. She tells me how burned out she's felt lately, with all her projects.

"I'm in need of a little fertile indolence," she says.

I look at her quizzically.

"It's when you shut down your brain. Every artist needs downtime to recharge. Doing nothing doesn't necessarily mean you're lazy."

A year later, when my office phone rings, I'm surprised to hear the voice of Uncle Len.

"I came across some of Ed's columns," Len says. "I hate to toss 'em. I thought you might want them."

"Sure," I say with a twinge of guilt, as though I'm sneaking behind my father's back.

"I was going through some old papers. Just trying to wrap a few things up before my surgery." He laughs.

"Surgery?" I can't tell if he's joking.

"Oh, just a little procedure. Anyway, let me know when you want to come by to pick up those columns."

After I get off the phone, I realize that too often I have let my father dictate which relatives I should remain in contact with.

Len stands in the driveway in another loud Hawaiian shirt — he seems to own an endless supply of them.

"Know why my hair is like an ocean?" he asks as I get out of my car.

"No, why?"

"It's waving goodbye!"

Len is as corny as my father. So why couldn't they have gotten along?

Recently, Len took an Alaskan cruise with another widowed dentist. He'd bought a video camera for the trip and asks if I'd like to watch his movie with him. He makes us highballs, his favorite drink, and narrates the footage of icebergs and mountains.

I want so much to ask why he and my father had a falling-out. "So," I say, loopy from the drink. "Uncle Ed's columns."

"Your aunt is the one who saved them," he says, handing me an envelope of yellowed columns, each one topped by Ed's mug shot.

"May I borrow these?" I ask.

"You can have them."

I tell him I will visit him in the hospital.

He says he doesn't have a good feeling about it.

"I'll keep you in my prayers," I say.

"Thanks, but I'm agnostic. How about another highball?" he asks. "You only go 'round once."

Jump Blues

IN JULY, THE *WORLD-HERALD* writes a story about the newly opened Stork Club, a swing and jazz venue in Omaha. It's a Friday night when I go there, nervously sitting in the bar alone, sipping a martini. I'm soon put at ease by my surroundings. It's as though I've time-traveled back to my father's era. The bouncers are decked out in zoot suits and fedoras. A jazz combo plays in the restaurant; in the main ballroom a big band performs Benny Goodman, Glenn Miller, and the Lennon Sisters. Women wear dresses and men wear suits, or at least dress clothes. T-shirts and jeans don't exist here. I sketch on bar napkins, taking in the music, imagining that I see my father and Uncle Ed playing together on the bandstand.

One Friday night at the Dubliner Pub, during a break with the County Corkers, an attractive woman approaches me.

"Were you flirting with me?" she asks.

"No," I say, telling the truth. Although I had noticed her. "Why?"

"Well, you kept winking at me."

"Winking?" *My Tourette's.*

236

She laughs a little. "Anyway, no big deal." She says her name is Joy.

"I have Tourette's syndrome."

"Oh." Joy shrugs as if I said "The sky is blue." "I know someone else with Tourette's."

"Really?"

"Yes. But I had something else I wanted to ask." Clearly, she's not interested in Tourette's. "I like your playing."

Now I wonder if she's hitting on *me*. If she is, I certainly don't mind. "Thanks.

"As a matter of fact," I say, taking the attention off me, "my father was a big-band drummer." I say this, for the first time in my life, with great pride.

"Well," Joy says, "I'm a singer, and I'm thinking about starting a swing band. Do you play other types of music?"

Why my Irish mandolin jigs would inspire her to ask is beyond me.

We exchange phone numbers and agree to talk on Monday. All weekend I think about Joy. I begin teaching myself jazz chords. I write my first swing song, "Goin' Downtown," about a boy and girl who have broken up and who now see each other on the dance floor, and through swing dancing they fall back in love. It's meant to be a male-female duet. Even though Joy tells me she intends to cover old standards, I can't help myself. What's the point of being in a band if I'm not playing my own music? To me, that would be akin to redrawing someone else's cartoons.

In my head, everything is planned. She'll hear my song. She'll love it. I'll convince her we need to do more original music. We'll fall in love.

I also rework into swing a blues song I'd written the year before. "Throw Me a Bone" is sung from a lonely dog's point of view. When I write songs, I imagine the characters in them in cartoon form. Likewise, when I draw cartoons, I hear my characters' voices; more often than not, my cartoons, although appearing in print, come with a soundtrack in my head.

I laugh at how I'm getting ahead of myself with Joy. On Monday, I call her, leaving a message. By Tuesday night, she hasn't called. Grunting, twisting my head, I force myself not to call her again. Wednesday comes and goes. By Thursday night, I still don't hear from her and call again. Maybe she really *didn't* get my first message. She seemed so positive about me, how could she change her mind like this? I leave another message. By the weekend, I'm heartbroken and discouraged.

Two weeks later, during a lunch break, I hear lively jazz bouncing off downtown buildings. I know that the musicians' association puts on concerts in the park over the summer; I follow the music. At first I hear a saxophone, drums, walking bass. Then a woman's voice, clear and energetic, soars over the music. It's Joy, front and center. Watching her sing, interact with, and play off these other musicians, I might as well be a dumped lover. I stay for the whole set, skipping lunch. I don't yet have my cartoon idea, which causes anxiety and some twitching. Nevertheless, this is my chance to talk to her, to find out what happened. At the end of the performance, I approach the stage.

"Hey, you," she says, struggling to pinpoint how she knows me.

"Nice show," I say sincerely.

"Thanks."

"Just curious if you got my call." I don't say "calls."

She pauses, says, "Oh, right." The moment of recognition comes across her face. "Yeah, I've been really busy. I'm singing in all these different bands right now." She motions with her head toward her band mates. "But, yes, we really should get together sometime." I take her at her word, but "sometime" feels too far away.

"Sure. Well, you have my number." I leave disappointed. On the walk back to work, a question seemingly comes out of nowhere: why can't I start my own band?

After returning to the office, I call a bass player I know, telling him I'm forming a swing band. Larry tells me he's awfully busy playing in pickup bands, but he's definitely interested.

"Who else do you have?" he asks.

I hesitate. "Just me," I say, laughing nervously.

"I might know a drummer," he says, "but it's going to be tough finding other musicians, especially in the horn section."

I tell everyone I know that I'm looking for sax and trumpet players. I post notices on the bulletin board of the music department at the University of Nebraska at Omaha, and at record and music stores. I frequent the Stork Club on Mondays for big-band night. I wait for the band's set to end, then ask the horn players if they or anyone else they know might be interested in my new band.

"What kind of charts are you using?" one sax player asks.

"Charts?" I say.

"You know, the music. Who are you covering?"

"Oh," I stumble. "Well, it's going to be original swing music."

"So who's writing your charts?" He seems unimpressed.

"Well, I don't actually know how to read music, so most of it is in my head, and . . ."

He turns away without a word.

Week after week, this interaction is played out with other musicians. I have no takers, though most of the musicians wish me luck.

I hear from a college student majoring in music who tells me she might be up for playing tenor saxophone. We plan to meet. In the meantime, every night I don't have Josh, I practice my guitar, then end the night at the Stork. One night, I approach the club's booking agent and explain to him that I have a new swing band, a band that won't just play covers but new songs, original songs — modern swing.

"Cool," he says. "You guys have a demo?"

"We're working on one," I fib.

"That's okay. Listen, I have some openings for shows in October. How does that sound?"

"Great." It's mid-August. What have I roped myself into?

• • •

Through word of mouth I find an alto sax player, a trumpet player, and a trombonist. Larry calls the drummer he knew in college. Two weeks before our first show, in early October, we finally practice as a group. We call ourselves the Prairie Cats. The night of our first performance, the Stork Club is crowded with friends and family and swing dancers in vintage attire. My parents are here; my father hoists a bulky video camera on his shoulder. When he puts down the camera and he and my mother dance together in front of the stage, I imagine how they might have looked nearly four decades before. After each song, my father cheers, "Hey, hey!" His voice is the loudest. He winks, gives a thumbs-up.

The Prairie Cats return to the Stork Club and begin to perform elsewhere around the city. This is where, and how, I like my parents best. Me onstage, my parents a safe distance away. Out there on the dance floor, in the audience, they appear happy and in love, a May-to-December couple who have raised five children and now have grandchildren. Up here behind the microphone, behind my gold electric guitar, I am safe. I write songs about love, the lost-love kind mostly, and when I perform these songs I think of my parents. How perhaps they have finally *found* love — with each other, all these years later.

The band is on break and I'm sipping a gin and tonic. In my other hand, a sweaty glass of water. I allow myself only small amounts of alcohol during shows. I must remain clear-headed, sharp. But I also don't go overboard to the other extreme. It's perfectly okay to have *some* alcohol. I am not like my father was.

A strong hand grabs my shoulder. My father. "Wonderful! Did you write all those songs?"

"Most of them," I say, turning around. A trickle of sweat burns my eyes and I wipe it with the sleeve of my suit coat, trying not to spill my drink.

"Your songs remind me of Hoagy Carmichael."

"Thanks, Dad."

"Yep. You would have been famous back in my day."

"Thanks. Say, where's Mom?"

"Oh, she had to call Grandma, to make sure she got back okay from her trip."

I know how it bothers my father that my grandmother takes regular trips to Las Vegas, a habit she formed in the wake of my grandfather's death. I am relieved when he changes the subject.

"Sure love the cartoons," he says.

I nod, taking a sip of my drink, chasing it with a swig of water.

"You know your mother and I met at a dance." He's nursing a Sprite.

"Yeah?" This is one of the missing pieces.

"Well, not quite like this." His hand waves around.

A couple of fans shake my hand. I introduce them to my father, but do my best to return my attention to him. I don't want to lose the moment.

"You sure have a lot of nice friends," he says.

"Thanks, Dad. So, a dance, eh?"

"What's that?" He struggles to hear as the disc jockey's music gets louder, a rockabilly number. He cups his hand over his ear, leans in toward me.

"The dance," I say loudly. "Where you met Mom."

"Oh, well, I was playing that night at the Blackstone Hotel and she was with Grandma. Grandma looked so young, I thought she and your mother were sisters. Of course I didn't know how young your mother was at the time." Again, all new information. I don't want him to stop.

The rest of the band is gearing up for the next set. "I'd better head back up," I tell him.

Why would Grandma go to a dance without Grandpa?

I return to the stage, to my guitar, to the music. Maybe I don't need to know *everything*. Maybe the journalist in me can take a break. It's better to leave my parents dancing, my father in his fedora and suit, my mother in her dress.

Out of Nowhere

MAYBE IT'S A RENEWED sense of nesting, but my parents do something I never would have imagined: they move. Not only do they move into another house — a cottage built in the 1950s — but the property they move to is nearly a half acre. Not far from our old South Omaha home, this new house is in Bellevue, near Fontenelle Forest, along the Missouri River. Here their spacious yard is surrounded by tall stands of pine, silver maple, oak, cottonwood, and weeping willow. In the morning, my mother says, when she drinks her coffee, she will look out the back window to watch deer grazing in the yard.

The house itself, although not much larger than the one in which I was raised, seems larger, if for no other reason than it's not full of junk. I don't ask how they can afford to buy this new house, although I guess that Jean left my father a little money. When my siblings and I visit, we give one another surprised looks. We're all, I'm sure, thinking the same thing: *It's a cruel joke. Why didn't you do something like this for us before we all moved out? Why now?*

My mother has decorated the new place in faux-cowboy style. A brown leather sofa and matching chair, cowboy boot logos burned into the cool, soft material, wagon wheels for arms. Does this furniture represent for her some long-held desire to escape the city?

"Isn't it beautiful?" she says, stroking the leather of the sofa, sighing with delight.

"Uh-huh," I say.

"You can find some really good buys at the Goodwill. Do you know what something like this would cost brand-new?" She waves her hand down as though slapping the air, a mannerism of my father's that indicates his disgust for playing full price for anything. Yes, she's always had to be frugal, but gone from her voice is the quiet disappointment that accompanied her shopping trips. There was a time when my mother lamented that she had to shop for her children's clothes at the "used store" or garage sales. Yet now here she is, a convert.

I am happy for her. In addition to the furniture, she has staked her claim on the walls and shelves with religious photographs, matryoshka nesting dolls Jeanie brought her from a school trip to Russia, paintings of flowers, candles, ornate jars of potpourri, photographs of her children at various ages. She is proud. We could be in anyone's house. If nothing else, if my mother never goes on vacations, if the upstairs and basement fill up, I hope she will always have the main floor.

"What about the other house?" Jen asks. "Is it for sale?"

"Not yet," my father says. "It needs work."

"We have to sell it," my mother says, turning worried. "We can barely afford maintaining one house."

This sparks an immediate discussion between Artie and Eddie, natural-born handymen, about what will need to be done. They inherited the mechanical, plumbing, and electrical genes from my father. I got his other genes.

"This is the house we never had," I whisper to Jen. I've begun to see, in recent years, how much Jen and I resemble each other.

She shoots me a scowl, her eyes deep under her brow. Her face straightens out, then cringes again.

"What about all the junk?" I ask out loud. "Maybe we could have an estate sale, get a dumpster for the rest, and—"

My father gives his bad-man face. "What the hell do you mean?" he says. Not even now, not even after all the good that has happened, am I safe. "That junk, as you call it, is gold. Do you hear?"

"Sorry."

My sisters glare at me as if to say, *Let Mom and Dad be happy.*

• • •

243

Three months later and the old house isn't any closer to going on the market. The attic overflows with clothes; the basement is still piled with old TVs and parts, musical instruments, garbage bags full of who knows what, and his 78 rpm records. The garages and the storage sheds remain full, too.

My father haunts the old place during the day. He rummages through boxes with his now bony hands, still attempting to sell TVs, cursing newer models that are beyond his technical reach. At my mother's urging, slowly, meticulously, he begins to sort his old records, moving them in small stacks to their new home. "I want everything in our house to be clean and orderly," he says. He also worries about leaving the old house unattended, fearing someone will break in and steal everything.

My little brother Eddie moves in to babysit the old house. In lieu of rent, he agrees to make improvements — pull up the carpet in the living and dining rooms, refurbish the bathroom.

My parents continue to scrape at the surface, packing in vain. When I call my father, he tells me he has a bunch of my stuff. Do I want it?

"Like what?"

"Oh, old records. Other stuff. I don't know. Artwork."

I try not to trip on anything as I maneuver through the old house. It is in transition, although an outsider wouldn't notice. Instead of TVs, the living room is filled with my father's records from the basement. This is his staging area, where he goes each day as if it's a job, sorting, listening to his collection to determine which records to keep, which to sell. He even found an ancient punch clock, which he keeps on the kitchen table. For all I know, he actually punches in every morning.

The old house has a way of depleting my energy. It's spring and the windows are open, letting in fresh air, particles of dust like millions of microscopic fish caught in a ray of sunlight beneath the ocean.

My father checks the condition of a record but quickly slips the black disc into its sleeve as if he is up to a secret.

"You really going to get this cleaned in time to put the house up by summer?"

"Oh, sure," he says.

The plan is to hold as many garage sales as it takes to rid the house of what my parents no longer want.

When I was a child, when my mother attempted to explain eternity, she told the story of a single dove carrying sand from a great beach, one grain at a time, across the ocean. Eternity, she would say, is how long it takes for the dove to empty the beach of all the sand. I think of this now as I watch my father blow dust from another record.

My mother is here today, too, in the kitchen, making a snack. For a moment I almost forget they no longer live here. "Hungry?" she asks.

I shake my head no. "Dad says I have a bunch of stuff to take home?"

"Boxes. Lots of boxes and bags. All kinds of things."

Where will I put it all? I've only recently moved into an old, small house in the middle of town, away from the suburbs.

I step carefully down the basement steps, which are lined with shoeboxes filled with trinkets, bags of knickknacks. I can see right off there has been movement, an almost tectonic shift, from one side of the basement to the other. Where towers of TVs, radios, and stereos once defied gravity, there is now empty concrete floor. Elsewhere, where paths and open areas once meandered, there are heaps of metallic objects too numerous to count.

Plastic garbage bags hang from the ceiling like heavy thunderclouds, marked JEFFREY'S DRAWINGS and JEFFREY'S ITEMS.

My instinct is to tear into these black piñatas, but I will wait until I get them home.

When I head upstairs, bags over each shoulder, my mother

asks, as though I've returned from exploring an uncharted cave, "How is it down there?"

Not knowing how else to respond, I shrug.

It takes three trips to get everything. At home, in my tiny, partially finished basement, I begin excavating. Drawings of rockets, paintings of trains and horses and kitties. Jimi Hendrix albums and Cream and Chick Corea and the Allman Brothers Band—a hodgepodge of tastes formed by garage sales and what I discovered at the mall record store. For the oldest of the albums, the flimsy covers that house the records are worn, a round line formed in the cardboard. I want to take credit for all of the wear and tear on these LPs, but many of them once belonged to strangers whose scratches and skips had become my own, part of the songs themselves as I knew them. It comforts me to study the albums I bought new with my own money. Even these records show wear. They prove that I, too, have a history. Many I will simply give away. I won't tell my father. Images of objects I'd hoped to find in the bags and boxes, but did not, flash in my mind. My Golden Books. My Matchbox cars and Hot Wheels cars—my favorite being the Jack Rabbit Special. My Major Matt Mason astronaut action figures. My prism. The *Dogie the Doggie News*.

It's past ten and I call my parents' new house to ask if there are more boxes. No answer.

I call the old house, assuming they are packing and cleaning, but Eddie tells me they left hours ago.

"That's strange," I say. "Where would they be?"

"I have no idea." He's always to the point, no nonsense.

My parents usually stay up late, but the only time they go out these days is when my band is playing. Even then, they don't dine out. Perhaps they turn off the phone before going to bed. What other reason could there be? When I call the next morning, my father answers.

"I called last night," I say.

"Yes? And?" he says melodically.

"Nothing. I guess I'm not used to you two being gone. Actually, I think it's nice that you and Mom are spending time together."

He groans.

"What?" I say.

"Okay. I'm not supposed to tell you. Your mother doesn't want you to know."

"She doesn't want me to know what?" My insides jump. Is someone sick? Dying?

"We were at the casino."

"The casino?" It's difficult to imagine them around all the smoke and noise.

"You heard me. Mom's going to crucify me for telling you."

Crucify? Mom? Is this how he perceives my mother? "I won't say anything. I just can't believe it, considering how critical of Grandma you've always been. I mean, don't you ever worry about running into her over there?"

A flash of silence. "Actually, we all go together."

"You and Mom and Grandma?"

"And Artie. Goddamn it! Why in the hell did you make me tell you?"

"Me? I didn't make you."

"You kept pushing, pushing, pushing. Just like you want me to get rid of everything I own. Well, goddamn it, I won't let any of my kids push me around."

"For God's sake, Dad, I don't give a shit if you and Mom — and Grandma — my God, I can't believe it — go gambling. It's your own business. It's kind of weird, that's all."

"Well, I know how much you hate casinos. You're always drawing cartoons against them."

"Dad, listen —"

"I don't have all day. I've got work to do. Oh, and I came across more boxes of your stuff."

"Thanks," I say.

"Besides," he says, "it's not like we're playing poker or the dollar machines. We're playing the nickel machines. A guy can be there all night having a good time on just a few dollars. Plus, they have a nice buffet. And it's cheap."

I stop by the old house to check in on Artie's remodeling of the kitchen. After Artie's wife became pregnant, it seemed a logical choice for Eddie to move out, making way for Artie and his new family. Then came the onslaught of Artie's health problems. The worst of it is his "brittle" diabetes — which, as Artie explains it, means that no matter how hard he tries to control his diet, his blood glucose levels are apt to fluctuate drastically. Although Artie works full-time as a pit boss at Harrah's Casino, he makes a little extra on the side selling used electronics. And like our brother Eddie, Artie has taken it upon himself to spruce up the house.

"Artie," I say, "you're pushing yourself too hard."

"I know what I'm doing," he says.

"But you're not taking good care of yourself."

"I have bills," he says. "Besides, I'm tough. I can still kick your ass." He pumps his fists, flexes his muscles. "Here, feel that," he says, nodding toward his biceps.

"I don't want to."

"C'mon."

I give in, squeezing his formidable muscle.

"See?" he says. "I'm just as strong — I'm *stronger* than I was when I would beat up all the bullies that picked on you."

"When you what?"

"You were in junior high and I couldn't stand watching you get picked on."

"I remember."

"Well, do you remember that kids left you alone after that?"

"Well, yes, but . . ."

"Let's just say back then I was kicking ass and taking names."

I say nothing more as he rolls down his sleeve. "Man, I used to hate how those kids treated you."

Floating

I'M PRESSING MY FOREHEAD against the tall window, imagining I'm floating above Manhattan at sunset. Below me: an endless forest of steel, brick, and concrete, the angular pinnacles of buildings gleaming orange in the fading light, obscuring the streets in purple shadow. If I lived here a lifetime, I would still not be able to learn the names of all the buildings. Bridges connect to boroughs I can't identify, a steady parade of microscopic cars and trucks inching their way, carrying invisible passengers to everywhere. It is quiet here at Windows on the World. Almost sacredly quiet. I, too, have arrived anywhere, everywhere.

I take a few steps back to catch my transparent reflection in the window. There I am, in my black-and-white windowpane suit (purchased for this show), my crisp white shirt, black-and-white tie, and black-and-white two-tone shoes. Behind me in the warm glow of the restaurant: the illuminated and well-stocked bar, the swanky drinkers. Farther off, but less clearly in the window, my band mates sort through their music charts, warm up their horns.

I refocus, gazing through my reflection, through myself. Back out into the world. Before the night is over, I will squint out a window as one of our trumpet players points toward the tiny Statue of Liberty. I will catch the silent explosions of a fireworks display far below. During the show, as I am strumming my guitar, I will watch over my shoulder as a June thunderstorm approaches from a great distance. I will not fear the weather. Here, I am above the lightning. Later, as the warmth of alcohol circulates through my veins, I will join patrons lifting colorful geometric glasses to their lips. I will watch dancers move. I will imagine we're all in a spaceship, the city's lights distant galaxies. If only my parents were here.

This is our last night in New York, our fourth show in the city. On the first night we played at the Hudson River Festival, the twin towers looming above. I craned my neck as I sang and played, knowing that in three days I would be singing up *there*. New York has welcomed us easily. In many ways, surprisingly, it took less effort booking shows in Manhattan than it sometimes does in Omaha. My father always said he'd had a similar experience, that Omaha was less welcoming to musicians than other places. "They sit on their hands in Omaha," he would say, "demanding you make them clap." Maybe it's the you-can't-be-a-prophet-in-your-hometown syndrome.

I turn from the window and glance to where Josh is sitting on the floor of the stage, leaning back against one of the narrow windows. His brown eyes and long lashes, framed by dark brows, survey the arriving audience. He, too, wants to play in a band someday. Is he dreaming about his future? Is he wishing his mother were here also? Does he forgive me for the divorce? He's fifteen; I won't embarrass him by smiling at him too long. He looks over, raises his eyebrows expectantly, wonders why I'm gazing at him. He relinquishes a misty grin. Behind him, the glittering city, and beyond, the entire country stretches out like a nighttime version of that Saul Steinberg *New Yorker* cover.

I venture to the lobby, and among a cluster of people I spot a man, his wife, and a boy a bit younger than Josh. Except that the man can't be my cousin Ed. My lasting memory of him is from the airport, 1969. He was tall then, his face chiseled in strong, handsome features. But I tower over this man, whose face is shielded by an unexpected beard.

"Jeff?" he asks meekly. He knows me, this stranger, right off. I swallow. "Ed?"

A shy smile reveals itself beneath his beard.

Instinctively, I hug him, wrapping my arms tightly, the bones

250

of his shoulders against me. He pats my back politely. I shake his wife's hand, then his son's.

When Cousin Sally called my mother earlier this summer to announce that Ed and his family would be coming to Omaha in August, my mother mentioned to her that my band would be playing in New York. As it turned out, Ed, a psychologist, was to be in Manhattan the same weekend, attending a conference. I've been anticipating this moment for weeks, but during dinner I am too nervous to speak. Every question I've ever had, every story about his father I've wanted to share, remains in my chest. I can't bring up Ed's father in front of everyone else. What if Ed doesn't want to talk about him?

"Tell me about Art," Ed says, grinning expectantly. "Does he perform much?" The beard has softened Ed's face; strands of gray have made inroads. I watch for, but do not see, tics in his face. His son's face is calm, too.

"Not really," I say. "I mean, he set up his drums in the basement of their new house, but he never plays out anymore. How about you?" I ask. "Playing much music these days?"

"Yep. Still pounding the keys. I have a regular gig with a jazz trio."

"What kind of stuff?"

"Well, I love Bill Evans," he says.

"Wish we had a piano. You could sit in."

"Wouldn't that be great, honey?" his wife says to him, her face full of color. She gives him a playful nudge.

"Tell us about your cartooning," Ed says, diverting attention from himself. "We see your work in our local paper from time to time."

"Well, I got syndicated last year, right after the election."

"That's wonderful," his wife says with the hint of a southern drawl. "Congratulations."

"Thanks." In the next room, our trumpet and sax players are warming up. My stomach is flickering with butterflies and tics.

251

"My father was with Scripps-Howard," Ed says, almost shyly.

"Yes," I say, lurching forward in my seat. "I know!" I catch myself, fearing I might have sounded rude, a know-it-all. I settle down. "I mean, I used to hear all these stories about him." I feel awkward saying this. I wish we had all night to chitchat about easy stuff before delving into a long conversation about our family, but I have to prepare for the show soon. Still, any disappointment I may feel about not having much time for a visit is made better knowing that Ed and his family will be coming to Omaha next month.

"You know," he says, "we came across something you might be interested in. Our other son was doing a research project on his grandfather. So we ordered some videotapes from the Kennedy archives."

"Really?"

"It's fascinating," his wife says. "They had all this footage from JFK's first televised press conferences."

"You can see my father several times," Ed says, "asking questions."

"Wow!" This is a revelation to me.

"With your journalism background," Ed says, "I'll bet you would enjoy it."

Journalism? This goes beyond journalistic interest. But how could Ed know what I've carried in my heart all these years? He couldn't possibly know I had long ago elevated his father to the status of a second, mythical father for myself. This tape is a treasure I didn't know I was searching for.

A Message from the President

THIS TIME, I'M MORE relaxed around Ed. Not that I'm not nervous—I am. Maybe it's the martini I allowed myself, arriving early at Mr. Toad's Pub.

"In New York you were telling me you really like Bill Evans," I say.

"Man, I could listen to Evans nonstop." Ed sips his beer. "Well, when I'm not gigging myself. Not to mention the day job." Ed's family is already in bed, exhausted from the flight and the day's activities, visiting relatives my father doesn't see.

I nod and let out a small laugh at this, but Ed is intense, off in his mind, thinking about music. I wonder whether he actually hears music when there isn't any. Just like my father does, like I do. Like Josh.

Omaha's Old Market district bustles with activity. My seat inside the pub allows a view of the passing scene, artsy women parading by in the sultry August air.

"What do you know about 'Flight of the Bumblebee'?" I ask.

"'Flight of the Bumblebee'? Well, I know it's not a song I'd attempt on piano."

I chuckle, poking at the olive in my drink with a tiny plastic sword. "Did you know that that was one of your father's favorites to play on the clarinet?"

"You know, I think I did know that."

We're both quiet.

I glance behind me, around the bar. The place is nearly empty, yet near the ceiling hovers a perpetual fog, the collected clouds from decades of smokers.

"I'm sure hoping Art will tell me a few stories this weekend."

It throws me off a little that he calls my father Art. Hardly anyone calls him that. "Me too," I say. "Before his memory gets worse." I say this in an effort to downplay Ed's expectations, to apologize in advance in case there's a blowup.

"That's too bad."

"Physically, he's great." I think of all his fake heart attacks over the years. "It's just that he's been forgetful lately." Maybe my father will forget how much hostility he has held in, his anger over Ed's last name.

I make a squeak in my throat. Like the sound a dog might make if someone steps on its paw. "Sorry about that," I say.

"Don't worry," he says. "It's no big deal."

"I have Tourette's," I say, shocking myself with my bluntness.

"Yeah," he says. "I figured."

This makes me wonder whether he noticed my twitching when he saw me at age eight.

"My father has it," I say. "And Jen."

"Well, it *is* genetic. You taking anything for it?"

I shake my head no. "Don't want to mess with the creativity, you know?" I take a long, hard swallow of my martini as Ed mirrors me with his Miller Lite, a wet napkin stuck to the bottom of the bottle.

"Has your father ever told you how our grandparents met?"

I shrug. "No." This is not a story I'd ever considered, a mystery I'd never before thought to ponder. Now I crave the answer.

"Sally tells me they met at a dance. In the old country, of course."

"Really?"

"Yeah, our grandfather was a bandleader. I'm not sure, but I think he also played clarinet. This would have been around the turn of the twentieth century. Anyway, our grandmother comes in with her date, and while they're dancing, Grandfather keeps looking over at Grandmother." I love the way he says "Grandfather." He makes it sound as if he knew the man.

"I have never heard this."

"So he's playing, watching. He sees Grandmother's date go off somewhere. Maybe for a drink. So right away he stops the song and calls another tune the band can play without him."

I imagine the band in matching costumes—ornate red vests, flowing white sleeves poking out. I can see the tuba and accordion players rolling their eyes, laughing. Maybe drunk.

"So," Ed continues, "Grandfather hops off the stage and goes over to Grandmother and asks for a dance."

"Really?"

"It gets better. Next thing, her date comes up, and of course he's not happy. So one of them—Sally wasn't sure—challenges

254

the other to a duel. Can you believe it?" He finally grins under that beard of his.

"This really happened?" I ask.

"That's the story."

"Did our grandfather kill the guy?"

"No, that's the funny thing. Grandmother pointed at her date and said, 'You. I came here this evening with *you*. I will only dance with *you*.' Then, pointing to our grandfather, she said, 'As for you. You're the leader of the band. Get back onstage and lead the music so my date and I can dance.' And that was that. Somehow, of course, they saw each other again. I'm not sure how that all happened. Maybe at another dance." Ed drains his bottle of beer. "Pretty wild, huh?"

"I don't know what to say."

"Sally has a lot of great stories."

"You know, I don't think my father knows that story. I'm sure if he did, I would have heard it by now. But sometimes he's really secretive about the weirdest things. That, or some things don't seem important to him. I can't figure it out."

Ed's not sure what to say about this. I hope I haven't made him resentful somehow. Like I should be grateful for having a father, even if he's forgetful or secretive.

"Well, I've been looking so forward to seeing everyone," he says. "What are the chances Art will play the drums?"

I think about my parents' new basement, how the drums are buried among my father's things. "You know, he really doesn't play much anymore."

"I'll bet I can convince him. Man, all the great stories I've heard about Art . . ." His voice trails off and he shakes his head a little, implying that my father has accomplished feats of heroic proportions.

Don't get your hopes up.

It is with great trepidation that I drive to my parents' house with Josh. I smile for Josh's sake, to act as if everything is okay. I do this a lot around him. I fight the urge to share with him my worries over how my father will treat Ed. If there is an argument, I will just say goodbye to Ed and his family and leave. I will not allow my embarrassment and fear to overshadow what hasn't yet happened. I glance over at Josh. The afternoon light flickers inside the car, highlighting the peach fuzz that has made an appearance on his fifteen-year-old face.

We get there before anyone else. My parents greet us at the front door as though *we* are the guests of honor. "Hey, hey!" my father announces in his circus voice. "Look who's here!" His smile is wide, gleaming under the brush of his wide gray mustache.

My mother hugs Josh and me. We're encircled by her lavender perfume.

"Hi, Grandma," Josh says, bashful from the attention. "Hi, Grandpa."

A Bing Crosby tape plays on a small cassette player. With all those stereos and record players, my father uses this dinky machine. My parents are cheerful. It occurs to me that Josh has never seen my parents arguing. These are not the same parents I grew up with. Do they simply put on a good show when others are around, or has age mellowed them?

In front of the fireplace I see a collection of instruments. A snare drum and one cymbal on a stand. A small Casio electric keyboard, three acoustic guitars with worn strings, and an electric guitar missing its electric parts. A trumpet—who plays the trumpet?

"Wow," I say, pausing in front of the makeshift bandstand.

My mother tries her best to smile, but worry washes over her face. Does she fear that this is the beginning of the end for her clean space?

When Ed and his family arrive, they are greeted pleasantly. Soon Artie and his wife and son are here, as are Eddie, Jen and her husband and daughter, and Jeanie and her boyfriend. The house is filled with the kinds of sounds I always wished to hear from my family. Laughing, children singing. No bickering.

In the middle of the commotion, I watch as Ed makes his way to the musical instruments. He's holding the keyboard, fiddling

256

with it, attempting to make it work. I walk toward him. No batteries, no power cord.

"That's okay," Ed says. "I want to hear Art play."

"Hold on," I say.

I find my father in the kitchen, sipping from a beer bottle.

"Dad?" I say, surprised.

"It's one beer," he says.

"I know, but—"

"I drink one beer. Per week. See?" He puts the nearly full bottle back into the refrigerator, stuffing the opening of the bottle with a paper towel. "I sip at it for a week."

"Oh," I say, relieved. I believe him.

"So are we going to have a jam session or not?" he says.

"There's no power cord for the piano."

"No problem! We have to have one around here somewhere."

"Well, Ed said it's not a big deal. He really wants to hear you play."

"He said that?"

I nod.

"Let me take a look for that cord," he says, slipping off to the basement.

I open the refrigerator door and examine the bottle of beer. There it is, almost full, the floral paper towel sticking out like a fake bouquet. From the other room, someone is banging on the snare drum unrhythmically. Someone else is tuning the sour guitars—Josh—getting them in sync. They might not have been tuned in years.

I go around the corner and see Josh, Artie, and Ed as they delightedly watch Artie's son bang away on the snare. Artie's son finishes his "solo" and everyone claps.

"Woo-hoo!" calls my father, striding up the steps like a young man. He comes into the room carrying a box full of jumbled cords, cables, and wires. "Surely one of these will work."

Josh and Artie take the box, rummage through it. Moments

later, the Casio is up and running. Artie plunks on the keys, cranking up the volume.

Ed sits at the edge of my father's recliner, balances the keyboard on his lap, extending his fingers, pressing the keys. He makes an adjustment, changing tones and settings, going from organ to marimba and finally to piano. I'm a little embarrassed that this was the best we could do for him.

He noodles up and down the tiny keyboard. Even his noodling sounds like a jazz solo. He looks up from the piano and finds everyone in the room watching him expectantly.

"Art?" he says. "You going to join me?"

"You betcha," my father says, slipping behind the drum.

"Jeff?" Ed says. "I see a few guitars here."

"Dad," Josh says, "I tuned the guitars for you."

I give him a wink. Not a twitch but an honest-to-God wink.

I pick up one of the guitars, hand another to Josh. He's eager to play. I hold the guitar against my ear to make sure I'm still in tune with the piano. The wood of the guitar is cool against my face, apparently still cool from the basement. I glance over at Josh, nod that the guitar is tuned perfectly, but he's already studying Ed's fingers, following along on the other guitar.

The Casio doesn't have much volume, so we all play softly. My father taps at the snare, his eyes closed. He doesn't twitch. Josh and I play rhythm. Occasionally, I fill in with a riff, playing off the licks that come from the keyboard.

I look up. Everyone is grinning.

Artie's son is slapping at the strings of a guitar, joyful in his noisemaking. Artie proudly watches his son.

After we eat barbecued hamburgers in the backyard, Ed asks if we'd like to see the videotape he's brought. Back inside, my father turns on the TV. Gone are his gesticulations of TV preparation, his adjusting. He simply presses the on button of the remote.

"Ready to go?" Ed asks.

"Yep," Artie says. He slides the tape into the player, and after several seconds of snow, the old CBS eye logo appears, filling the screen. An announcer, whose voice is as plain as the black-and-white picture, declares this will be the first televised presidential press conference.

I look to my father. His eyes are watery. The kids in the room squirm, and Artie's wife takes them into the kitchen for a treat.

President Kennedy enters the auditorium, which is filled almost entirely with white middle-aged men in dark suits and narrow ties. After brief opening remarks by the president, the tape unexpectedly skips to a scene of a reporter standing, adjusting his glasses as he asks a question about Cuba. His chin juts confidently.

"That's your brother," my mother says to my father.

The president gives his response.

"We went through hours of press conferences," Ed explains, "to find the parts with my father."

Again the tape jumps ahead. There is some confusion as to whom the president is addressing—is it the White House reporter Marianne Means or Uncle Ed? My father scoots forward on the sofa, cupping his hands over his ears.

Another day, another press conference. On and on the tape continues, showing Uncle Ed addressing John F. Kennedy. We listen as the president considers each question and answers with precision and confidence.

Another press conference. This time the president makes his way across the stage, his face grim, somber.

"Good morning," he says, his demeanor all business. "I want to first of all express my regret at the information I've just received in regard to the death of our colleague in these press conferences, a fine newspaperman, Ed Koterba, who I understand was killed in a plane crash last night. He was a most outstanding newspaperman associated with Scripps-Howard. We want to express our sympathy to the members of his family and also to the newspapers with which he was associated. I want to say personally that I'm extremely sorry to have heard the news."

Sharply, the image goes to black. A beat later, white snow.

259

My father doesn't say anything; neither does anyone else. We are silent. One of the kids is crying in the kitchen, and the sound of Artie's wife attempting to soothe her son is all we hear.

Somehow I'd expected the tape to go on, as though both men, Uncle Ed and JFK, were alive in some parallel universe. I hadn't counted on the president's pronouncing "Koterba" correctly. I almost hadn't counted on Uncle Ed's dying again.

Grounded

How," asks Artie, "were you able to escape?"

"What do you mean?" I dab a French fry in ketchup. He's asked me to meet him at this Burger King near my parents' old house, now his.

"I mean, how did you know to escape from Mom and Dad's when you did?" He leans forward, his elbows on the table.

What I see is a man with broad shoulders and cantaloupes for biceps who has lost almost all of his hair. A man who must rely on a cane to get around. A man who once broke high school football records, now barely able to walk.

"So?" he asks again. "How did you do it? I mean, you were looked at like the black sheep of the family for a long, long time. I remember how angry and hurt Mom and Dad were that you never came around. And I was, too. I thought you were a real asshole. But now I can see why you had to do it. You had to get out to save yourself. I couldn't. I don't know what stopped me. But I couldn't leave. It never occurred to me that I *could*. If even for a short time." He slaps at the table. "Damn it," he says, smiling, "how the hell did you know to get out?"

I shake my head. "I don't know," I tell him. "I honestly don't know."

"Man," he says, "you are awfully blessed."

• • •

260

Beyond Artie, out the window, a commotion—people running, gathering along the street.

"What the heck?" I say, urging Artie to turn around.

"Let's go," he says, groaning when he attempts to stand too quickly. "Goddamn neuropathy," he says under his breath, limping slightly.

We make our way up the street to where the crowd has formed. A police car has arrived, its red lights flashing. In the distance, the wail of a fire truck, a rescue squad.

"Excuse me," Artie shouts. He is always more bold than I. "What happened?"

A woman turns around, says something that sounds like "The sky."

As we get closer we see a crumpled motorcycle in the street. I scan the street, the curb, searching for the injured rider. Nothing. I call the newsroom on my cell phone to report the accident, in case someone missed hearing it on the police scanner.

"The sky?" Artie says. "Why the hell would that woman say 'the sky'? What does that mean? Do you think the motorcycle fell from the sky?"

"What?" I say, hanging up. "No, that's not what she said." Yet a part of me wonders if it's true. I believe in a world where anything can happen. Anything is possible.

We both stare up into the purple night.

"I mean," Artie says, "maybe there was no driver. Maybe the damned thing fell here somehow."

I ask someone else. "Excuse me, ma'am. Do you know what happened here?"

"Yeah. This guy crashed his bike, then took off running past the Burger King."

This guy.

Artie and I look at each other and laugh.

"Shit," Artie says. "Maybe the guy stole the bike. Maybe he ran right past us! Just think. If we had seen him, maybe we could have stopped him. We could have taken him down." His eyes light up.

"Maybe, Artie," I say. "Maybe."

I receive a call from Artie at work. I always worry when he calls, fearing he isn't well, that he needs to go to the hospital.

"Jeff," he says.

"You okay?" I always ask this first.

"Oh, I'm fine."

"Good," I say, worried that I don't have an idea for today's cartoon. It's already one in the afternoon.

"Yeah, well, you'll never guess what I found."

"I have no idea." I doodle a cartoon face.

"You're going to be really surprised," he says, as if he's my father and I'm a child.

"Really?" I allow myself to get excited.

"It's something you used to play with. You had several of these."

"Several?" I say, searching my memory.

"Well, you know how we're remodeling the kitchen? We were cleaning out the old cabinets and guess what we found?"

"I have no idea."

"An Etch A Sketch."

"Oh."

"*Oh?* Jeff, it's an Etch A Sketch from when you were a kid. It still has one of your drawings — do you remember drawing a skyline?"

I say that I do.

"Well, it's still intact. It's a damned good thing we don't have very many earthquakes around here, buddy boy!"

As much as I'd dreamed, as a child, of reaching into space, into the past, to listen as my father sang on the radio, my father had, all along, been reaching into the future, saving my drawings, saving everything.

"Jeff?" Artie says.

"Yes?" I look down, not realizing I'd begun sketching a cityscape.

"That's pretty freakin' cool, huh?"

"It is, Artie," I say. "It really is."

Acknowledgments

With heartfelt gratitude, I wish to thank my literary agent, the amazing Amy Moore-Benson, for her encouragement and wisdom, and for her unwavering belief in this book even when *Inklings* was nothing more than an inkling; Becky Saletan, for her enthusiasm and invaluable insights and guidance; everyone at Houghton Mifflin Harcourt, especially Larry Cooper, Martha Kennedy, Brian Moore, Carla Gray, Taryn Roeder, Loren Isenberg, and my editor, the talented Thomas Bouman, whose spot-on suggestions instantly made me a better writer.

Over the years I have been blessed with countless friends, teachers, and mentors who have patiently given of their time, lending advice only when asked, sometimes holding my feet to the fire, but always cheering me on. In no particular order, my sincerest appreciation to Christine Starr, Stephen S., Timothy Schaffert, Alex Kava, Marianne Moore, Angela Glover, Liz Hruska, EmJay, Rivkah Sass, Abe Sass, Cassie McElroy, McGraw Milhaven, Bill Johnson, Mike Drelicharz, Wayne Walls, Rebecca Rotert, Woody Howe, Harold Andersen, Sandy Asirvatham, Jesse Lee Kercheval, Sally Arteseros, and Sharon Stark. In addition, to my current and former colleagues at the *Omaha World-Herald,* I say thank you: John Gottschalk, Terry Kroeger, Geitner Simmons, Mike Reilly, Mike Kelly, Virginia Bensheimer, Jim Anderson, Chris Olson, Todd Von Kampen, Jason Kuiper, John Malnack, Jeff Beiermann, Jolene McHugh, and Chris Machian. Extra-special thanks to Frank Partsch — I continue to learn from you every day. And another extra-special thank you to my friend Jen Stastny for her sharp eye, her tough questions, and her profound generosity (and also for answering my e-mails at all hours). And in a category unto herself, my steadfast friend, muse, and trusty wordsmith Trilety Wade, whose inexhaustible support as my official first reader, and devotion to this book, I will carry in my heart forever. I couldn't have done it without you.

Finally, to my supportive family, I say thanks: Stacey, for her love, counsel, wisdom, patience, encouragement, and funny voices (say hi to Mr. Pick); Josh, for his boundless optimism and love, for his smile, and for his gift of music (not to mention teaching me a thing or two about really complicated guitar chords); Sally Cohn and Ed Morgret — the miles may separate us but you are never far from my thoughts (and I promise I *will* visit); Jennifer and Jeanie, I am proud of you both for your inner strength and wisdom, and for all you have taught me about coffee; Eddie, whose brain does not come with an off switch and never seems to run out of great ideas; the incredible, indestructible, and big-hearted Artie, whose diligence, generosity, and loyalty provide daily inspiration. Most of all, I am truly grateful to my parents, not only for allowing me to write about them, but for their countless sacrifices, for their enduring love, and for instilling in me an appreciation for creativity.